IN WHOSE EYES

In Whose Eyes

*The Memoir of
a Vietnamese Filmmaker
in War and Peace*

by
Trần Văn Thủy
as told to
Lê Thanh Dũng

Edited and adapted by Wayne Karlin
Translated by Eric Henry and Nguyễn Quang Dy

University of Massachusetts Press
Amherst & Boston

Copyright © 2016 by University of Massachusetts Press
All rights reserved
Printed in the United States of America

Originally published 2013 as *Chuyện Nghề Của Thủy* by Văn Hóa Phương Nam,
Ho Chi Minh City, Vietnam. Translated and adapted by permission.

ISBN 978-1-62534-252-2 (paper); 251-5 (cloth)

Designed by Jack Harrison
Set in Times New Roman with Latin Wide display
Printed and bound by The Maple-Vail Book Manufacturing Group

Cover design by Jack Harrison
Cover photo of the author by Trần Thế Dân, taken during the war and damaged by mildew
due to conditions on the Ho Chi Minh Trails.

Library of Congress Cataloging-in-Publication Data
A catalog record for this book is available from the Library of Congress.

British Library Cataloguing-in-Publication Data
A catalog record for this book is available from the British Library.

Portions of this book, under the title "Excerpts from the Memoir of Trần Văn Thủy," were
published in the online journal *War, Literature & the Arts,* vol. 26 (2014).

An Apologetic Dedication

My friend Lê Thanh Dũng and I have made this book to express our gratitude to various elders, colleagues, viewers, and friends, both inside and outside the country—people who have believed in me, supported me, and encouraged me throughout my career. I am sorry that, for certain very delicate reasons, I cannot provide a full list here of the names of my benefactors—people who have left in my memory a belief, however fragile, that in this world there are still many kind and decent people.

—Trần Văn Thủy

Since a long time ago, our elders have taught us: decency used to exist in every human being, every family, every lineage, and every nation. Let us patiently wake up this quality and place it on the ancestral altars or the national grandstands, for without this, even the greatest effort and the best vision of a community would be nonsense... Let us focus our children and even adults on learning to become human beings, decent human beings, before hoping to turn them into people of power, wisdom, or superiority...

That is why, in the final analysis, there is no profession, no work, and nobody in this world who can become decent without starting first from human love, from the appreciation of human life, and from concern for human suffering.

—From the film *The Story of Kindness*, 1985

Contents

Introduction xi
Wayne Karlin

A Friendship xvii
Trần Văn Thủy

I. War

1. The Swimmer   3
2. The Measuring Stick and the Mirror   10
3. Do You Feel Honored?   14
4. Going South   21
5. Rebirth   26
6. The Beauty and the Bullet   35
7. Carrying the War Home   47
8. An Uneasy Homecoming   56
9. Letters from the Fire   68
10. The Trans-Siberian Express   71

II. Peace

Preface   81
11. Hanoi in Whose Eyes   84
12. Untie the Bonds of Writers and Artists   94

13. The Story of Kindness   99
14. Kindness Repressed   106
15. Kindness Abroad   114
16. A Violin at Mỹ Lai   124

III. To the Ends of All the Seas
Preface   137
17. A Letter   140
18. A Birth   152

IV. The Labyrinth
Preface   163
19. An Unpleasant Occurrence   167
20. Immense Sorrow Is Forbidden   170
21. The Language of My Land   176

Epilogue
A Few Words to Thủy's Daughter   187
Final Words by Lê Thanh Dũng   190
A Note from the Translators   192

Awards Presented to Trần Văn Thủy for His Films   195
Acknowledgments   197
Notes   203
Index   211

Illustrations follow page 98

Introduction

WAYNE KARLIN

Since I began to return to Vietnam after the war, I've met many veterans who fought on the other side. My deepest friendships within that group have been with a woman who had been a teenager in the "youth volunteer brigades" on the Hồ Chí Minh Trails and later became a fiction writer, and with the filmmaker Trần Văn Thủy, whom I call anh (brother) Thủy. I think there are several reasons for the particular intensity of these relationships. Both began when the other person and I came to know that we had been in certain places, at certain times, when we literally had had the opportunity to kill each other, or at least watch each other's deaths with satisfaction or indifference. The realization that I would have "wasted," as we called killing during the war, not only these people I had come to cherish but also the books that one of them came to write, and the films that the other came to create, left me with an ache of grief, as if I really had killed them, had subtracted those gifts from the world. Our friendships grew from that ache, from the need to mourn and then bury the war by acknowledging what it had cost our hearts. But they also grew from a recognition of the common need we had as artists who came out of that war to try to wrench some meaning from that terrible, transformative experience.

Once, as anh Thủy and I were sitting on one of the huge roots of an ancient banyan tree that stood alone in the middle of some golden rice fields that were about to be harvested, he told me how afraid he had been of the American helicopters—a fear shared by my other friend, who had been hunted by them, and who had seen her friends die under the triple canopy jungles that concealed the Hồ Chí Minh Trails. To them, I had been the brush of a predator's shadow, or a helmeted, carapaced form hunched behind a machine gun. To me, they had been targets, faceless abstractions like blurred ghosts in a deadly landscape that could reach up and kill us. Actually, during my time as a helicopter gunner, I never served on what we called a gunship, those aircraft whose task was solely to strafe and kill. The helicopters I flew in deposited troops and aided those that remained—sometimes rescuing them, sometimes resupplying them, and often removing the wounded and the dead, the detritus of war. But if we were shot at or if we saw the enemy on the ground, we tried to kill them. "I would have killed you," I said to Thủy as we sat on that gnarled banyan root, and I thought of shooting down on places such as this, and I could see his face, as I had my other friend's, as if it were forming and rising up to me from that earth.

This kind of vision has seized me more than once during my trips back to Vietnam, as if the present were just a diaphanous veil thrown over the war. But that image of faces coming into focus as if in a lens, sharpening from the abstract into the human, has come to embody for me the other root of our friendship in addition to the commonality of the war: the need I find in Thủy's art to reveal, as this book does, the human faces, faces as scarred and as beautiful as that of the female sniper Văn Thị Xoa, the subject of one of Thủy's films during the war. Half of the sniper's face was stunningly beautiful, and the other half had been destroyed by a bullet. I met Văn Thị Xoa in 2004, when Thủy and I took a group of NYU film students through Vietnam. She asked me where I had been during the war and said that she would have shot me. She then held my hand and would not let go for half an hour, her trigger finger twined around mine, as if to immobilize both. Hers is the face we see in the mirror at three in the morning, those of us who were in the war—or maybe everyone can see it, if they look hard enough, the way Trần Văn Thủy does.

Another image. Thủy, starving, thirsty and filthy after hiding in a tunnel and being forced to flee for days from an American operation that had swept unexpectedly into an area where he was filming. He and the two guerillas with him stop at a river and strip down to bathe, only to be spotted by an enemy artillery observer. The three jump out of the water and run for their lives as American artillery shells, rockets, and bombs explode all around them: what must seem to Thủy all the might of a superpower trying to, very personally, wipe out one skinny, hungry, naked Viet Cong[1] armed only with a camera. If anyone ever made a film about this filmmaker's life, it should start there: Thủy scurrying about, barely avoiding the destruction hurled down by overwhelming power to try and erase that stubborn and brave little human figure armed with nothing but a camera, still relentlessly recording the force that is trying to destroy him. It is a scene that always evokes to me some essential truth about the man and his art.

Thủy had come to the war, as most of us did, when he was very young. After an abbreviated period of training in how to aim, focus, and shoot a camera, he was infiltrated into South Vietnam down the Hồ Chí Minh Trails, armed only with a Bolex and a vague assignment to film the war—a task he accomplished through on-the-job training. Most of the other cameramen given that mission (and many of those who helped them) died doing it; in these pages Thủy recounts his own many close brushes with death and the miraculous ways he survived them. Fate made him a filmmaker not only because he had to learn to quickly select and frame images and scenes, instantaneously turning them into stories, while he was under fire but also because in witnessing the terrible cost of war, he came to understand and accept his own responsibility to capture it in the gimlet eye of his lens, to bring back the images branded into his mind and share them with those for whom the war was being waged.

All of which is to say that Trần Văn Thủy's career as a filmmaker began with the war not only because he was handed a camera but also because the war clarified in him a deep love for a country whose sacrifices demanded outcomes worthy of their cost, a spiritual belief that the miracle of his survival obligated him to be a witness to his times, and a hatred for the degradation of human beings. The many films Thủy has made since then take on the dehumanization of violence, the "iron hat" of repression and censorship, corruption, social inequality, and the hatred that still divides Vietnamese from each other. But they also reveal the spirituality that is still at the heart of Vietnam: the strong who live at the broken places, the wounded yet beautiful, the gentle saints and the sweet clowns, the compassionate and the faithful. Thủy shows what needs to be changed while at the same time showing human beings whose own lives reveal that change is both desirable and possible.

What other filmmaker has ever titled a film *The Story of Kindness?*

"Decency exists in every human being," says the narrator at the beginning of that film, "in every household, in every lineage, and in every nation. Let us be persistent in protecting and awakening this quality; let us place it on our ancestral altars and national podiums. For without this quality, even the most powerful efforts and noblest aims of a community will come to nothing. Let us first of all lead our children, and our adults as well, into the study of how to be human beings—decent human beings—before hoping to train them to be people of power, ability, or distinction."

Kindness, like several of Thủy's other films, was initially banned at home and forbidden to be shown abroad—in this case because of the inequalities revealed in a supposedly egalitarian society. There have been Americans and Europeans who, seeing Thủy's films, are so surprised the documentaries have not been censored that they take their existence as a gage of the amount of freedom of expression that was allowed in Vietnam. What they do not know, and what Thủy dares to recount in this book, is how much resistance there was to those films: how they were banned; how many times Thủy was followed, surveilled, and pulled in for questioning; and how he was called "unpatriotic" by people who do not understand what patriotism means to veterans such as Thủy, which is the debt that the losses of the war imposes on its survivors. "I love this land," Thủy has said, "and I want to make this land even more beautiful. I am consumed with the wish to make human life worthy of the sacrifices that have been made for it. . . . All the films that I have made, all the things I have written, all the lonely roads I have walked on, all the desperate situations I have endured have arisen simply because I love my country."

Throughout this memoir, we see not only Thủy's physical courage during the war, the way he put his body on the line to capture the truth of war through his lens, but also his insistence ever since then to keep telling the truth, at whatever risk or cost to himself, about the Vietnam that owed it to the dead and the maimed and the haunted and the degraded to become truly united and live up to its ideal, the promises Thủy sees written in the country's history and culture. Thủy's story, like his films, is particular to Vietnam; his story, like his films, is universal. It is the story of an artist's struggle to prevail over threats, pressures, and temptations and to live as a person of moral integrity and human kindness, and it is the story of what divides us from each other and what can bring us together. "Making a documentary film," Thủy says, "is not just a matter of saying what you think, but of touching on the things that are troubling people; you must touch on the deep places in the destinies of human beings, and make people reflect on these things. That is the code, the key that opens the path I travel on."

For me, reading his words in these pages has been like once again sitting with him on the great root of that ancient tree that stands like a silent witness to his story.

I invite you to have a seat next to us and to listen as well. It's a hell of a story.

A Friendship

TRẦN VĂN THỦY

In 2002, the BHD company (the name comes from the initials of the founders), made a feature film titled *The Song of the Stork*. Investing in a production such as this was doubtless an important milestone for BHD. The owners of this independent film production company were a young couple, Nguyễn Phan Quang Bình (nicknamed Bình Boong) and his wife Ngô Bích Hạnh, and their three daughters, the three "Dans" (D): Nguyễn Phan Thảo Đan, Nguyễn Phan Linh Đan, and Nguyễn Phan Thi Đan. Bình's mother, Phan Thanh Hảo, has been my friend from my days of poverty and obscurity—the period of *Hanoi in Whose Eyes,* so full of uncertainty and hardship. I had known the two young people from the time they were little, and I quietly admired them for their innate abilities and spectacular initiative. After the initial filming of *The Song of the Stork,* Bình came to my house one day to discuss ways of fixing it. He said that the person playing the role of the war correspondent, who provides the voice-over for the film, was too young. Bình said that his mother and father-in-law, Ngô Thảo, a People's Army veteran, had suggested that it would be more appropriate to ask "Uncle Thủy" (me) to play that role. "You are old enough," Bình said, "and you were actually a war correspondent for many years. I accepted their invitation in a casual manner, never imagining that, thanks to them, I would soon have a very sincere and straightforward American friend, Wayne Karlin.

I said to them, "I've made documentary films all my life; I haven't the talent to dream up stories the way feature filmmakers do. So in the part I contribute, please allow me to tell only true stories—stories of real experiences that I actually had in wartime, without following any script at all." Also, the film included a story line about an American veteran meeting a veteran (me) from the other side of the war, so I asked that, if possible, the role of the former American GI who was to be my interlocutor be played by a former helicopter gunner. You should be aware that in the war zone of the South back then, I was most afraid of helicopters, not infantry soldiers, B-52s, B-57s, or artillery. I was afraid of helicopters, because they could finish us off in an instant, anywhere. They would chase us like a cat chasing a mouse, and our death could come in the blink of an eye.

Bình and Hạnh agreed! Only a few days later they invited me to their house on Lê Ngọc Hân Street so I could meet my "costar." I was astounded—not just taken by surprise—when before my eyes stood a former American GI, towering and gentle. At first he seemed to be a bit uneasy, for he had indeed been a gunner on a helicopter in South Vietnam in nearly the same time and place I had been. His name was Wayne Karlin.

Wayne, Bình, Hạnh, Phan Thanh Hảo, and I chatted for a long while. The next day, we went to the film locations—beneath a banyan tree, along a village road, atop a river dike during the harvest season, and next to farmers harvesting and threshing rice and spreading straw to dry. As Wayne and I strolled along these backdrops, we spoke only of things we had actually experienced in our own parts of the war. I didn't hesitate to tell Wayne how I feared and hated his helicopters more than anything, and Wayne confessed that from up in his helicopter, he would shoot at anything that looked like an enemy soldier on the ground.

Later, when I went to the United States in 2002, I worked with Wayne and other friends to compile a book in which Wayne repeated what he had told me that day, and added a further passage: "When I met him [Trần Văn Thủy] in Vietnam, and he confided to me how afraid he had been of helicopters back then, I was deeply saddened by the realization that if I had seen him on the ground back then, I would have shot him dead without the slightest pity or regret; and if I had done this, humankind would have suffered an immense loss."[2]

As a veteran of the Vietnam War, Wayne brought a great deal of experience and vision to his career of writing and teaching. Together with two other Americans, he and I took seventeen American students from the Maurice Kanbar Institute of Film and Television at New York University's Tisch School of the Arts to Vietnam for hands-on training. These youngsters were all American, but they came from different backgrounds: some were white, some black, and some yellow. Three were of Vietnamese background. Their point of entry to Vietnam was Nội Bài Airport near Hanoi. On their first night, they gathered in Sóc Sơn, north of Hanoi (at an educational training center), and built a campfire; then they went to Hanoi and visited the Temple of Literature and various museums. After that, they came with us on a tour of all of the regions of Vietnam. They were equipped with four cameras and other professional equipment. Our aim was to have them use what they filmed to make four documentary films about Vietnam on their return to the United States.

Wayne knew all of the wartime sites, battles, and stories by heart. His memory was marvelous. He gave explanatory lectures to his students whenever we came to well-known places in Central Vietnam, such as the Bến Hải River, Cồn Tiên, Dốc Miếu, Khe Sanh, Tà Cơn, Gio Linh, and Cửa Việt ... Thus the students had many notable experiences that would leave lasting impressions on their young minds.

Wayne had an unconditional faith in the explanatory lectures I gave to the students, but not exactly because I had experienced the war, or survived it, or because I was a documentary film director who had won international prizes—perhaps Wayne needed me on this trip simply because he cherished me, a friend whom he had come close to killing with the muzzle of his gun on the helicopter back then.

We took the students to many other places, and they conscientiously recorded scenes and stories. On the last night we had a dinner party at the New World Hotel in Saigon. It was truly a touching farewell party. At the end of the party, someone suggested that the students be allowed to freely roam the streets of the city, but I made a counter-suggestion: that they move to the top floor, where we would divide them into four groups, each with a camera. Each student in turn would express his or her feelings with regard to the Vietnam journey just completed. Each would be filmed at close range, one after the other, as they spoke. I could never have imagined what would happen or what the students would say. We all know that whenever Westerners, old or young, talk on camera, they will be self-confident, natural, and straightforward. These students were no exception. They all talked about their thoughts and feelings before and after they set foot in Vietnam, and their thoughts were extremely sincere and moving. Some wept as they spoke, others standing nearby wept, and even the person handling the camera wept at times. Wayne said, close to my ear, "There is no writer who can express such genuine, accurate, and moving things."

I said to the students, "Tonight you have done a wonderful and significant thing in speaking of your thoughts and feelings about war, and about the Vietnam War, before and after you came to Vietnam. As students learning the film profession, you must surely all understand that the hours of film you have just shot on these four cameras can serve to communicate the themes of your films. They can serve as opening words, or concluding words, or also as commentary. There is no writer, not even Wayne, your teacher, who can do better than that."

The students all loved and valued me, and some called me "Father." Before we parted, many students embraced me and sobbed, and they left behind farewell notes full of love.

As for Wayne, before he took leave of me, he gave me a sweatshirt on which were embroidered the words "College of Southern Maryland, CSM 1958"—a souvenir of his school, where I had visited him. He also gave me a photograph.

It was a black-and-white photograph in a wooden frame, twenty by sixteen millimeters. In it is Wayne as a youth, sitting in a helicopter, wearing an armored vest and a flight helmet, with his arms cradling a fast machine gun. It is a wartime photograph taken when he and I were in the war zone at the same place and the same time. How could such a photo be a gift from one to the other? It shouldn't be given—it would reawaken such painful memories. It couldn't possibly be given! But Wayne gave me that picture anyway.

As a documentary film director, I understand that there can be no image that is "forbidden to use"; the problem is one of placement, the words used to accompany it, and the meaning of the image in context.

I held the picture in my hands and then was very moved when I read the inscription:

For Anh Trần Văn Thủy. I'm glad I met you now, and not when this photo was taken.

Hòa bình ["peace"], your brother, Wayne Karlin.

I
WAR

1

The Swimmer

When I was a child, my family fled to the countryside after French soldiers came to our hometown and tried to kill us.[1] In the place we came for refuge, the person who cared for, fed, and taught me and my brothers and sisters was a wet nurse, a country woman, whom we called "Auntie," "Auntie Nhuận," out of love and respect. I remember a lullaby she used to sing to us:

> *Oh stork stepping sideways on the riverbank,*
> *Oh stork, how can you cast aside your mother's care?*
> *I ask you who was it that bore you,*
> *And why you cast her off and failed to nourish her.*
> *Remember former days when, going everywhere,*
> *She caught shrimp to keep you fed?*
> *You're ungrateful as a stone, oh stork,*
> *Your father's care, your mother's love, do you remember it?*

The words of this lullaby are closely tied to the months and years we spent in that small village surrounded by bamboo palisades, blending in my memory with the sound of swaying hammocks and afternoons when sunlight turned the rice fields to gold. Every evening when the gardening, rice husking, and rice pounding was over, and when the chickens had gone to their coops, Auntie Nhuận would set up a hammock on the porch, and would lie on it, telling us stories. Back then I was quite unaware that she was illiterate; I saw only that she had an endless fund of stories and poems in her memory that went on night after night.

And so one night, beneath the mysterious night sky full of twinkling stars, a big question mark concerning the nature of the finite and the infinite suddenly arose in my childish imagination, and I began to question my auntie as follows:

"If I go to the end of our village, what village will I come to, Auntie?"

"Our village is called An Phú. If you go to the end of An Phú, you'll reach An Lễ.

"And if I go to the end of An Lễ, what village will I come to?"

"If you go to the end of An Lễ, then you'll come to An Phong."

"And then what places will I come to?"

"After An Phong, you'll come to An Nhân, and then An Đạo."

"And if I go the end of An Đạo, what will I come to?"

"If you go to the end of An Đạo, you will come to the sea."

She explained these things to me with confidence. I was filled with endless admiration at the breadth of her knowledge. And then suddenly I got up and asked her, "And if I go to the end of all the seas, where will I come to, Auntie?"

In the depths of that dark night, my auntie was silent. From the time that I first started to understand things, I had never seen my auntie so downcast. In a voice full of sadness she answered, "Even I have no idea where you will arrive if you go to the end of all the seas."

I gradually grew up and gained a wider understanding of the world, while my auntie quietly passed away during my years abroad. She had no children, so her grave was desolate and lonely. Once, while lighting incense by her grave, I sorrowfully whispered the following words to her: "Oh, Auntie, I love you, for until you died, you never knew where a person would arrive after going to the end of all the seas. Now I know the answer, Auntie. If you go to the end of all the seas, passing all the oceans and all the continents, going on and on without stopping, you will at last return to your own homeland, to your native village, Auntie! I'll save some money to make a better grave for you. And please allow me to put on your headstone these words:

Here my auntie rests in peace,
An old country woman who could not read,
She was my first teacher."[2]

Like many other naive children in those days, I believed that the face of the earth was flat, like an enormous mat that went on and on as far as your eyes could see. That was the cause of my perplexity—if you just kept on going and going, where would you get to? One day, my teacher brought a globe of the earth to the class, and only from that point on did I realize that the earth was round. But at such a tender age, I surely could not imagine where someone might arrive after endless travel.

In my journey through the destructiveness of war and the winds and waves of life, I learned a great deal. I traveled to many places, heard many stories, and made the acquaintance of many people, until my hair turned gray. Only then did the answer to that childish question occur to me as a truth about my life: my endless travels had ended where they began, in my homeland.[3]

The year was 1946. The Franco-Vietnamese war erupted in Hanoi and then spread rapidly to all of the provinces. My home was in the town of Nam Định. One day French soldiers climbed over the surrounding wall and fired randomly into our house. They fired into the second and third stories, and even into a couple of passenger vehicles sitting in the front yard.

Abandoning his spacious villa with its yard and garden, my father led the entire family to a place of refuge in the countryside: An Phú village in Hải Hậu. A life of misery and privation began, and eventually the war found us there again. And yet, in spite of that, and even though it lasted no more than two or three years, my life in that farming village in the Red River Delta sowed beautiful memories in a six- or seven-year-old boy's soul that would never fade for the rest of my life. The melody of some country songs sounded to me like the heartbeat of the countryside. Though in later years, I would hear them sung again and again, they would never seem as beautiful and touching as those I heard and sang as a child.

Auntie Nhuận's husband and children had all died in the terrible famine in the year of the rooster (1945).[4] She couldn't read even half a word, but was a treasure house of traditional tales, such as "Tống Trân and Cúc Hoa" (a verse narrative about a husband who seeks his deceased wife in the other world), "Phạm Tải and Ngọc Hoa" (a verse narrative about a domestic love story with many supernatural elements), "Hoàng Trừu" (a verse narrative about the relationship of a Chinese prince and a Vietnamese princess), and many others. When the destructive land reform policy was implemented,[5] the authorities attempted to imprison my father and then force Auntie Nhuận to "denounce" him, saying that he had cruelly exploited those who worked for him. Auntie would have none of this, and replied that my father was her benefactor—during the famine of 1945 he had helped many survivors and seen to the burials of countless unclaimed corpses, as well as donating money for food to help people building a dike in his district in order to stave off more hunger.

Auntie Nhuận was a kind and honest person. Mr. Song, a paternal cousin who, with his wife and children, shared the house with them for a time, had a bit of gold that he feared might get lost in the upheavals, so he secretly buried it beneath one of the pillars of the house. Later, when he moved back to the city with his family, he confided this secret to Auntie, telling her the spot where the gold had been buried, and entrusting her with the task of digging it up and sending it to him. Auntie Nhuận used every possible means to have the gold conveyed to the city and delivered into his hands intact.

Both Auntie Nhuận and my father were born in 1902, when the French built the Paul Doumer (now Long Biên) Bridge in Hanoi. When she was sixty-two or sixty-three years old, my father bought a burial casket for her, and he even crawled in and lay down in it to try it out. Everyone in the house was, as was expected, aghast with horror, but they were also amused. Auntie used the casket to store rice. It was not until twenty years later (in 1983) that she died, beloved and grieved by all. Her death anniversary is the first one in the year in our family: the twelfth day of the first month of the lunar calendar, as recorded in our book of family records.

Auntie Nhuận left a deep impression in my soul. She looked after all five children in the family, one after another, as if they were her own, and they all loved her like a mother.

Auntie Nhuận was also the source of the title for my book *If You Go to the Ends of All the Seas*. It came from the question I posed to her when I was a child that she was never able to answer.

In 1949, French troops and local soldiers under French direction conducted a sweeping operation through our refuge in Hải Hậu. Rifle fire rang throughout the area, *rat-a-tat-tat*. The villagers ran in all directions. Women and girls, afraid of being captured and raped, smeared dirt on their faces and hid in the rice fields. My sisters did the same. My elder brother Trần Văn Vĩnh, fourteen years old, was shot dead. The bullet hit his heart, shattered his chest, and sliced through the woven reed bag on his back, making a dozen holes in the mosquito net he was carrying in the bag. Anh Động, the eldest son-in-law, carried Vĩnh's body on his back, crossing the rice field and a river, finally depositing it at the base of a banyan tree at the beginning of the village. The night was pitch-black. Here and there in the distance, we could still hear the *rat-tat-tat* of gunfire, and somewhere the dim light of a kerosene lamp kept struggling in the wind, showing the shaking figure of my father now lying down on the ground to embrace his son's corpse, weeping and weeping . . .

The funeral was hurried; the family borrowed Mrs. Ngũ's casket to bury him that same night. Poor Vĩnh, he was so kind, so good at school, and so loving to his younger siblings. Had he lived, Vĩnh would surely have been a firm source of support for me later on, though he was only four years older than I was.

After his death, my father decided to take the entire family back to the city, even though it was still occupied by the French army.

That was in 1949. My brothers and sisters recommenced their studies at school. In Hanoi, my eldest sister lived with her husband and children at 41 Ngô Sĩ Liên Street, across from the gate to a Chinese pagoda. When summer came, I went up to Hanoi, where I roamed around and practiced swimming at the Ấu Trĩ Viên (now called the Children's Palace). There I had a teacher and swimming classes. By age eleven, I was very skilled at swimming; I could do the breaststroke, the backstroke, the crawl, and more.

In Hanoi, many children did the same, but in practicing swimming, I never dreamed that as a little imp I was training myself in an essential skill, without which I would have been dead dozens of times as an adult on the battlefield. Our elders have a saying: "If you *are blessed*, you'll have children who know how to swim; if you *are cursed*, you'll have children who know how to climb."[6]

(Now, at seventy-something, I still swim fifteen or twenty hundred meters every day, without feeling any fatigue.)

We kids would roam around the streets, from Ngô Sĩ Liên, along Sinh Từ to Hàng Bông (Cotton Goods), Hàng Gai (Fishing Nets),[7] and Bờ Hồ (Lakeshore), all the way to the Children's Palace—just as if these places were next door to where we lived!

My youth included some experiences related to my later professional activities. As a result of my father's decision to *dinh tê* (a transliteration of *rentrer*, "to return to a city under French occupation"), I saw a great many films as a child during the period between 1949 and 1954. I was so in love with films that I spent all the pennies I could save in movie theaters. That is how I came to be familiar with such figures as Tarzan, Zorro, Charlie Chaplin, and films such as *Rashomon, I'm Trying to Feed My Child* (a Japanese film), *Bicycle Thieves, Samson and Delilah, Quo Vadis?, Ivanhoe, The Three Musketeers, Les Misérables,* and *Gone with the Wind* . . . as well as many other classic films. I even collected photos of all of the famous stars of that time, such as Robert Taylor, Clark Gable, Victor Mature, Lana Turner, and Elizabeth Taylor . . .

The first movie theater that I ever stepped into was the Bắc Đô (Northern Capital) on what is now Hàng Giấy (Paper Goods) Street. Something I have never forgotten happened that day. We had come to see *Tarzan*. When we little kids stepped into the theater, the lights had been turned out and the show was already in progress. We held on to each other's shirts as we sought places to sit down. It was so dark, we couldn't see a thing. Feeling about with our hands, our eyes glued to the screen, we stealthily sat down on seats that seemed to be nothing but hard edges. We couldn't understand why the seats seemed so uncomfortable, but we ignored our discomfort as we watched, transfixed by what was on the screen. Only when we stood up at the conclusion of the film did we see what the problem was: the theater manager had not bothered to set up all of the chairs, and the ones we had tried to sit down in were all upside down! We should have pushed them aside and sat on the floor. No matter; I'd been willing to pay the price in pain in order to become lost in the scenes playing on the screen.

I was also in love with the popular music of the day, such as *nhạc tiền chiến* ("prewar" music, a darkly soulful genre), and knew many songs by heart from childhood on. Later on these romantic songs would be strictly forbidden—people were sent to prison just for gathering and singing these songs to each other. This would prey greatly on my mind. I also pursued, though in vain, a course of study on the Hawaiian guitar with the musician Đoàn Chuẩn in 1958–59. Just recently, in 2010–11, I made a documentary film about the troubled history of what is known as "yellow music" (a term that in government parlance means "degenerate music").

After high school, I enrolled in a museum course in anthropology organized by the Ministry of Culture. The venue was 22 Hai Bà Trưng Street, formerly the Department of Museums and Preservation. It was directed by Đặng Xuân Thiều, a cousin of Mr. Trường Chinh (a former party chief). This course was to train activists for missions in the mountainous regions of the Northwest inhabited mostly by some of Vietnam's tribal minority peoples.

I completed the course and went north.

2

The Measuring Stick and the Mirror

The natural surroundings of the mountains where I was sent were of extraordinary grandeur, reflecting the awesome, limitless power of the Creator. The rivers rushed on impetuously like waterfalls, humming and resounding throughout the day and the night, from one generation to another, from one century to another, from one millennium to another, since the creation of Heaven and Earth. The stones, as small as marbles, or as big as a room, were all utterly smooth and round. When one watched the rising sun from a mountaintop, the jutting peaks of the layered mountain ranges below looked like the backs of so many camels lying at rest on the ground.

The year was 1960. The Thái-Mèo Autonomous Region, called that because it was the home of the ethnic minorities of those names, embraced eighteen districts, later organized into three provinces.[1] Those of us sent out to Lai Châu were regarded as people endowed with a spirit of volunteerism and able to endure difficulty and hardship. There were twenty of us, but some returned to the lowlands, some went on leave, and some went on other missions . . . leaving only me and Đặng Trần Sơn to go all the way to that location with Lương Quy Nhân, the chief of Lai Châu's Department of Cultural Affairs. The two of us were thus regarded as the first staff to join that nascent department.

Our "headquarters" were initially established in the mansion of Đèo Văn Long, once the king of the Thai region, located at the three-river crossing where the Nậm Na and Đà Rivers converge to form a larger river flowing into the lowlands. On the other side is Mường Lay. The entire multiroom mansion of the Thai king had been abandoned—it was now only a place to tether horses before crossing the river.

One room in the villa had a great square window through which the spectacle of peaks, rivers, clouds, jungle rain, mountain winds, glowing sunsets, and long, deep nights was like a series of pictures floating past the frame, now fast, now slow—as if they were scenes projected on a screen going on ceaselessly from day to day and month to month.

Of all the people who passed through this crossing—laborers transporting goods on horseback, or Xòe (a popular dance of the ethnic Thais, usually performed with fans or hats) dancing girls in the heyday of the Thai king—where are their souls now?

On the wall, hanging on either side of the window, were a measuring stick and a mirror. With no conscious intent whatsoever on the part of this curious young man, these things—the measuring stick and mirror next to the window—came one day to symbolize honesty and integrity in my dreamy imagination. And that thought began gradually to merge with my experience of the great hardships and upheavals of life, even when my hair had turned gray and my eyes had dimmed. Was this an omen appearing already in my early youth in the abandoned mansion in the Northwest so long ago? A square "picture screen" with vivid "film scenes," a measuring stick, and a mirror . . .

Đặng Trần Sơn and I would go into the jungle day in and day out to gather firewood, descend to a stream to fetch water for cooking rice, and then focus on our assignments. At night, fearing that tigers might come to stalk us, we would bang bamboo pipes on the floor in rhythm and sing at the top of our lungs. It was a beautiful stretch of life that contributed much to the character of two youths just setting out in their lives.

It was just like these familiar lyrics of bygone days: winding paths that seemed to have no end, going up and down rolling hills, twisting and turning. Sometimes, next to a stream, you could hear the leisurely sounds of a water-powered rice-hulling apparatus *thump-thwack, thump-thwack*, a sound that went on day and night, *thump-thwack, thump-thwack,* as slow and measured as the sound of time itself. This machine "worked" by itself all alone, without the shadow of a companion. The owner of the rice-husking apparatus might have been nearby, or hours away by foot. There were people passing through who would sit down and help turn the rice or scoop it out if the grains were sufficiently white already, and then pour in more unhusked rice. The rice was placed in plaited backpacks lying right next to the mortar.

Every now and then, we would come upon an empty thatched hut by the path, inside of which clusters of bananas hung, along with sweet potatoes or cassava roots, bamboo shoots, ears of corn, batches of eggs, and even chickens. Whoever needed anything could simply take it and leave some money in an adjacent basket.

I don't know how the simple people native to that locality referred to these places—perhaps they cared little about giving them a name. Later, when the Kinh people (lowland Vietnamese) went up there, they invented a name for them with a nice revolutionary flavor: "voluntary shops" (*quán tự giác*). Having been given such an attractive name, these places soon breathed their last and "voluntarily" died, because the goods inside them disappeared, and the money baskets remained empty. Anyone who knew and saw those lovely little shops along the wayside will surely feel some pain and regret when they remember the term "voluntary shop."

The thatched shops are shattered now and the water-run rice mortars abandoned. We Kinh people are like jungle demons; wherever we go, places endowed by nature with interest and beauty go to ruin, or are made to look more "interesting" and "beautiful," before they . . . die. The innocent soul of the jungles and mountains has been frightened away. Ah the Kinh . . . they are terrors to the jungles and mountains.[2]

November 26, 1960, was the day that I turned twenty. At a little past 4:00 in the morning, I began to climb the Mường Mô mountain slope. Not until midday did I reach the top and gaze at the distant houses down below, where some columns of blue smoke were rising. This was where the district office of Mường Tè was located, but one had to walk on until dusk to get there. Mường Tè was the district most remote from Lai Châu and also the northernmost point in the country. People say that when a rooster crows there, the sound can be heard in three countries. There were no decent roads, only trails traversing slopes and streams. This was the land of the most primitive tribes in northern Vietnam.

I was on an anthropological mission: my task was to seek to understand the nomadic tribes of that region and to produce written accounts concerning them. The location names there sounded strange to the ear:

Ca-lăng, Té Xứ, Pa Ủ, Pa Về Xủ, Mali Pho, Mali Chải. These places were then inhabited by such ethnic peoples as the Hà Nhì or U Ní, the Khù Xung (Suffer Together), and the Toong Lương (Yellow Leaf). In my various expeditions, I lived with "primitive" folk who wore only bits of grass to cover their lower bodies and nothing above. They kept some tools for making fire with flint, cut bamboo for simple dwellings, gathered banana leaves to shield themselves from the rain and the sun, and cleared patches of jungle large enough for their groups to reside. They were still attached to cave-dwelling ways of life. When food grew scarce with the disappearance of fruits, tubers, and game, and the thatch on their huts had turned yellow, then they would move on.

In 1960, when frontier troops first came upon them, these people were still living in a very simple manner. They used water only to drink; there was little concept of bathing. In the clearing where they lived, they used thick bamboo stalks to construct a frame platform for me to sleep on, while they themselves lay on the dirt below. In the evenings they would make a fire, call and croon a bit, and then stretch out next to each other to go to sleep. On nights when I grew wakeful, I would see the fire nearly extinguished, while my hosts lay embracing each other in a circle around it. They practiced group marriage, and their children belonged to the whole group; no one had any idea to which parents they belonged.

I investigated the lives, activities, habits, and origins of several other ethnic peoples as well, and made careful notes for anthropological reports that I sent back to Hanoi.

3

Do You Feel Honored?

Mr. Lương Quy Nhân, the chief of Lai Châu's Department of Cultural Affairs, was a very good, kind man of Thai ethnicity. He was also a poet of some reputation. Later on, he became a deputy chairman of Lai Châu Province. When he first came to Lai Châu to assume his duties there, he fell ill and grew feeble. Though I had no medical training, I had to give him injections.

Đặng Trần Sơn and I did everything necessary to start up the department, drawing up a plan for establishing offices, a plan for training procedures, a set of guidelines for regional activities, personnel recruitment and instruction, a plan for setting up a performing arts troupe, and so on. In addition, I often organized mobile cinema and cultural teams, traveling to remote mountainous places to set up photo exhibits, song and dance performances, and films for the local people. Gradually, I became aware of the great effectiveness of film, a medium inherently more powerful than lengthy speeches or explanations. Film acted quickly and strongly on viewers, especially films dealing with science. From that time on, I had a liking for the way the medium could be used to express thoughts and feelings on particular problems.

I wrote a letter many pages long to a provincial leader asking for permission to return to the lowlands and study film, so as to come back later for continued service in Lai Châu. But, as it turned out, my soon-to-come studies in film school and my later journey to the south were done in obedience to official decisions, and had nothing to do with my own plans or those of the province I served.

Among other duties, I acted as the department secretary, so all office correspondence passed through my hands. Thus, one day I saw a notice about a film course with the curious name "Fighting America for National Salvation." I spoke to Mr. Lương Quy Nhân and asked him for permission to attend the course.

"Oh, sure—it'll be fine if you go!"

Such was Mr. Lương Quy Nhân's belief in others. I often met "gullible" people like him in my life. I use the term in jest. Such humane and virtuous people helped me when I was most in need.

"Then how do we go about it?" I asked my boss.

"Well, the document's right here—it shows that the highlands are regarded as a priority. Shall I make the decision, then?"

Mr. Nhân signed the document and various other papers as well, including the one to terminate my salary. He said, "If you can join the course, fine. If not, tear up all the papers and come back here."

"Our Kinh people are almost never as open-hearted as that," I thought to myself.

The roads leading from Lai Châu all the way to Hanoi were very hard to traverse, especially since American planes had begun attacking the area. From Lai Châu I walked to Tuần Giáo, then at Tuần Giáo I had some business that required me to walk back to Điện Biên, which cost me an entire week. At that time, the town of Điện Biên was just a dirt road with a row of thatched dwellings on either side. There was no such thing as a shop to eat at; in the early mornings there were a couple of peddlers selling *bánh cuốn* (steamed rolls) and *xôi* (sticky rice) as snacks for travelers; but as soon as the sun began to beat down, they disappeared so as to avoid American airplanes. Sơn La and Mộc Châu were also very primitive and neglected.

This was in the middle of 1965.

With a worn knapsack on my back and a cloth bag hanging from my neck—the bag that the artist Đặng Trần Sơn had used originally to carry painting supplies—filled with snacks protected with a lining of banana leaves, I went on, eating by hand as I walked, stumbling along the rough hilly roads of the Northwest. I would walk by day and sleep in hamlets near the road by night.

On reaching Thuận Châu, I managed to hitch a ride in a vehicle and arrived in Hanoi a few days later. I went to Cao Bá Quát Street, where the cinema headquarters were located and where students were being recruited. I reported there and presented my papers and was immediately told, "The entrance exam was already held two weeks ago—you can't do anything without that!"

So the game was over! I would have to tear up all my papers and return to Lai Châu, where I would resume my routine work. But, as I considered this, I had a second thought—and began to hope that somewhere in Hanoi there might be some hidden opportunity.

I had no acquaintances, and looked dark and rough, like a zombie. I ventured to knock on a few doors, but the officials I spoke with all said the same thing: "I see, but you must take the exam!" I spent a week wandering around. Finally, I went to the Cinema Department on Hoàng Hoa Thám Street to see if I could find any official there to whom I could present my case and make an appeal. I saw a man with white glasses awkwardly making his way down the sloping street, and found it a bit difficult to guess what sort of person he might be.

"Excuse me, sir, I've just come from the mountains and have a problem; can you help me out?"

"What's your problem?"

After I explained, I said, "Can I ask you sir, what your position is here? And your name?"

"I've got no position or power at all. I'm Nông Ích Đạt! I'm from the highlands also. I see you're in a tough situation—you've been running around here for several days—so things must be really bad for you, right?"

He took my hand and said, "Follow me."

We went up a flight of stairs and stood before a man who I later learned was Mr. Trần Đức Hinh, deputy director of the Cinema Department, principle of the Cinema Academy and the person in charge of the new training course.

"Mr. Hinh, this fellow has just returned here from the Northwest. He's got a bunch of files and documents directing him to come here. The distance was great, and there were bombs dropping all along the way, so he didn't arrive until the deadline was past. If you don't give him some consideration you'll be making a mistake. Let me tell you right now that mountain folk like me can't be found anywhere even if you go digging for seven days. This fellow is Vietnamese, but he lives and works up there in the mountains. If a Nông, or Lò, or Ma tribesman (names of ethnic minority peoples) isn't available, then you've got to give this fellow a chance and train him! Now that his paperwork's done and his salary terminated, he'd be out in the streets like a beggar! He's been running around here for days already."

Mr. Hinh said, "All right, let me see what can be done."

It was due to sheer luck or God's blessing, that I ran into Nông Ích Đạt—otherwise, I wouldn't be sitting here today recounting these tales. Those icy-faced bureaucrats always despised mountain folk as if they were garbage.

(Much later, feeling sick and tired of life and desperate in spirit, film director Nông Ích Đạt and his wife took sleeping pills to commit suicide—but they didn't die! Others managed to rescue them. But they didn't live very long after that anyway. Everyone felt pity for this kindhearted, innocent man.)

Deep in my heart, I thought I would return to the mountains at the conclusion of my studies anyway, having no intention to compete with city folks in the lowlands. I was self-conscious about my place in society and suffered from the feeling that I was inferior to others.

Mr. Hinh wrote a note as follows to Trương Huy, the school's manager of academic affairs: "Please give careful consideration to this case. In the opinion of Mr. Nông Ích Đạt, this case should be reconsidered, because this man has just returned from the highlands."

Mr. Hinh instructed me to come to 33 Hoàng Hoa Thám Street, the location of the film school. There were just some thatch-roofed houses there, and a large open field.

In the end, I was accepted by the school with the following condition: "You didn't take the qualifying exam, so the school has no idea what your abilities may be. Try doing the coursework—if you do it well, fine; but if you fail and are disqualified, we will return you to the Department of Cultural Affairs in Lai Châu." In such circumstances I had no choice but to behave and do the work in an obedient, painstaking manner.

The course began in August 1965, seven months after American ground troops landed in Vietnam, and was to conclude in August 1967. I had taken only the first half of the course when an urgent directive came from the party's Central Organization Department and Central Reunification Department saying that six cameramen must be sent immediately to the war zone in the South.

The school had 120 students at that time, divided into four groups pursuing different curricula: producing, script writing, filming, and directing. I was taking the filming course. We did our training outside the city at an evacuation site.[1] On days off, the other students would return to Hanoi, while I would remain at the school, focusing on the course materials.

In the first year we studied theory without equipment. Only on two occasions did I get to touch a film camera: an ancient 16-millimeter Admiral from Czechoslovakia. I was never allowed to shoot a scene, but I was allowed to press some buttons on the machine on two occasions. The first was to test the telescopic lens, aiming the camera at the same subject and trying the telescopic mode, the normal mode, or the wide-angle mode to see how the image would change. The second time was to test the sensitivity of the film. Using light speed settings of 21, 18, or 17 for alternately strong and weak lighting, I opened the lens cylinder, pressed buttons for "sufficiently bright," "excessively bright," and "insufficiently bright," and then developed the images to see what the results were.

Given such a primitive level of skill, it wasn't possible back then for someone to even apply for an entrée as an assistant cameraman in a film production company in the North. In spite of that, many of the people who participated in this training course became successful—too many even to list their names—and would contribute significantly to the achievements of Vietnamese cinema. Nowadays, classmates from those times meet annually to reminisce about the period of evacuation to the countryside and tell stories about their teachers and friends.

One day in the middle of 1966, as the war raged on, Mr. Nguyễn Đức, secretary of the school's party executive committee, called me into his office and said, "The school board and our friends feel that you have made good progress in your studies and have demonstrated a serious attitude." He mentioned that the leadership needed people to go immediately to perform missions in the war zones in the South—whether in the 5th zone (the Central Highlands), the Mekong Delta, or in Quảng Trị (just south of the 17th parallel)[2] was as yet unknown. "How do you like the idea?" he asked. "Is it okay with you? Do you feel honored?"

I said, "Thank you for the attention you have bestowed on me and for calling me in for a chat. I lived in the Northwest for five years and have grown accustomed to hardship, so I shall have no reluctance to go to the war zones. But I wish to complete my studies. Then you can tell me to go wherever you wish. Another thing to consider is that when Lai Châu sent me here to study, they hoped that I would return there to continue my services.

"You asked if I feel honored by this. I would like to reply that I do not feel honored, because the last five or six years of hard work and privation in the Northwest have already given me the highest degree of honor. But if the leadership wishes to give me this new assignment, I will obey the orders, though my wish is to complete my course of study."

Mr. Đức said, "According to regulations, you must all be party members.[3] The others, like Hiến and Sửu, are already members. As for Trâm and Trường, they're from the South, so it's not a problem. Only you aren't yet a party member. We'll look into this. Your attitude is good. Your admission to the party will be a mere formality."

"If you have come to this decision, then there's nothing more for me to say."

This "special favor" troubled me and caused me many sleepless nights. I thought that my "improper" family background would make admission to the party next to impossible. Being a party member or not wasn't important. Far more worrisome was that someone going to my native village to investigate would discover my "improper" background—and then I wouldn't be allowed to continue my studies; in other words, even my cinematic career would be ruined.[4]

I spoke frankly to Mr. Nguyễn Đức, saying, in effect, "Let me complete my studies; I don't care where you send me afterward. My family background isn't simple."

Mr. Đức said that the board would take care of this.

The man who took my papers back to my place of origin to check out my background was Mr. Võ Hoàng Khả, a party cell secretary. He was a southerner dispatched by the army to join the training course as a student, a pleasant man.

Only much later, when I had survived the war and returned to the North, did Mr. Khả tell me how he had met my father in Thượng Trại Hải Hậu (where my family was evacuated; my home was still in the city). When my father learned of the background check, he shook his head in deep melancholy.

According to Mr. Khả, when he told the local officials of the check, they flatly objected. "This family just won't do!" they snapped. Mr. Khả replied that the leadership required that all people going to the frontline be party members, because it was so fiercely dangerous there, especially for cameramen—very few of them would survive and return intact. I had no idea what kind of report Mr. Khả made to the school, but they went ahead with the plan to admit me into the party.

My admission was smooth and speedy—the only hitch was that the next steps were all rushed forward. I was urgently sent to Hòa Bình Province to join a group assembled for training for the journey to the South (known as *đi B,* or "going to the South").[5] So there was no time for any admission formalities at the cinema school. Only when we were in Hoà Bình preparing to depart in a vehicle for Quảng Bình did someone read out the admission decision to me.

From then until now—late 2012—no one at all in the rest of my family has been allowed to become a party member, including a dozen or so brothers, sisters, and in-laws, among whom several have worked for dozens of years in government. My younger sister applied to two schools, the Hanoi music school and the army music school. Though she obtained very high scores in the qualifying exams for both schools, she was not admitted to either due to her "improper background."

Going South

The group in which I went to the South had more than fifty doctors, some of whom had just graduated, and seven young men with cinematic training, including two who were originally from the South: Trường and the ophthalmologist Đặng Thùy Trâm, who would become famous after her death.[1]

Later Trường defected to the other side, and spoke over the radio. I even heard his voice coming down from a helicopter, addressing us by name: "Come over to the open arms that await you with the government of national legitimacy . . ."

Trường's was a long and sad story. He had many problems before the departure for the South; recounting them all here would be a distraction. When he reported to 51 Trần Hưng Đạo Street in Hanoi for transport to Hòa Bình, we all sat in a *đít vuông* ("square-backed") jeep used by junior officers in the Soviet army, while *đít tròn* ("round-backed") jeeps were used by more senior officers. Trường's young and pretty wife clung to him and wouldn't let the vehicle start. Trường indifferently patted her on the shoulder and stroked her cheek, saying, "Well, that's enough, go back now." And so the engine sprang to life and we started off.

That image has remained imprinted on my memory—it is a terrible image. After the end of the war in 1975, I went to the South many times and looked for Trường, but couldn't find him. Among the journalists, artists, and filmmakers, there were many people who defected in response to the "open arms" call, including even Mr. Lê Bá Huyến, who had studied in Russia and was the assistant director of the well-known film *The Rising Wind* (*Nổi Gió*).

After a whole month of eating good food and doing nighttime training exercises, such as climbing up and down mountains with heavy back loads, we set forth from Hòa Bình, traveling by day and resting by night. We cooked food along the way and shared our meals.

Many things happened on the way as we trekked along the steep and winding paths that led to the South, but what I remember most of all concerned Dr. Đặng Thùy Trâm. The people in the group were all young intellectuals with minds that were pure and full of merriment. We loved and respected each other very much.

As we were passing through Lao territory, I began to feel something unusual in my stomach. It had been hurting for a long time, but I knew that if I reported this fact, I would be accused of ideological deviation, of wanting to take a "U-turn" back to the North. I gritted my teeth and bore the pain without saying anything. I refrained also from confiding in anyone, and had already managed to cover a long part of the journey. Once when walking along a level stretch, I was suddenly convulsed by a severe spasm of pain in my stomach. I collapsed into a sitting position on the side of the path and unfastened my backpack. Dân, Sửu, Hiến, Trâm, and others rushed to give me encouragement. I told them all to go on ahead; I would rejoin them after resting a bit. But I was in such pain that I lay back on the grass—I could no longer sit.

The man in charge of our group was Chuyên, a man from the 5th Zone (Central Highlands). He was about ten years older than the rest of us. Seeing me sprawled on the ground in agony, he said sarcastically, "My, oh my, when going into a land of death, how many kinds of pain appear!"

Looking stern, Thùy Trâm said, "You are a doctor—how can you say that?"

Trâm told me to lie back, then rolled up my shirt, applied a plaster bandage, then gave me three shots of atropine around my navel. The atropine was only to induce numbness and reduce pain.

After more than two long months of arduous and rapid travel, climbing up and down mountains and crossing rivers, we arrived at the jungle base camp of the 5th Zone Propaganda Unit, a high mountainous area in Quảng Nam close to the Laotian border. Trâm and others had to go further; we, however, remained at that location.

Everyone in Trâm's group went ahead, but Trâm lingered, reluctant to leave us. Finally Dân, myself, and a few others who had been close to each other throughout the journey gathered around to bid farewell to her. We never met her again afterward, and we could not communicate with each other, though Trâm's image remained always in our minds: a gentle girl from Huế, a good friend.

And so the war ended, and the diary of Đặng Thùy Trâm resurfaced, was published, and became a very popular book. Because I had been close friends with Trâm on the journey to the South, I have taken a keen interest in this event and have my own thoughts about it.

I don't know who first said that when soldiers from the other side killed Đặng Thùy Trâm and found her diary, and an American soldier was about to burn it, Trung Hiếu, a sergeant in the Army of the Republic of Viet Nam (ARVN), said, "Don't burn it, there's already fire in it."

In Vietnamese, that word "fire" connotes a kind of ideological rhetoric. Is it true that Sergeant Hiếu said that? It's a little hard to believe that he used such political language. With bombs and bullets exploding on all sides, who could have had time to read it and learn what was really in there? Could a sergeant who, as we have come to know, was not fond of socializing, and was a person of very few words, have said something so rhetorical, so theatrical? Especially in the midst of a fierce battle?

Whoever has read this diary, with its unpolished, sincere language written by a good, gentle girl will have found that it overflows only with private thoughts and feelings. If it has fire, it might have been added by someone infatuated with "stage operas" [i.e., agitprop].

When Đặng Thùy Trâm was praised and blown up to heroic proportions, and when thousands of articles about her followed, Thanh Thảo, a poet from Quảng Ngãi, the place where Trâm met her death, looked at her story from a different angle. This is what he wrote:

> I was unable to keep back my tears when I read the last line of the letter that Đặng Thùy Trâm sent to Khiêm, her sworn elder sister, dated May 20, 1970: "If, in the days to come, when our land is at peace, you return and find that I am no longer among the living, will you remember your petty bourgeois younger sister? If so, then please light a stick of incense for me." Thus it appears that right up to the moment when she was about to sacrifice her life, Thùy Trâm was still troubled by the term "petty bourgeois," an expression that people had clearly used more than once to define her, and to such an extent that at last she had to accept this definition, with bitterness.

But what is a "petty bourgeois?" It has been a long time since I've heard the term used, perhaps because the people who used to define others as such have "bypassed the petty bourgeois phase," so as to advance straight to a "fully bourgeois" status. I in fact remember now that when I was an inexperienced newcomer to the war zone, I was very displeased when a person would use that term behind my back; naturally it was to classify me as a "petty bourgeois." But what on earth did it mean? In those days, all I had, aside from my "teeth and testicles," were two uniforms, an undershirt, and a few shorts—thus I often had to do "plain" laundering, washing these things with water alone, for there was no soap. I existed simply—where was there any money to buy soap? Taking stock of all my "property" at that time, I can't see anything at all of sufficient value to give me the privilege of being referred to so generously as a "petty bourgeois"!

Since Thùy Trâm entered the war zone four years before me, she no doubt had far fewer possessions than I had. The class of people regarded as "northern intellectuals" who entered the war zone, as we did then, had no possessions other than a bit of knowledge provided us by our schooling, and, as a slight addition, some private thoughts and feelings. Our thoughts and feelings came from our hearts. We didn't (or didn't yet) know how to lie, or how to repeat what others said so as to benefit from it. We lived on scanty, shared rations and said what we thought. We had no thoughts at all that might be considered incorrect; the only thing was that, just like Thùy Trâm, we were very allergic to lying and cheating, and to ways of living, speaking, and thinking that we thought were not honest. There were many instances of "mean" behavior in the midst of that great war—that could be accepted, because it was a simple life. There were "mean" people right on the battlefield, where life and death were but an inch apart. That too had to be accepted! But when these "mean" actions and "mean" people struck and mocked gentle, honest, and innocent people who didn't know how to defend themselves, then it was very painful. How cruel it was that those people who were defined by the rhetorical term "petty bourgeois" happened to be the victims of murky, dishonest, below-the-belt blows and mockeries. Being a nice yet straightforward man, I was often in a rage due to these blows and mockeries.

Now, reading Thùy Trâm's dairy, I feel even greater compassion for her. Not everyone could surmount such painful tests.

If Trâm were still alive today, I'm sure she would not let the diary be published. She would live in obscurity—who knows, perhaps like Sergeant Nguyễn Trung Hiếu, living beyond Time. In times like ours, people like Trâm would lead sad lives. The road of advancement, from infirmary chief to hospital director, deputy director or director of the Public Health Department, and so on upward would without doubt have been very difficult for a person like Trâm. Even if she had had a distinguished record that showed she was both "red" and "skilled," a person so absolutely pure and honest would have found it hard to achieve success. So I believe that if she were still alive, she would suffer.[2]

Thảo is a person whom I value and respect for his talent and integrity. I shared many deep recollections with him when I went back to Quảng Ngãi with a film crew to make the film *The Sound of a Violin at Mỹ Lai*. Having both been in the cruel and bloody battle zone, he and I had deep-rooted recollections that only people like us who have taken part in wars could fully appreciate.

Actually, the feeling that war is heroic can only exist for brief moments; few who have really witnessed its terrible ravages can tell war stories in a heroic mode. In fact, in many interactions with an audience, I said that it would have been best if we had managed to avoid that bloody war altogether. I spoke thus because I had escaped death a thousand times, but not so that I could survive to sit around here bragging.

Don't suppose that I'm speaking satirically—if the poor soul of Đặng Thùy Trâm were here, I'm pretty sure that she would confirm that there were lots of people many times more heroic than she. That view is not at all wrong—the only difference is that those people don't have dairies; and secondly, they have not yet died.

5

Rebirth

No sooner did we step into the "battlefront" than we had to throw ourselves at once into . . . hill farming!

In the 5th Zone battlefront area, we had to put up not only with *pháo bầy* (coordinated artillery barrages from warships and firebases, all falling on one location), CBU bombs,[1] B-57 and B-52 bombers, and mopping-up operations by the Americans, but also with many other things no less terrible, such as hunger, malaria, disease, and scarcity. We lacked everything: food, clothing, medicine, and even light, because we had to be active at night, working in the deep jungle, hiding in underground shelters that were wet, humid, and moldy; we even lacked air to breathe.

Whether you were a journalist or an agitprop artist, nobody cared. You had to produce your own food for self-reliance for six months, cultivating land to grow corn or rice for the rest of the year, while the army would supply food for six months only. In the 5th Zone, food rationing was reduced further to five months, and in film units, it was reduced by another ten days. This meant that every year, we had to grow "self-reliance" crops that would last for seven months and twenty days.

One of our most terrible experiences during the war was hill farming. I would fall into a rage whenever I thought about it. If they wanted us to grow crops, then why the hell didn't they just let us stay in the North and do it in Hòa Bình, instead of coming all the way down here to suffer? Many people died of hunger. The people in our film unit had to forage for food all year long, clearing a number of hills that were so large and far apart that we couldn't hear each other even by hailing; then, after the clearing was done, we had to wait for the grass to dry out, so we could set fire to it. In burning grass, we were inadvertently telling the enemy where we were. Yet we kept on doing it diligently, enduring hunger to clear the hills for farming, and burning whatever we could. Afterward we used sharpened sticks to punch holes in the ground in which to place corn seeds; we worked in pairs, one person punching the holes, and the other putting in the seeds. This primitive punching-and-planting routine made us dizzy. With the war raging on, and with equipment and manpower invested at great hardship and sacrifice, we had to throw everything aside to be preoccupied with food! Then after all that work, we had to wait for the harvest, wait for the corn to sprout and bear ears, so as to have something to put in our mouths! That hill farming took up so much of our time that even on fine days when there were events worth filming, we were unable to touch our cameras.

Compared with my companions on the same journey to the South, such as Dân, Hiếu, and Sửu, I was lucky, in that I was able to leave the Trung Son mountains and go down to the lowlands not long after crossing the 17th parallel, while Trường and Trâm had to continue further to the South.

Going down to the lowlands was dangerous, but at least there our stomachs stayed pretty full, for local people would feed us. We had to move furtively, but once we had something to eat, we recovered a bit. Since there was much fighting going on there, we also actually had some stories to film. Of course, it was more dangerous and closer to death.

After wheedling my superiors, I was given a very good 16-millimeter camera, a Paya Polex, with thirty canisters of film. As I didn't know much about film stock, I was quite reassured when those superiors told me, "The film stock you received consists entirely of Agfa color negatives produced in West Germany; it's really good. The film and camera were all left behind by a Chinese film crew—there's no way we could have imported such equipment." Who could have known that this excellent Agfa color film would later on plunge me into misery!

I have many recollections of the days when I shot the film *People of My Homeland*. There was an old man who did paintings there, Teacher Niên, an educated man. He had translated propaganda pamphlets aimed at South Korean troops into Mandarin.[2] Later on, a spy reported his activities, and the Koreans killed him.

I stayed at the old man's house many times. He had a son who had gone to the North, and who later became a ranking official. After 1975, another son, Mr. Toàn, older than me, became the head of the Education Department in Duy Xuyên District. From time to time, he wrote me letters couched in very affectionate terms.

The Thu Bồn River has a vast sandy islet in the middle where the Chiêm Sơn Bridge crosses over it. South of the bridge lay the village of Xuyên Trường. The old man's hamlet lay right next to the Thu Bồn River.

During the war we had to be careful—wherever we were, everything had to be within arm's reach; we couldn't leave our pants in one place and our shirts in another. There would be no time to gather them—we had to scoop everything up in a few seconds and run at top speed—whether down to the river or down to an underground shelter depended on circumstances. The problem was not about our possessions, but rather that things left behind were evidence that someone in the area was protecting the Việt Cộng, so houses would be burned and people killed.

When I first came down to the lowlands, I was a good-looking young man. With a movie camera on my back, walking down to the marketplace in the liberated zone, people would call me *thằng tây con* ("little expat"; literally "young Westerner"), since I looked so bewildered . . . Once we were sleeping next to Bàn Thạch Market when an artillery barrage started. At such times you have to roll to the ground at once or crawl into a shelter, but I kept lying in my hammock. Mr. Tý—a local man who acted as guide, protector, and mentor for me—said, "You must be crazy!"

"How so?"

"Get down from the hammock and crawl into the shelter now!"

Later Mr. Tý said, "Why are you so careless?"

When artillery barrages came, I felt no urge to lie down—I was merely bewildered because I thought that my body would be the same size, whether standing or lying. I hadn't the slightest idea what to do, because nobody had trained me for those circumstances.

The whole area to which I was assigned was devastated, houses blown apart, pigs and chickens on the loose. Because of this, Mr. Tý took pity on me and followed me around protectively. Speaking with some superiors, Mr. Tý said, "If you don't let me go with him he'll sooner or later end up dead! He doesn't know a thing!"

It was tense and ferocious, with never a moment to relax. We lived in perpetual fear. Among the people in our group, there were Sơn, a teacher from Hải Phòng, and Ba, a local guerilla who had a Lambretta [pedicab]. Another person who was very important to my moviemaking in the 5th Zone was the above-mentioned Mr. Tý—he was born in the Year of the Rat (Mậu Tý), and his pen name was Triều Phương. He was a poet and educator who for a period of time was the head of the education department of a district, and at another time was the head of the performing arts troupe of Quảng Đà Province.

His wife, chị Hai Hoàng, and her family lived in a disputed area near Núi Bà market, where she ran a good business. The local authorities knew that her husband was a Việt Cộng (VC) and her family used to house VC soldiers sneaking in and out, but as a smart business woman, she managed to survive and got away without arrest for quite some time. Finally, though, she was caught and imprisoned for aiding and abetting the VC.

This man Tý took pity on me, and followed me everywhere after getting the approval of our superiors. Later on, Tý wrote me many letters, even after I had returned to the North. His letters were immensely touching, and his children still preserve them.

Wherever we went in those days, we first had to check out the locations of the entrances to the shelters—hidden tunnels and spider holes—before washing, seeking food, or discussing work. We couldn't do anything before knowing where the shelters were. Once in Xuyên Trường, near the house of Teacher Niên, we had gathered together to pass the night exchanging jokes, when at about 4:30 the next morning, a swarm of choppers flew right over our heads; we knew immediately that American troops would soon be pouring out of them. And this in fact was what immediately happened; there were so many troops that they could have encircled the whole area holding hands. They started a sweep operation, moving into the village. Anh Sơn, the teacher from Hải Phòng who had lain chatting with us during the night, was shot dead the moment he ran out of the house. As we scattered after him, we could see him lying face-down, his upper body submerged in water. When I recalled this later on, I was always obsessed with the thought of his parents—what would they have felt if they had seen that tragic sight?

Having no time to flee further away, we ran for the hidden tunnel entrances. The tunnels all had ventilation holes hidden in clumps of bamboo or reeds, but it had rained the previous night, and the ventilation holes were plugged up. I had jumped into a one-man spider hole, followed by Mr. Ba, and a moment later Mr. Tý jumped in as well. There we were, the three of us crouched in a small shelter made for one person with the ventilation hole blocked. With the entrance cover closed, we could hardly breathe; I was unaccustomed to this.

Down in the spider hole, there was only a brief interval before I began to suffocate. Unable to bear it any longer, I said, "Anh [Brother] Tý! Let me get out!"

I thought that if I remained inside, I would surely die—die like Lê Anh Xuân (a war hero). If I crawled out, they might not see me; if they saw me, they might not fire; and if they fired, they wouldn't necessarily kill me.

The sound of helicopters. The sound of people shouting. The sound of gunfire and exploding grenades. I don't know when I lost consciousness. When you can't get oxygen, death comes in a strange manner; you have to experience it to know what it's like. It felt like a steel band around my head growing tighter, ever tighter, ever tighter. My brain was about to break apart. When I started to lose consciousness, I had only one thought: "This is too shameful, too illogical." I could imagine all other types of privation in life: food, clothes, medicine, love, sunlight—but I could not imagine the lack of oxygen.

When I pleaded to get out, Mr. Tý said, "Impossible! If they find out, they'll burn the house and kill everyone up there, not just you."

But finally Mr. Tý couldn't bear being in that hole either; he knew that remaining in it would end up in an awful death. As a local man, Mr. Tý was familiar with these games, and, as the last to enter the shelter, he was still clear-headed. He gently pushed the cover up a bit. When I came to, I saw that he was propping up my chin and pressing my nose to the slight opening. Awakening thus in Mr. Tý's arms, I was very moved.

It was then about 10:00 a.m. I said, "Enough, anh Tý—let's just get out!"

"Impossible!"

"Let's do this, anh Tý. We can't bring up all our gear. If we're still alive, then we can come back to find it. I'll leave everything here; just let me get out. Whether you two come with me or not is up to you."

I raised the cover and tumbled out, leaving my hat, sandals, film and camera, and everything else. After crawling a few meters from the underground shelter, I turned over on my back and gasped. I was in a field of the leafy grass that people used to thatch their homes. Never before in my life had I felt that air was so precious, so sweet!

A moment later, I felt someone bump my foot. Mr. Tý had come up. A few minutes later, Mr. Ba emerged as well. The three of us lay stretched out next to each other. The grass field was a few hundred meters wide.

The sound of gunfire had died down. A group of American soldiers carried a big mirror out of a house. They slapped soap on their faces and shaved, then opened some cans and had a meal. One thing at a time; just the style of Americans. We'd all go to perdition if they saw a few Việt Cộng fellows reflected in the mirror.

The three of us lay on our backs gazing at the sky, filling our lungs with delicious air. A woodpecker was hopping about on a chinaberry branch, *cheep, cheep . . . cheep, cheep.*

It was so happy, so free—not miserable like us.

Tý thrust an M26 hand grenade into my hand. Quietly, I asked, "How do you throw it?"

"You remove this wire pin and then throw it. Don't let this lever spring off in your hand, or we're all goners."

After crawling some distance with the grenade, I found that it greatly impeded my progress, so I gave it back to Mr. Tý. I had never received any training in weaponry.

I wore only a pair of shorts and a short-sleeved shirt. I followed the other two, crawling like a centipede, without hat or sandals, through orchards, through ditches, through water buffalo stalls and latrines, my hands and feet all scratched up.

"Where are we crawling to?"

"Up to Dựng Mountain."

"When will we get there?"

"It's not far at all, a few kilometers only."

Though we were moving through an area under the surveillance of American and ARVN troops,[3] there were times when we could stand up and walk. We made good time, and by the time we reached the mountain slope, afternoon was shading into dusk. The three of us were all wearing the same "uniform": shorts and short-sleeved shirts, dirty and ragged, and with nothing in our stomachs.

By nighttime, we had crawled to Mount Dựng. This was a mountain formation that jutted out into the ocean, very near the infamous place known as the Vĩnh Trinh Dam, where a massacre occurred in the time of Ngô Đình Diệm, the former prime minister of Vietnam.

We came to a cave—it was a sort of crevice where the rock had split horizontally. Inside there were spots where water had collected, and spots that were dry. It was high enough only to sit or lie in. Silvery moonlight and chilly mist flowed into the cave. When we first entered it, it seemed utterly silent, but after that we heard whispering into which were mixed the dialects of North, South, and Central Vietnam, the voices of other fighters hiding in the cave.

Around 4:00 a.m., I said, "Anh Tý, let's just go on. One way or another, they'll discover this place. If they spray us with flame throwers, we'll all be burned up."

We started to crawl out. But where could we go? Wherever we went, we would end up being in the same area. All that day we wandered through abandoned fields and houses, great numbers of them, all utterly desolate. There were even some bonsai and some stately old trees around the houses, but the dwellings themselves had become gaunt, empty shells. And there was nothing whatsoever to eat. When night came again, we didn't return to the cave but sat at the edge of a rice field. The mosquitoes swarmed; the only way of dealing with them was to break off a leafy branch and keep waving it back and forth until the branch lost all its leaves, and then break off another branch and do the same; otherwise the mosquitoes would suck us dry.

Finally, after six days, we came to a large stream. This was a semi-mountainous region; the banks were steep on both sides. The three of us stripped and went down to the stream naked, so as to bathe and wash our clothing to relieve our itching. Suddenly, thunderous artillery fire began raining down on the area where we were bathing, and we ran for our lives, still naked.

We thought it would be simple—just keep running along the sloped riverbanks—we'd be safe. But we had no inkling that the stream was on the enemy's maps. The spotters could peer down at us through their binoculars and call in artillery to fire on us at the coordinates. Artillery fire followed us wherever we ran—I don't understand why we all survived intact. Later—perhaps when we ran beyond the range of their observation, or of their coordinates—they ceased firing.

We ran on to the Vĩnh Trinh Dam. Right next to it was a railroad. People had removed the railroad ties to build an A-shaped shelter. The three of us crawled into it.

Only a few minutes later, the enemy started bombarding again. Helicopter gunships came and strafed mercilessly. The bombardment hurled dirt from the hillside over the roof of the shelter and then blew the dirt away to expose the roof again.

The Americans had so many bombs and shells that they could waste them. Smoke from their explosions obscured everything, turning the sky black. It was around eleven or twelve o'clock at night. We were hungry, tired, despairing, and desperate.

For six or seven days, we had eaten nothing. What was there to eat anyway? So we sneaked back to the village of Xuyên Trường again, where we met some guerillas. As soon as they saw us they yelled, "*Get out now!* The enemy is all over the place here!"

They turned on their flashlights, and we saw each other's faces for the first time. We all looked like zombies, eyes white, teeth white, and faces full of mud and dirt, blackened by smoke from the bombs. In later years, Mr. Tý would write about all of these things in his letters.

I was consumed with anxiety, fearing that my film and camera would be ruined.

"Is there anything to eat?" I asked the guerillas.

"Not a thing."

"Then where are we to go?"

"You must turn around and climb past this mountain. Then go back until you reach Xuyên Thanh village."

It was the middle of the night. Our stomachs were empty, our feet were waterlogged and bleeding, and our clothes were ragged and drenched. Where would we find the strength to go on?

"We're horribly cold. Do you have any pieces of dry clothing?"

"Yes, right away, right away," said one guerilla.

With this, he withdrew a dagger and sliced off a few broad banana leaves, made holes in the middle, and put them over our heads. Then he folded over the front and rear halves and used banana tendrils to tie them around our waists. Thus we all had leafy "overcoats." This done, he shouted, "Move!"

The three of us then groped our way back through the gloomy shadows of the night across Mount Dựng and at last reached Xuyên Thanh village. Tý said, "Let me lead the way." There were again culverts and ditches, stalls for water buffalo, and latrines . . . Tý led us into the home of his elderly paternal aunt. She looked at us as if we were three ghosts.

"Come on in then, get washed up first, then come into the kitchen to get warm by the fire."

She went off to cook rice. And then we ate it with *mắm* (a sauce made from fermented bonito). We had never had anything so delicious in our lives!

On the afternoon of the next day, we returned to Xuyên Trường village, this time taking with us a few packs of steamed rice. All around, there were burned houses, dead bodies, sounds of people calling to each other, sounds of weeping and mourning. The place was devastated, destroyed, in pain . . . I made my way back to the grassy field, opened the cover of the underground shelter, and found the film and camera, and the rucksack with my clothes still intact.

It was a cruel and terrible war; people suffered, and the film and camera also suffered. Bombs and shells plowed up the earth, everything got buried or flooded, and people wandered about in all directions.

6

The Beauty and the Bullet

The Chiêm Sơn Bridge across the Thu Bồn River was a railway bridge, second in size only to the Long Biên Bridge up in Hanoi. The guerillas planned to blow it up, and I had to submerge myself in the water to film the explosion. When it came, great waves swelled up and rolled toward me, one after another, and I had to hold the camera high up to keep it clear of the waves. Once the filming was complete, I had to move immediately, knowing that the fighter-bombers would come right away and artillery shells would rain down. Just as I started to move, my foot struck against something hard down in the mud. I had just enough time to dive and pluck it up. It was a steel box. On opening it, I found it was filled with gleaming bullets. I asked a guerilla how long the ammo box might have been there, and he told me that two years earlier the enemy had conducted a sweep through the area. It occurred to me at once that I could use this steel box to carry film. Pouring out the bullets, I saw that they were bandoliers meant to be wrapped around a person's torso.

So an American ammo box became my film box. It was a fine box; after I put the film in, there was some leftover space on both ends, large enough to stuff in some roasted rice as a safeguard against humidity.

There was no way I could carry such a great quantity of film on my back to all the places I went to during my time in the lowlands. It would be like having an entire studio on my back! So it occurred to me that I must go in search of more of the same kind of ammo boxes. Once the film was shot, I could throw it in a box and bury it wherever I happened to be. Identification signs for the burial spots would be big trees, river bends, and boulders . . . But then the surface of the earth could be turned upside down by bombing. Burying film in that manner was extremely risky, as it could be lost at any time, and then what could I say to my superiors? But, miraculously, even though I shot a huge amount of film during all those months of wandering here and there, I was able to dig up all of it, wrap it up, and, at the conclusion of my mission, carry it back intact to the mountains.

I recall that during my years of filming in the battlefield, I often found it strange and illogical that I had not yet died! Surely, it would have made sense to die hundreds of times!

Another day, we were coming downstream, moving along in the Thu Bồn River, when we saw a band of guerillas just then coming up from the opposite direction, talking and laughing noisily. As I gazed into the shallow water, intent on my wading, a pair of white long legs suddenly appeared. I looked up and saw a girl, the only girl in the group of male youths. She was wearing a tight pair of shorts, revealing smooth, tanned legs, supporting a tall, slender figure. Her face was refined, with an aquiline nose, and a pair of bright eyes . . .

But only one side of that face, as beautiful as an angel's, was intact. The other half was horrifically deformed. I learned later that she had been injured by a bullet hitting her squarely on that side of her face.

The girl gazed straight into my face. Our eyes met for a second. Then she shifted the Garand rifle on her shoulder to her back, turning sideways and kicking the water with her long legs with a swirling motion, like a ballet dancer, sending sprays of water in the air. Countless pearl-like drops of water flew up, making gleaming arcs in the air as they fell under the early sun. And a clear, spontaneous peal of laughter resounded on the wavy surface of the river.

Hỷ, our photojournalist leading the way, said, "That's Xoa, Văn Thị Xoa, chief of Xuyên Châu village militia."

I was terribly obsessed by her beautiful yet half-destroyed face. Now, forty-five years later, I still, at this very moment, remember the exact sound of her laughter. It was a laugh unlike any other I have heard in my life; it seemed tinged with some kind of thirst for revenge.

Half of her beautiful face had been shattered and deformed by the bullet wound, so the girl would have to live with that for the rest of her life. The pride of her beauty had been snatched away. Her hope for love and a happy marriage had been ruined. Her burst of haunting laughter reflected the hidden pain of a deeply wounded human being, with a sense of loss, bitterness, carelessness, and desire for revenge. I learned later that she had trained herself to be a sniper. I thought that without the war, without the wound, she could have enjoyed a happy, normal life, like anyone else. But the war had robbed her of all that, and left her with lonely, impoverished prospects.

A few days later, I suggested to my colleagues that we organize a shooting sequence about Xoa and other guerilla girls of Xuyên Châu. Dozens of people gathered to do this, but before we could begin, artillery shells began to rain down on us, forcing us to run in all directions. The whole area was devastated. Only after another three months was I able to communicate with them again. I suggested to Mr. Lai, the Duy Xuyên District party secretary, that he let Ms. Xoa go down to my place near Bàn Thạch Market so we could film her there. Mr. Lai was so conscientious that in spite of the intense and desperate fighting all around us, he sent the village militia chief all the way to our location, so we could make a film.

But, split off from her own unit and her familiar surroundings, with no Thu Bồn River or green fields of mulberry, Xoa was no longer the dynamic, natural, enterprising, self-confident Văn Thị Xoa that she had been before! We tried one approach after another, but she was still stiff and dry, lifeless. Finally I had to give up after three days and return her to her unit.

Only long afterward, when we went to Xuyên Châu, where Xoa and her unit were active, to make a film on the spot, did we succeed. Only then did the image of Văn Thị Xoa become vivid, as was seen in the film we made of her.

One night, Anh Tý and I left the sandy seaside area in Thăng Bình District to go up the hills in the opposite direction. We were accustomed to traveling at night to avoid encounters with enemy troops. We came to a very broad river. This was the Châu Giang, a name that Tý used to name his first son.

To this very day, after the passage of nearly half a century, I still remember the mysterious sensations of that night by the sea, listening to the breezes chasing each other over the tips of the *phi lao* (seaside pines), and smelling the warm salty aroma of the ocean. Peaceful, reflective moments such as those were very rare. Suddenly Tý asked, "Do you see those lights on the other side of the river?"

"Yes, certainly."

"That's Bà Market. My wife and family are all over there. It's been a long time since I've gone back to visit my wife."

"So could we take this opportunity to make a quick visit then?"

"Let me see. If I went alone, it would be all right, but with you along, I'm afraid something would happen, and then we'd be in big trouble."

"Are there enemy soldiers there?"

"No. By day, the enemy's there, but at night we're usually in control."

"Then let's go. I too would like to visit your family and meet your wife."

We decided to swim across the river. To call a ferry would be dangerous. If someone should inform on us, things would be insecure. So we stripped off all our clothing, wrapped our gear and cameras in many layers of nylon, and then, arrayed like the legendary Chử Đồng Tử (i.e., a stark naked fisherman who turned into an immortal saint), gently put our wrapped bags into the black water, pushing them ahead as we swam. We didn't make a sound.

By the time we reached the middle of the river, a swarm of small fish, imagining that we were some kind of exotic morsel, began nibbling enthusiastically on the area of our bodies that should not be touched. The tickling sensation was hard to bear, but we continued to swim as if nothing were happening.

On reaching the other side of the river, about a kilometer away from the lights, we put on our clothes again and arranged our gear. Taking my hand, Tý pushed me into a clump of shrubbery and told me to lie low, so he could go in first to test the situation, after which he would come back and get me.

I sat without moving in the shrubbery while the mosquitoes bit me to death. About half an hour later, Tý returned and said, "Things are very quiet. Let's just go in."

The family of anh Tý's wife was moderately prosperous; they did business in Bà Market. They had a two-story house; on the lower level they sold herbal medicines and miscellaneous goods, and there were many bedrooms on the upper level. We bathed and brewed some tea. Moments later, a little boy came up. With respectfully folded arms, he said, "Mrs.

Hai Hoàng wishes to invite you two gentlemen to come downstairs and have dinner."

We went down and saw a tray of hot *trứng vịt lộn* (half-hatched boiled duck eggs) and glasses of cold beer to start with, and lots of other dishes arranged in the middle of the room. And so the two "ravenous ghosts" got to eat their fill, making up for their endless days of hunger and misery.

Next morning the local militia posted guards in the area to keep a lookout for the enemy, so we were able to film the activity going on in the marketplace. Such crowded, merry scenes were very seldom seen in the "liberated" areas. Chị Hai Hoàng went out to the market, where she stood out as an elegant beauty arrayed in off-white silk. I don't understand why the enemy didn't come that day to search through Bà Market. We later departed peacefully amid the fond good-byes of chị Hai Hoàng and her family. Those memories remained deeply implanted in my mind and subsequently turned to sorrow when I learned chị Hai Hoàng was arrested and imprisoned. Anh Tý sent me a poem he had written to his wife in prison, as follows:

WAITING
(written for Hoàng)

I wait for you as dusk awaits the wind
To disperse the clouds, reveal the starry sky.
Sails spread before the wind, returning to the pier,
As lines of windswept pines confide in whispers to each other.

After the war, Mrs. Hoàng and her children became close friends of my family and have remained so until the present day. She and her children have been to Hanoi a couple of times to stay at my home, and I have also gone back to see them.

Underground tunnels and shelters were closely bound up with our lives in that region. Some shelters were dry and others were wet, with toads, snakes, and centipedes. Sometimes we remained in shelters for days—we had to use these places for purposes of elimination too, and then breathe in the aroma of what had been "eliminated." Yet, that was not the worst. In some areas, the surface of the earth was barren, so the shelters couldn't be dug in the usual manner. The entrance had to be dug underwater at the edge of a stream or pond. To enter them you had to plunge beneath the water and then go up vertically, as in the lairs of otters. Every time you wanted to enter one, you had to feel around with your hand to find a cave, like a cave for crabs. The "tunnel rats" on the other side also regularly submerged themselves in the water and felt around with their hands to identify the entrances.

Sometimes at night we got word that enemy scouts had crept into the area. It would be silent, with not even the sound of a dog barking. Within five or seven minutes we had to wrap up our gear and crawl noiselessly out to the river. The things that filmmakers like us brought along were not weapons but cameras and film, both exposed and yet-to-be-exposed, and clothes as well, including the clothes we were wearing. We would wrap up all these things securely in a few layers of nylon, until they were like rubber floats, so we could submerge them in the water and conceal them for later use. Then, arrayed like Chử Đồng Tử, we slid easily into the water and lightly pushed the buoyant nylon sacks ahead of us. On reaching the entrance to a tunnel, we would pause and take in a great breath of air, so we would have enough oxygen in our lungs to push our gear downward, move it five or seven meters forward, and crawl into the tunnel. I was quietly grateful for all those days in my childhood when I had run away from home to practice swimming at the Children's Palace in Hanoi in 1954. My film passed through countless jungle rainstorms, watery submersions, underground burials, storage in tunnels and shelters, and traversals of streams and rivers.

It must be added that a photojournalist filming scenes in a war zone must necessarily put his life in danger, going to places where the fighting is most intense, choosing locations that command the widest view from different angles; standing in high places, so as to capture the best pictures. But he must not die! His film must not be damaged. His duty is not to gain victories in battle, nor to use his body to support a machine gun or to block the gunfire from a bunker. His foremost duty is to live, in order to shoot scenes and bring the film back to the studio for processing—only then does he fulfill his duty. Death would be totally useless: all the hard training, all the expensive equipment, all our important stories and unfinished work would be as if cast into the ocean.

As a rule, people who survive aren't honored to the same extent as people who die, but no one is so stupid as to choose death. Naturally, death carries the possibility that you may gain a heroic name, be praised to the skies, and be remembered for generations. Putting it this way may sound very rude and naked, but it is the truth, a very cold, hard truth. In a war zone, with bombs falling and bullets flying everywhere, life and death are not up to individual will or wisdom alone but are also up to fate, to God's will. A great many of my colleagues didn't come home from the war but departed this life forever, leaving gaps that cannot be filled among their families, relations, and colleagues, from the North to the South. There are a great many such cases, but here I will recount only the story of one colleague who was closely associated with me, immersed in the affairs of the same war zone, in the same time period.[1]

Compared with my other colleagues, I made Nguyễn Giá's acquaintance late, and perhaps knew him less well.

It was in 1967, at the headquarters of the 5th Zone party committee, when we heard that Nguyễn Giá, who had just completed a course of training in Russia, had come to Quảng Đà. I had never met the fellow before, but I'd heard many stories about his courage. What sort of person was he? How had he managed, all alone, to cope with these terrible war zone conditions? We didn't say anything to each other, but we all understood that Nguyễn Giá had decided to throw himself into an uneven fight. It was also in mid-1967 that I was lucky enough to obtain a camera and film, bid farewell to hillside farming, and come down to Quảng Đà. For many months on end, bombs rained and bullets flew, and the enemy came through on sweeping operations. I had met thousands of familiar and unfamiliar faces, but I had not been able to meet Giá. Such was the harshness of the war in Quảng Đà. Sometimes we would be only one rice field, one small canal, one secret tunnel apart, and then, in a flash, an artillery barrage would start, enemy troops would pour out of helicopters, and bullets would fly all about—and then we would disperse in all directions.

When we had filmed the final scenes for the film *The People of My Homeland* in Duy Xuyên, we were subjected to a ferocious sweeping operation the like of which I had never previously experienced in my life. I could never have predicted that it was just in that moment of supreme peril that I saw . . . yes, without doubt, it was Giá! Helicopters swarmed like flies over our heads, and the shouts of Americans resounded in all directions leading into the village. From Mt. Dụng outpost, the ARVN troops descended, kicking over the fences. Bullets kept whizzing by at belt-level and above. I had again taken shelter in a secret tunnel and had started to suffocate. I had been dragged out by the armpits to an open place so I could breathe, when someone cried out, "Look, there's Giá!"

I tried to raise my sagging body and look up. The actual flesh-and-blood Giá was rushing by in a bent-over posture, about ten meters from us. He was about my age, a bit dark, well-built, attired in rural green "pajamas," and had a sack on his back, probably for a camera. What underground shelter had he just darted out from? How did he intend to escape from the enemy encirclement? It was all like a hurriedly taken snapshot.

My films were shot, so, after bidding farewell to my friends, and to Anh Tý, I followed some liaison guides up to the base camp. There was no more hope of meeting Giá. I had gotten only a glimpse of him! He seemed like a tough guy.

Perhaps nowadays, because living and working conditions have changed, and people can travel around by automobile or aircraft to make a film, the need to meet others in the profession is not so strong. But back in those days at the front, meeting with colleagues and hometown compatriots was a big comfort.

The road through the piedmont area up to the base camp was remote and endless. On the afternoon of the fourth day, at a liaison station, I received an order from a leader in the regional party headquarters: "You are to return at once to the Quảng Đà front."

"To do what? My films are all shot."

"This is an order from the regional headquarters. Your mission will be given to you later."

"I don't have a single scrap of film left."

"Just return. We'll talk about film later."

So I had no choice but to turn around. To tell the truth, I had no particular reluctance to return—at least I was familiar with the roads and underground shelters there. Furthermore, that fellow Giá had just returned from Russia, but had chosen to stay in Quảng Đà also. The only annoying thing was that the bosses hadn't told me what to film or where to get film.

On the eve of Tết Mậu Thân (New Year 1968, the Year of the Monkey), war journalists of every sort (newspapermen, broadcasters, news agency reporters, photographers, and filmmakers), as well as musicians and writers, regrouped or, more correctly, were herded into a large underground bomb shelter. This was perhaps the largest and most unexpected gathering in the war. A commander read out an order for a general offensive and uprising throughout South Vietnam.[2]

I had not yet understood anything when suddenly I saw Giá. He looked exactly the same as he did when I had seen him running at full tilt during the attack at Xuyên Trường. He was sitting in a corner of the shelter, still with a bundled sack on his back. His facial expression was natural and relaxed, as if he had never run from a sweeping operation. I approached him.

"Giá, right? I'm Thủy."

"Yeah, yeah . . . Triều Phương [anh Tý] told me you'd gone back up to the base camp, right?"

Giá's voice sounded like that of someone from Lai Xá.[3] But this was not a time and place for us to chat socially. So I said briefly, "The order that was just read isn't for me—I can't film with an empty camera."

"Don't worry, I'll give you some film," he offered. "I have a little black-and-white film, but I've left it all this time in Điện Hồng."

Giá was without a doubt someone from Lai Xá, very kind, no-nonsense, and reliable. He pulled me out of the shelter and the two of us suddenly craned our necks to look up at the sky. The night before Tết and the sky so full of stars? Or was the sky in the central region always like that? There were surely no stars in the Hanoi sky at this time. Giá rushed ahead, and I followed him, almost running. High over our heads, some high-flying B-52 bombers glistened like stars.

Seconds later, a long, horror-filled wail filled the air, and the earth was lit up, shaken violently, and consumed in flames.

"Where are we going, Giá?"

"Up to Điện Hồng!"

If we'd been in Hanoi, I would have concluded that this fellow was a psychopath. Điện Hồng village was way up in Điện Bàn District. We had to swim across the Thu Bồn River, stumble up and down steep paths, roll and crawl in the pitch-black night for twenty kilometers!

After having crawled in and out of several partially blown-out tunnels, we found the one where Giá had his film stored.

As Giá crawled out, I touched the bundle of film that he was holding in his arms.

"Is this all you have?"

"Yeah . . . they said they'd send some more later. Go ahead and take half of this."

The "half" that Giá referred to was half of a canister containing three hundred meters of 16-millimeter film. I've always been a cunning fellow, but Giá was so sincere and generous. How could someone up in Hanoi have made such a promise to him? In a few more hours, Tết would arrive, and gunfire would erupt throughout the South, instead of the usual Tết cease-fire, just as our superiors had announced.

The two of us hugged the three hundred meters of film with no cassette and no bobbin (to divide the film into smaller sections) in our arms. How could we film? Giá was a newcomer, but he already had many local friends and acquaintances. He took me along as he groped around for a while and then crept into the house of a blacksmith.

This gentleman woke up at once, as alert as if he had never closed his eyes (only later did I learn that people living in areas subject to bombs and artillery were accustomed to waking up without any yawning or stretching). In accordance with Giá's requests, he pulled out a set of tools: flare canisters, pincers, punches . . .

Giá placed a bobbin before him to use as a model: a Paya Polex movie camera bobbin. The blacksmith was utterly zealous—he went to his work with a habitual disdain for the modern manufacturing techniques used in civilized countries. As for us, we were hungry and tired, and could think of nothing better to do than to sit stupidly and wait.

In the end, the handmade bobbin was finished. Aside from their differing colors, it was hard to distinguish what this blacksmith had made from the product made in Switzerland. I noticed that Giá was sweating profusely, though the night was now advanced, and it was beginning to get cold. He opened his back sack, pulled out his camera, and put the handmade bobbin inside.

We were all nervous about the outcome. We wound up the spring on the camera and pressed the start button to see what would happen. The machine ran and whirred for a spell, making our eyes brighten, and then . . . it got stuck and stopped. He tried fixing it this way and that way, taking it out and reinstalling it, but the machine still would not run satisfactorily; it would run for a number of seconds and then get stuck again. But it was late, and we had to say good-bye to the blacksmith.

When we thanked him and shook his hand, we could see that he had never previously accepted defeat in the face of modern technology, not even that of the machines all around him, making such a clamor in the sky and earth for so many years. Giá was sad and deeply worried, more than I was. We miserably searched for expedients until the hour of Tết arrived. Then from here and there, the roar of gunfire began to encircle us.

The Cẩm Nam River is south of the old town of Hội An (now a popular tourist destination). The place is right next to the sea, so by about 4:00 a.m. the light was clear enough to distinguish people's faces. Hundreds of big and small boats filled with people were advancing toward the town with drums and gongs. Our superiors had told us to go and "capture those in power." Giá rode in one boat, and I in another. When the boats had departed from the pier for a few boat-lengths, I saw him waving his hands toward the sky as signal. I didn't understand what he meant. I saw only that gunfire from the city was coming at us thick and fast. Someone shouted, "That's our fire, we're in control of the town! We're firing to mislead the enemy!" (Only later did I learn that the man was lying.) And so, after the shouting, the boats kept crossing the river en masse. Gunfire from the town rained down on the river, with high-speed automatic gunfire spewing at us like red water drops sprayed from a hose. A number of boats took hits, foundered, and sank.

Sounds of people shouting and cursing . . . Some boats turned around, but the gunfire was fiercer than ever. I have never afterward been able to remember how we returned to the southern bank. So Giá and I were separated again and wound up in different places.

After the second wave of the general offensive, the other side counterattacked fiercely. Then came the third wave. The liberated zones gradually shrank, until nothing of our territory was left in Quảng Đà. It was perhaps for this reason that when I left the base camp and was on my way to the North, I unexpectedly ran into Giá again at the edge of a jungle. We were overjoyed. When Giá learned that I was going to the North, he couldn't restrain his tears, and he embraced me—embraced the scrawny, stinking bundle of bones that I had become. As for Giá, he looked older, thinner, and shrunken. "With such bombing and gunfire, his mere survival must be due to the blessings of his ancestors," I thought to myself. The two of us spent the night together. When morning came, Giá found two tins of rice somewhere and pushed them into a tubular bag for me, but I declined: "When I reach the way stations, there will be something to eat."

Giá gave me an enclosed letter and a small pack of gifts for his wife and children. We walked together for a long stretch before parting. His eyes swimming with tears, Giá said, "I'll return later—please remember to tell my wife. The thing is, I can't go back empty-handed. I must film something or other, you understand?"

That was my third and last meeting with Nguyễn Giá.

His life was full of setbacks; no sooner did he make his way to some location, then that area would be subject to ferocious sweeping operations. The first load of film he sent back to the North for processing went "foul"—the film flicked by with no images. When he went with Lê Bá Huyến, Huyến was captured. When his first child was born, he never got to see the infant's face.

And after all this, most tragically of all, he died in Quảng Ngai while shooting the last millimeters of the film to which he had so devoted his heart and soul.

7
Carrying the War Home

After the Tết Offensive in 1968 came the second and third wave of counterattacks by the other side. We were dispersed, devastated, broken up. We kept running and kept suffering repeated blows.

My mission was to protect the film I had shot and carry it back to the North, where I was supposed to deliver it to the Cinema Department without allowing any part of it to be lost or damaged. At that time, I was thin as a rail and sick with malaria, and my hair had fallen out, leaving only stray wisps. Someone said to me, "When I sit near you, I smell the odor of death." That was chị Tú, the younger sister of chị Thúy Bằng, the wife of the musician Văn Cao (the author of many famous songs, including the Vietnamese national anthem). She was at the time working there with her husband in the news agency of 5th Zone.

Let me tell the story of Trần Thế Dân. Much earlier, Dân had studied cinema and photography at a film school in Beijing, and spoke excellent Chinese. After graduation, he came back to work at the National Feature Film Studio in Hanoi and later became vice director of the Cinema Department, and then deputy general secretary of the Cinema Association. Everything Dân thought and did for himself and in his family was in complete conformity with the rules he had been taught at school. He was always thoughtful and so kind by nature that he was liked by everybody.

I have many fond memories of our times together in the war zone. Dân cared for me wholeheartedly, especially after I fell ill. Once he had me lean against a pillar while he gave me an injection. When he withdrew the needle, I fainted and fell down to the ground. Dân hastily picked up the tube of medicine to see if he had administered the wrong substance—but it was only vitamin B1 . . .

Once Dân cut some slices from his last piece of ginseng for me. It had been given to him by Mrs. Hảo, the wife of the musician Nguyễn Văn Thương (author of the famous melancholy song "Đêm Đông" or "Winter Night") and the sworn elder sister of Dân.[1] At another time when a mission took him to a neighboring area where crops were grown, he carried back a bunch of water spinach to give to me. Since he was on the road for three or four days, almost all of the water spinach dried up and withered, so we had to sort them out bit by bit to see which stems were still edible. Later, when I set out for the North, Dân shared some rice with me.

Dân was completely deaf in one ear, yet he was given the "special favor" of being allowed to go to the war zone. When there was an explosion, he had to turn around in a circle to determine what direction it came from. For the same reason, Dân could not go down to the lowlands where bombs fell everywhere and where one could meet with enemy troops at any time. He remained in the highlands and made the film *The Wild Game Hunters of Mount Đak Sao,* which won a gold award at a film festival held in Moscow. Very few people, if any, could have done that, given such bombing, starvation, and illness.

The counterattacks of the other side after the Tết Offensive in 1968 pushed us into Laotian territory. Every time we changed location, our unit had to carry along some sick or disabled men. My presence had become a burden for my colleagues—nobody would be able to carry me around on their back or on a stretcher. And besides, the quantity of film was so great that it appeared necessary to see if it could be turned into movies or if the negatives held images or not.

The command therefore decided that I must go back to the North via the Hồ Chí Minh Trails through the Trường Sơn Mountains. If I had been healthy, it wouldn't have been necessary for me to return to the North—someone else could have carried the film back there for processing, postproduction, and "montage," and my role would simply have been writing explanatory notes and names of locations concerning each section of the film.

Such was the background at the time of my return. But later, when I got back to Hanoi, I would be regarded with suspicion by some, because there were quite a few cases of *B quay* (meaning a "U-turn" made by people who were scared of the war and turned around to go back to the North) before completing their duties. They made up excuses that they were too sick or handicapped to go on.

When I set out, I left everything I had behind for my colleagues, including my best rucksack. I took along only a cloth bag, which, filled with rice and tied with a string, became a sort of makeshift rucksack. I left my *hung go* (cooking pot) behind as well, taking only an empty can with a steel wire wrapped around it for cooking on the way, and two sets of uniforms. It was hard to say when I would reach the way stations,[2] so my colleagues gave me a *ruột tượng* (a long tubular bag) with rice contributions from the others, a can from some, or half a can, or a handful from others. At that time, I was so weak that whenever I urinated, I had to hold on to a tree for support. So how could I carry all these things? My colleagues let me try by loading them up on my body, which now looked thin as a chopstick. When I stood up, the rice bag slipped down to my feet, for I had no hips or any protrusions for it to hold on to. And when I put the rice bag on my shoulders, I couldn't bear the load and fell down, though the rice wasn't that much, just a few kilograms. Yet, I had to carry a few dozen canisters full of negatives up and down jungled mountains.

So I went.

My colleagues walked with me for some distance to see me off and encourage me: "Go, and do your best, okay?" That journey allowed me to understand how powerful spiritual motivation can be.

I wasn't dragging my corpselike body back North just to rest, eat good food, and get medical treatment. The yards and yards of film on my shoulders were filled with so many images of so many people, so many stories, so many battles. I was carrying all of their lives with me . . .

On the way up to the way station network, I had to cook food for myself. I was so sick that whenever I ate, I would vomit and have diarrhea. It was miserable. But when I mixed the American orange juice packets with spring water, I could drink it right away, and this helped the diarrhea as well. When I started running a high fever from malaria, I put on all my clothes and carefully wrote the following note, which I placed in the film pack: *These are all film negatives shot in the war zone, not yet developed. If they should fall into your hands, please take the utmost care to preserve them and deliver them on my behalf to the office responsible for Cinema. They must not be opened.*

When seized with high fever on the way, I spread out the nylon tent and lay on it, half exposed and half covered, with my arms protectively wrapped around the sack of film, lying right on the trail, which was no more than a meter wide, so that if I died, anyone passing by would see me.

I had seen dead people by the wayside many, many times. Once when I went to get cassava tubers on the hillsides, I saw someone on a hammock groaning miserably, still with hat, canteen, and a backpack . . . and on the way back, I saw only a twisted corpse, with no possessions left. I had seen such deaths, many of them, time and time again.

I thought that if I died, anyone who happened to run into my corpse would know what I was carrying. I lay there burning up with fever and groaning, as drops of rain fell here and there on the top of the tent. Many people died from malaria like that, not just from bombs and bullets.

And then I heard the voices of people conversing in the distance and the sound of heavy footsteps as if from young and healthy people, probably from paramilitary volunteer youths or frontline workers.

As the footsteps came closer, I was overjoyed. Their voices were enthusiastic as if they were young and strong. One person came up to me: "Oh, there's a fellow lying here; perhaps he is dead already." Another person lifted the flap of the tent. Our four eyes met. "Hey guys, he's still alive." They closed the tent flap and went on their way.

On one occasion, while I was traveling with a small group going North, I became too weak to keep up with the others and told them, "Go on ahead, just make marks along the way for me to see—I'll get to the way station without getting lost." The night was black as ink; another fellow and I went along, groping our way forward in the dark, and I had no idea how we could finally make it to our destination.

This fellow was a disabled soldier. Of those going back to the north, nearly all of us were disabled, missing a foot or a hand, sick with malaria, some carrying children with them . . . we were in fact a band of disabled troops.

The soldier I was with had broken a foot and a hand. He said he was good at swimming. I too was good at swimming; I could cross any river no matter how fast the current. As I have previously observed, I owed my life to that critical skill. The soldier could wade across a stream if it was shallow, but whenever it became so deep that he had to swim, he would look pitiful as the current swept him away with only one hopelessly working hand. How can you swim with just one arm and one leg? The dividing line between life and death is indeed that fragile.

After we caught up with the group again, we found our way was blocked for fifteen days by a large group of enemy special force commandos that had been dropped into the area. The first day, we each ate one can of rice; the second day, less than one can; the third and fourth days, half a can; after that, not a grain was left. We had to gather wild roots, such as taro, to cook and eat. Later on, I would shudder whenever I smelled it. Taro is similar to the elephant ear plant. We would cook the leaves until they turned into a horrible sort of soup, and add a pinch of salt and glutamate powder. And this was the food that everyone ate, both the sick and the healthy.

Our group included all sorts of people—men and women, old people and children. One woman had brought along a four- or five-year-old child—I still remember that his name was Vĩnh, little Vĩnh. Everyone in our group loved both the mother and the child. We gave them the best spots to sit and, whenever there was anything to eat, shared it with them. A liaison soldier caught a stone crab when crossing a forest stream and brought it back for the child, for the boy had nothing to play with. He used a long cotton thread to tie one of the crab's claws at one end, and tied the other end to the stake to which my own hammock and that of the mother and son were tethered. I lay on my hammock and gazed down at the child playing with the crab.

When night came, my hunger and thirst became unbearable; I was overpowered by a desire to eat something. There was some roasted rice in the sack with film, but I wouldn't have dared to eat a grain of it, even if I had to die of hunger. The roasted rice was there to protect the film from moisture. Then I remembered that a crab was tied to one end of my hammock. An "ideological struggle" (a much-used term at the time) took place in my mind—should I steal the crab, so as to roast and devour it?

After thinking this over and over, I decided finally to eat the crab. When the mother and child had fallen asleep, I crept out of my hammock without a sound, opened my backpack, and took out a water-filled canteen. The water had been obtained for me by the liaison soldier, as I had no strength myself to go down to a deep stream. I scooped up a little salt and put it into a Chinese metal bowl.

Then I carefully disengaged the crab from its string and stealthily brought it down to the kitchen hut. The cooking hearth still had some red embers. I took a little water and washed the crab clean. Then I stirred up the embers and placed the crab on top, turning it over again and again until it was roasted brown. I was consumed with hunger, so I no doubt did this hurriedly. I broke off the crab's smallest leg, dipped it in salt, and put it in my mouth. I chewed and chewed it, then washed it down with a mouthful of spring water. I went on in that manner until I had eaten the biggest claw, and then each other part, washing it down with a mouthful of water. I took that crab apart and ate its upper shell, and finally its body, throwing away nothing! It took me half an hour or so to devour the whole crab.

Having finished, I quietly sneaked back to my hut and crept without a sound into my own hammock. The following morning, the little boy burst into tears because he had lost his crab. I felt utterly ashamed.

All of us in the group kept together as we traveled. We exchanged items of clothing for cassava and honey: a pair of long pants for a few cassava tubers, and a shirt for half a liter of honey. I gave the boy some cassava and honey. If God has allowed little Vĩnh to live on, then by now he would be close to fifty.

Actually, in situations of absolute want and hunger, such as this one, human beings sometimes start behaving like beasts. At night, for example, someone might steal some honey from my backpack, spilling it on the ground.

I must add that the ethnic peoples living in the remote areas of the Trường Sơn Mountains led a poor and miserable existence in no way different from that of the Khù Xung and Toong Lương peoples with whom I had lived in the Northwest in former days. They lacked everything, including the simplest scraps of clothing, and needles and thread. Normally, bringing gifts for our highland brethren and sharing a few things with them would be a source of happiness, but we were too hungry, too sick and weak, for this—so we had no choice but to seek anything available to exchange, so that we might have something to fill our mouths with. The tribesmen didn't know how to measure, count, or make calculations like us Kinh Vietnamese. A spool of thread could be exchanged for two cassava tubers, but if you unwound a spool and divided the thread into lengths of two outstretched arms apiece, the tribesmen would still give you two tubers for each length. And so our "beastly" natures turned imperceptibly into blood and flesh—our own.

It strikes me, remembering those days, that no matter how unfortunate my life became, I managed to live on, and even got to travel to many far-flung places.

About thirty years later, when, as an invited guest, I sat in lavish banquet rooms in Paris, Tokyo, Sydney, London, Boston, and New York with important dignitaries such as officials from the French foreign ministry, the mayor of Yamagata, Australian and Japanese cinema directors, a British House of Commons member (Mr. Chris Moulin), famous American movie directors, and even presidential candidate John Kerry,[3] I would still occasionally remember my feelings of shame in those days—especially the dark night when I had stolen a crab from little Vĩnh to roast and eat it, or the days when I had lived like a hungry ghost in the Trường Sơn Mountains and broke rolls of thread into arm-length spans to exchange for two small cassava tubers given me by the impoverished, swarthy tribesmen. I wish I could turn all these things into a feature film . . .

But then people would say it was all made up.

When we reached the headquarters of Đoàn 559 (the name of the army battalion in charge of the extensive system of Hồ Chí Minh Trails from North to South), my strength was utterly exhausted, so I had to remain there, unable to go any further.

At the time we arrived, everyone had left their huts to work, and there were so many huts that I had no idea which I could enter. Finally I lay down in the corner of a deserted hut and covered myself with a reed mat.

I was awakened by a shout: "Who's this guy? Why's he still lying here at this hour?"

A polite voice gave a reply: "Sorry sir, this is not someone from our station. He's a journalist from the front. He's ill with fever, so he's staying here."

"Then something must be done—why do you let him lie here? Move him to the infirmary!"

"Yes sir, but he keeps stubbornly hugging this bag, saying it's the film he shot at the front that he has to bring back to the North."

"That's all the more reason why he can't stay here. You must find a way to take him back to the North."

After the man had left, I stuck my head out and asked the soldier, "Who is that man?"

"He's the chief!"

"What's the chief's name?"

"Mr. Đồng Sĩ Nguyên!" (the famous commander of Đoàn 559).

After that, I was treated with some concern, not because of my personal condition but because of the stack of film I was holding on to.

The next morning, someone said to me, "There's an automobile." I thought he meant some small vehicle. It turned out to be a truck. The back of the vehicle had no roof, as was the case with all vehicles that went to the front. A huge diesel generator filled almost all the space in the back; it was tightly secured with steel wire to guard against shock and to keep the machine from shifting position and causing the truck to turn over. Someone found a canvas mat, to cover the spot on the floor of the truck near the cabin, making a sort of nest, and said, "Here you are, your place is up here."

The canvas was dirty and torn, and it stank.

"How about the cabin?"

"There's no more room in there."

Later, I found that there were two others in the cabin aside from the driver. I hugged the sack of film and lay on the filthy nest, raising a corner of the canvas to shield myself from the sun and rain. When there was anything to eat, the people in the cab would throw some of it to me.

As the truck crossed the Bến Hải River to the northern bank,[4] I lay on my back gazing at the canopies of trees speeding over my head. Using my depleted strength to crane my neck to look over the side of the truck, I saw a distant church spire . . . a village . . . I was overjoyed, thinking that if the truck would stop, and if my legs were strong enough, I would be able to walk there. I recalled how in the war zone I would hide behind gravestones in a cemetery and gaze at cars and Lambretta scooters zooming past only a few hundred meters away, while having no way at all to go up to the highway and set foot in one of those vehicles. That was why gazing at the scenes around me now made me feel strange.

And so, after several more days and nights, we reached Unification

Park in Hanoi. Someone banged the side of the truck with a heavy thud, and shouted, "We've arrived, get down!"

The truck had come to a stop by an entrance into the park along Nguyễn Đình Chiểu Street near what is now a club where *chèo* opera is performed. Back then the park was very simple; it had no walls or fences . . . Later on, people were unable to imagine how I could have gone straight from Đoàn 559 headquarters to Unification Park. I myself also found it unbelievable.

As a rule, people coming back from the South were supposed to be issued some money and clothing on crossing the 17th parallel, but I never got the slightest glimpse of any station there, and never received any rations, any clothing, or funds. It's not as if the three people in the cabin were mistreating me either when they threw me down from the truck. The war was like that.

As I was getting down from the truck, hugging my sack of film, one fellow said, "My house is on Bông Nhuộm (a downtown street). When you're feeling better, let's get together." And so we parted ways.

I sat on the sidewalk, thinking. They should have taken me back via the way-station network. That way I would have arrived at the Ban Thống Nhất (Department for Unification, in charge of receiving returnees from the South) or the Ban Tổ Chức Trung Ương (Central Department for Organization) or the K25 Rehabilitation Camp, or any other comparable organization, where I would have been welcomed and given food and clothing, with all appropriate paperwork and formalities.

But now they had thrown me into Unification Park! What could I do in a situation like that?

An Uneasy Homecoming

I sat at the curbside for some time, dazed, with no idea where to go, or where to find the Central Organization Department, the Department for Unification, or any reception center. I didn't have a cent in my pocket, and I looked like a zombie. I was too weak to go anywhere. With great effort, I dragged myself to a park bench nearby. Sitting there, I thought of my girlfriend Hằng, who was somewhere in the city.

I had gotten to know Hằng (who eventually was to become my wife) before I went to the South. We fell in love through friendship and mutual respect. If I had remained in the North, we would have been closer still, more committed, and probably become man and wife at an earlier point in our lives. But at that time, dumped unceremoniously into Unification Park, I felt a pang of loss when I thought of her and saw young couples strolling here and there; I felt inferior and painful. Unification Park was a place where Hằng and I had gone for a walk before I left for the war front. But now look at me! Even a street beggar could not have been more dirty, foul-smelling, and empty-handed. At the time of my departure for the war zone, there was little hope for anyone to survive the experience and come home. When I went to the South, my mother was so worried and grieved that she lost her mind, placing a teapot on the stove and throwing ashes into it for tea, and forgetting to add any water to a pot full of rice when she put it on the stove to cook.

Since my elder brother Vĩnh died, I had become the oldest son, but I had left home at a time when my parents were already aged, and my younger siblings were still too young to make a start in their lives. Yet I had to grit my teeth and go. What else could I do? So I don't like the nonsense stories that people make up nowadays, with such catch phrases such as "I was heroic, I hated the enemy, I had this point of view, or that political stance, et cetera." But if I were to speak my mind honestly and frankly, people might look at me as if I were a madman.[1]

Before I departed to the South, then, I had thought very hard and decided to speak to Hằng as follows: "Look, my dear, in the places where I'm going to, the fighting is so terrible that out of ten people who go there, very few come back alive. And this happens especially to cameramen like me, because my work is to film the war. I'll have to stand up to shoot the fighting, not hide in shelters or trenches. Many cameramen have died. So, don't wait for me. We must say good-bye now, and farewell for good. You'd have your own life to carry on. Every girl has only one spring time that must not be wasted . . ." She wept and didn't know what to say.

Having said all this, I also wrote her a letter with the same content and had Đặng Trần Sơn deliver it to her home. Though my heart was in pain, I didn't really want to make the girl I loved wait for me so hopelessly. Thus I made this painful decision so we wouldn't be bothered with this later. After that, there was a long absence of news, as I had gone to the South where I could die any moment. That was how we parted. And the war went on.

And now I had returned to the North, utterly sick and broken, like a beggar without anything: no home, no job, no money, no status—nothing. And my life was still at risk: What if my film couldn't be developed? What if I should be sent back to the South? I couldn't afford to think about marriage, or about Hằng, especially when I heard friends saying she was going to get married. Though I still missed her, I decided to try to forget her.

Then one day (later on, after a lengthy illness), as if arranged by fate, I suddenly ran into Hằng at a busy intersection near Điện Biên Phủ Street, on my way back from the Việt-Xô (Vietnamese–Soviet) Friendship Hospital for a checkup. She was riding a bicycle, along with her new boyfriend, who had been one of our classmates and would later go to study at the same cinema school in Russia where I would also go. We chatted casually for a while and then parted, though I noticed Hằng was obviously very moved and confused.

Only a few hours later, she came rushing back to see me at my temporary residence for war veterans at 103 Quán Thánh Street. Hằng sobbed on and on as we talked. And from that day, we started to see each other more often, as she decided to leave her boyfriend, though it was very difficult for the three of us. And in early 1970, we decided to get married. The wedding ceremony was very simple. I know Hằng really cared for me, for she decided to drop everything to come back to me when I had nothing to my name to offer her. She put up with everything to support me during the most difficult time of my life. I am deeply indebted to her.

As I lay helpless in Unification Park, I remembered that my elder sister's home was on Hoà Mã Street nearby, and reasoned that it would be best to go there first. My sister Muội had married a man named Mạc, so we called her "chị Mạc" ("Sister Mạc"). She was born in 1939, so she was a year older than me. She was the last child of my father's first wife, and was a full younger sister of my brother Vĩnh.

Looking at the cyclos passing by, I wasn't sure that any of them would give me a ride.

"Xich lô ["Cyclo": pedicab] . . ." I called out.

The driver gazed at me fixedly, then went on, peddling silently down the street.

An older driver came peddling by.

"Bác Xich lô!" (Now addressing him politely as "uncle.")

He looked at me hesitantly.

"Uncle, I'm going to Hoà Mã Street, number 52 . . ."

"You have money?"

"Certainly. I don't have it on me right now, but my family has it over there. It's not very far."

As I was about to step into the cyclo, he removed the mat on the seat. Too bad! The mat wasn't all that clean after all . . . so I had to sit on a bare wooden plank. With my shrunken hips and the protruding bones of my behind resting directly on the wood, I felt pain throughout my body whenever the pedicab gave me a sharp jolt.

We reached number 52. I saw sister Mạc walking around right inside the steel fence. I called out, "Chị Mạc!"

Four eyes gazed at each other. She didn't even ask "Who's there?" but instead quietly retreated into the house. The cyclo driver asked, "Could you be wrong?"

"No, that's my sister! Uncle, do me a favor—knock properly at the door and call for Mrs. Mạc. Tell her that a close relative of hers is here."

The cyclo driver did as I instructed. She stepped out of the gate again and stood for a moment, fixing her gaze on me. When she recognized her younger brother, she was utterly confused, and the driver didn't know what to do either. She led me into the house and drew out a plank bed for me to lie on. I noticed that the plank had Chinese characters on it—it had formerly been half of a set of paired-couplet placards (*câu đối*—Chinese inscriptions on a pair of vertical planks often seen on both sides of the family shrine). During the land reform, our family was so afraid of being denounced as rich that we had sawed off the planks and made a bed from them—on the other side, the old inscriptions were still there.

My brother-in-law Mạc had gone elsewhere. My sister and I lost ourselves in conversation. We spoke incoherently, but the cyclo driver was nevertheless able to catch the drift of everything we were saying. Suddenly I remembered that he was still waiting.

"Can you give me *ba hào* [thirty cents] to pay the driver?" I asked my sister.

"I'm sorry," said the driver. "I thought he was a returnee from a reeducation camp or an escaped convict so I didn't really want to take him. Now that I know the story, I just want to help. I won't take any money."

We tried very hard but he refused to take the money. Then he bade us good-bye and slowly peddled away. I told my sister, "I came back from the frontline, but they just dumped me down at Unification Park. I don't know where my offices are. Let me stay here for the time being, while I find out where they are."

My brother-in-law Mạc returned. "Oh, what happened? Let him take a bath first!"

He gave me his two best suits of clothes. Back then each person was allowed to purchase only five meters of cloth each year. I have never seen such a generous brother-in-law in all my life—and he was like that from the beginning. Later, when my father breathed his last in 1975, this brother-in-law held him in his arms.

Brother Mạc sorted out my stuff and took out all of the boxes of film. As for the other miscellaneous items, such as an empty can and an old cloth sack . . . he threw them all into the garbage. He heated a huge pot of water, just like the ones used to boil *bánh chưng* (special sticky rice cakes cooked for Tết), so I could bathe and put new clothes on. Then he ran over to the office where he worked, the city busing management board, and made a phone call to Nam Định.

My father was a big man, 1.8 meters tall, with a resounding voice. He very seldom shed tears. From Nam Định he went straight to his daughter's home, where he saw his son lying there, with two feet as white as paper from being immersed too long in streams and rice paddies. He knelt down, embraced my feet, and wept . . . That was only the second time in my life that I saw my father weep. The first was when he embraced Vĩnh's body on the day he died in the French sweeping operation of 1949.

In any case, I had to make contact with my office. I had no idea how to begin. Anh Mạc made a few phone calls and found all the contacts for me. Nearly an hour later, an official jeep arrived.

They delivered me straight to the Việt-Xô Hospital. From the emergency room to the transfusion room, I kept on hugging the sack of film. My red blood cell count was two million and eight hundred, and my weight was forty-two kilograms. For three months running, they gave me blood transfusions and protein injections! Only after half a year of medical treatment did I return to a roughly satisfactory condition.

Almost immediately on my arrival at the hospital, I tried to contact the Cinema Department concerning the film. As far as my position was concerned, I belonged to the Unification Department, but this department didn't have a clue about film.

When the Cinema Department learned that a journalist just came back from the front with undeveloped film, they immediately sent someone to the hospital to receive the film, but I refused to give it to him. It had to be someone with a clear responsibility and position. This was no joking matter.

Mr. Nguyễn Thế Đoàn arrived. He was the chief of film-developing technology; only *he* could be given the film. He is a person I'll never be able to forget. He was from the South, and was at the forefront of the revolutionary film generation. He was famous for filming the Second Party Congress in Việt Bắc (the Northern war zone controlled by the Viet Minh), and for other scenes showing Hồ Chí Minh visiting workers, meeting farmers, riding a horse on a mission, crossing a stream, walking through jungles, doing martial exercises, playing volleyball, and so on...

There are many interesting and lively tales concerning his filming of these scenes that have never been recounted. These rare and precious materials have been widely used by later generations in all conceivable places, times, and programs, but often without attribution to him. In January 2009, he was awarded the second-class Independence Order of Merit, but this recognition came late and was devoid of the publicity and pomp accorded to other creative artists.

After I had given my film to Đoàn, there were some rumors that my report should not be believed: "What sort of filming did he ever do—he just kept pressing the 'go' button to use up all the film, so he could flee back to the North; there are no pictures at all in that film." In fact nobody believed that I was able to film anything, as my studies had been interrupted and I had no experience, other than pressing the button a couple of times. "And as for Agfa or ORWO color film, he doesn't have a clue!" they said.

After discussing all the technical problems with me in detail, and inquiring about the source of the film, Mr. Đoàn said, "Put your mind at rest, and concentrate on your treatment. I'll do my best to develop the film!"

I didn't really understand his anxiety. Developing film is a normal procedure in the industry, especially for "masters" like him—so why would he have to "do his best?" Mr. Đoàn took the film back for development testing. I had already marked the segments that could be used for testing.

The first time he tested a twenty-minute segment only, which means he developed it in a bottle, a bowl, or a small vase.

"Thủy! The good news is that the film is very clear, and not mildewed! But the color isn't appearing," he announced.

"Please help me. Frankly speaking, if you can't develop the film, I'll be dead meat. They don't believe I've shot anything, you know that!"

Mr. Đoàn only gave a hesitant shrug.

There was an order back then that film brought into the war zone could not remain in great three-hundred-meter rolls but had to be divided and loaded into boxes with thirty-meter bobbins, ready to be put into cameras, so as to avoid doing it in humid underground shelters later.

The film that I had shot was Agfa color film, and it was loaded correctly in nice boxes, according to specifications. That gave them the idea of throwing away the film I had used so as to use the boxes for fresh film to be sent into the war zone!

Mr. Đoàn was extremely upset. He said that many people had told him that "that fellow Thủy" wasn't capable of filming anything, so he shouldn't waste his time for nothing trying to develop the film. He came to the hospital and said to me, "I think there must be something in that film, that's why I'm determined to develop it. But since the film you shot was Agfa color, it has to be developed in a special way. Where on earth did you get this film? We never sent this kind of film to the South, and have never used Agfa color before! We only use ORWO color, and in the war zone, we only shoot black and white—we have never filmed in color!"

I said, almost in tears, "How could I know, brother? I went there and did hill farming, then asked for permission to film the war. They gave me a camera and some film, so I just went and shot these war scenes—how could I know anything about Agfa and ORWO?"

Mr. Đoàn explained that Agfa was made in West Germany, and ORWO in East Germany, and that we were able to develop ORWO film only.

Good grief! And so, after three long years, extending even beyond the Tết Offensive of 1968, running here and there, filming scenes amid bombing and shelling, a horror that went on day after day, only now had I learned this absolutely elementary, absolutely crucial fact.

But if I had thought back then while I was in the combat zone that all the reels of film that I carried on my shoulders as I plunged into the war, amid bombings, taking the utmost care with each image and each scene, would later not be able to be developed, would I have had the courage, the recklessness, to record the war at close quarters, as appears in my film, with tanks, infantry soldiers, and even war planes zooming toward my camera lens?

Absolutely not!

Lying in the hospital, I kept reflecting uneasily on what had recently transpired. In the war, I had faced death many times—from malaria, hunger, and exhaustion—before I was sent back to the North. Though I could scarcely stand or walk, I had managed to keep intact all of the boxes of

Agfa color negatives, and had been confident that this would be the first color film to come from the 5th Zone.

I felt so bitter!

For three long months Mr. Đoàn wrestled with the film I had brought back, but he still couldn't develop it.

The rumors became almost "official": "Trần Văn Thủy is just a con artist; what could he have filmed? When the war got too hot, he just pressed the button to use up the film he had been issued and . . . *B quay* [ran back to the North]." In that period, *B quay* was the most serious offense, and wasting precious film by shooting scenes just to use it up was a crime that would make a prison term almost certain.

It was difficult in those days for people to believe in each other. What could I use as evidence? That was what made me miserable as I lay there getting blood transfusions and other treatments in the Việt-Xô Hospital: How could I prove that I had shot the film for real, that I had done it carefully, and at the expense of the sacrifice, devotion, and even blood of many people?

One afternoon during visiting hours, Mr. Đoàn came to the hospital to see me. He was the one who understood better than anyone else the dangers I faced if the film I had brought from the war zone couldn't be developed. He said, "I don't know why I trust you. I believe that you shot the film for real, but we aren't able to develop West German Agfa color negatives. I've tried every possible method already. I don't dare hope anymore that the film can be turned into a movie, but if I can just get images from it, that will be enough for me to clear your name."

I was worried and brokenhearted. Throughout that time, even though the hospital gave me medicines and nutritional supplements, I kept getting thinner and couldn't sleep at night. I feared that if Mr. Đoàn lost his will to help me, my life, like the film, would be ruined.

Mr. Đoàn continued wrestling with it for several weeks, doing further experiments on his own. He came up with a new chemical solution, and even constructed a wooden mechanism to develop the film by hand.

One day he said, "Hey Thủy, we'll have to resign ourselves to developing the film in black and white only. It will be "inversive development"; in other words, given direct exposure of the images, the positives will appear directly."

Though this is what Mr. Đoàn planned and envisaged, it was still several months after I had returned to the North before he actually started developing the first reel.

Only later did I learn that the process called "inversive" involved two exposures to light. The first was exposure while shooting the film. After that it would be processed in some kind of chemical solution, then brought out for a second exposure, after which it was taken into a darkroom and processed again in another solution; only then did the "positives" appear.

But, perhaps because Mr. Đoàn's assistants thought that this material contained no images, or that the images had no value, they did their work sloppily, and didn't allow enough time for the second exposure, so that the "positives" appeared prematurely. The result was that what should have been black appeared as white, and vice versa; so, for example, you would see black skies, white coconut trees, and black airplanes—and aside from that, many scenes were marred by flickering.

When I met Mr. Đoàn, it was the first time we knew of each other; we were neither close, nor bound by favors, nor by any design for reputation or profit. How could he have thrown himself so wholeheartedly into this work, and how could he have been so concerned on my behalf? I saw that, aside from his instinctive sense of responsibility toward his work and toward films born of the blood and fire, the bombs and bullets of war, he also felt a deep sympathy for me because of my years of suffering the deadly horrors of the war zone, and because of my emaciated and sickly condition at the hospital, desperately awaiting his news day by day.

He was the person who believed that "the film had images," and he understood better than anyone that if he could not develop the negatives, then the "author" of those negatives would be thrown in prison. At that time, I was already subject to irregular treatment, reflecting policies concerning people who had come back from the South. When I had departed for the South, my salary had been fifty-two *đồng* per month. Now, after four or five years spent amid bombs and bullets, and reduced physically to the state of a zombie, my salary was still fifty-two *đồng*.

All I could do was wait desperately for news from Mr. Đoàn's developing room.

And then one day Mr. Đoàn sent me the news: "Hey, Thủy! We've got results! Come take a look!"

He had a person meet me at the hospital and take me directly to 42 Yết Kiêu Street, where the Liberation Film Company worked on the campus of the College of Fine Arts. I remember that at this first draft viewing, even Mr. Hà Mậu Nhai, the director of the Liberation Film Company, was present.

Frankly speaking, I was shocked to death when I saw the film. I was immensely indebted to Mr. Đoàn; nevertheless, the quality of the images was very different from what I had imagined when I shot them. Where were the somber purple horizons looming behind the barbed wire of the enemy outposts? Where were the scenes of eggfruit trees burned half-yellow and half-green, the lines of the evergreen willows, and the silvery waves of the rivers?

And these scenes were not my work alone!

There were hundreds of people in the film, but only two of them survived. One is Ms. Văn Thị Xoa in Duy Xuyên District, and another lady in the performance troupe. As for the rest, they are all dead. Mr. Hy, the photojournalist who accompanied me from the beginning, is dead. Mr. Tý, who took over from Mr. Hy the job of guiding me around, carrying my film stock, and who went everywhere with me day and night, devoting his life to my film work, who mixed milk with beer for me to drink when I had abdominal pains, is also dead.

It was anh Tý who arranged for me to meet all of the personages in the film—if he had not done this, I would have had no idea who was who! Or what was happening where! Thanks to him, I got to know these people and their fates, so as to put their life stories into the film. I silently cherished a deep feeling of gratitude toward him, and thought that if the film could be produced, I would surely put his name in the film as its coauthor. But in conditions of such hardship and danger, how could I be so sure that it would become a film that I could speak of in advance? So I just kept the idea in my head and prayed to God that the film would survive, and that I would survive! After I returned to the North, my motivation for producing the film was partly to pay my debt to all my friends in the war zone, and especially to Mr. Tý (Triều Phương).

Although I was frustrated and exhausted, Mr. Hà Mậu Nhai was especially enthusiastic. He looked at me with affection in his eyes and encouraged me: "Let's edit it. Keep going!"

Later on, he was the one who did everything necessary to contribute to the final success of the film after a long saga.

And thus I was rescued from criminal accusations, such as being a "con artist" or a *B quay*. Nevertheless, the images in the film were a disappointment, though only from a technical point of view.

I sat down in the production room, which was also at 42 Yết Kiêu Street on the campus of the College of Fine Arts. At first I rejected all of the scenes that had been corrupted by improper development; that is, the ones that looked like negatives, and also the ones that flickered. It was painful, as if a knife were cutting my entrails.

Mr. Đoàn thought about this a good deal, and after a few days said to me, "Thủy—I have a very strange feeling about those 'corrupted' scenes that you've removed!"

I was startled at his observation. After several days and nights of agonized obsession with this problem, compounded by intense feelings of regret, I acted on Mr. Đoàn's suggestion, trying to incorporate those corrupted scenes in a long sequence of fierce fighting. This made an unexpectedly strong impression. When postproduction was completed, the film appeared in its first prototype.

The first screening was at 22 Hai Bà Trưng Street. Present at the showing were the musician Phan Huỳnh Điểu (the author of some famous songs), Mr. Hà Mậu Nhai, Mr. Khánh Cao (father of the cinema artist Trà Giang), and other film and arts people from the 5th Zone.

When the film was over, everyone was shocked! They couldn't imagine a film so strange. Nobody would believe it was made by an unknown fellow with no professionalism such as me, who didn't know a thing about film, who had grown corn and manioc in the hills to eat, who wrote his own script, did his own directing, shot his own film, dug underground shelters to hide the film, and carried the film back to the North for the Cinema Department!

Yet it had become an actual film! And won an international prize!

Later on, at an international film festival, the Soviet filmmaker Mr. Roman Karmen, who at that time was on the panel of judges, asked me, "The scenes that looked like negatives and flickered—did you make them that way intentionally for effect, or was it the result of faulty development?"

I had to tell him the truth. "It was precisely those scenes that produced the deepest impression on the judges," observed Mr. Karmen.

On that occasion, I could never have imagined that two years later I would be a student of Roman Karmen for five years at the National Institute of Cinema in Moscow.

9

Letters from the Fire

After the first showing at 22 Hai Bà Trưng Street, everyone was stunned, and then merrily congratulated me. But one person sat in silence without saying a word.

Trần Hữu Nghĩa worked in the delegation of the National Liberation Front[1] at 19 Hai Bà Trưng Street, just across the street from number 22. Nghĩa was a cousin of Triều Phương (the son of his uncle). We had known each other for a long time, and I had invited him to come see the film. Only after everyone had left did he speak:

"Anh Thủy, I'm deeply moved at this marvelous film you have made about my homeland [in the South], and at your acceptance of my homeland as your own in *The People of My Homeland*. When I saw Triều Phương's [anh Tý's] name appear next to yours as the coauthor of this film, I was in such pain that I wanted to cry, for he never got to see the film . . . Triều Phương has just died, you know!"

I was shocked and almost paralyzed. After all of the efforts we had made, after all of the dangers we had come through, now the time had come to pick the fruit of the trees we had planted, but Triều Phương was no more! Like so many others in my group, he had disappeared!

His death anniversary is on the fifth day of the fifth month of the lunar calendar. When he departed this life, he left two young and helpless sons and his wife, who was still in prison.

All I have of anh Tý now are his letters. I was afraid they might be lost, so during my years of study in Russia, I took them with me and kept them carefully.

In 1988, when I went to a film festival in Đà Nẵng, I visited the grave of anh Tý. He lay next to his younger siblings, Sửu and Mão, in the [War] Martyrs' Cemetery of Duy Xuyên District. As we stood before the incense and the soul of my deceased friend, I gave these letters to anh Tý's children, so they could keep them as a precious record of the handwriting, feelings, and thoughts of their father in the midst of the war, when they were still only a few years old. A couple of decades had passed, and this was the first time in their lives that they got to see their own father's handwriting, and hear the stories about his life during the war. When they read the letters, they dissolved into tears, especially Cẩm Linh.

Dear Thủy
I read your letter hungrily. I miss you in a way hard to describe (it's like what one might feel for a departed lover). The day you were digging the shelter, I missed you so much that I tried to come see you. But Hy was nasty and wouldn't let me; I was very upset . . . My wife raised a hen waiting for your next visit to eat—that hen is still there. When people saw me, they always asked about you, even people in Bà Market. You have left in my heart the image of a sincere friend, to whom I have been most deeply attached since I first started to experience life. As I miss you so much, I often wonder wildly that if one of us died, how the surviving person would think about the dead one (as I'm writing this, artillery from Bồ Bồ and An Hoà positions keeps shelling sporadically, shaking the underground shelters). One day I dropped in to see Mrs. Hảo. I didn't want to stay long, because I heard little Thắng asking about you. I remember the day we lay there in a secret shelter with an empty stomach, holding each other to share the warmth. That memory is a beautiful experience! But now you're gone, no longer sharing the fire with us . . .

My life these days is full of hardship, you know. I'm no longer witty, no longer naughty. There were days I had to run around finding food for the unit. I'm worried that if you see me again later on, I'll no longer be the same fellow I was when you knew me. I've forgotten everything, except you. Yesterday, I stopped over at Sơn's grave to burn some incense, I felt I've become too soft, perhaps too sentimental. Something to love and to remember would enrich one's life.

Perhaps I miss you more than you miss me.

Whenever I saw anyone coming from the North, I would ask for you. On one occasion, they told me that you had come to talk at the artists' association, thus I learned you had managed to cross the line of fire [bombing raids] by B-57s and B-52s. If you talked about the South at the artists' association, then you must surely remember me and the day we lay holding each other down in a secret shelter. I remember very clearly your green undershirt produced by "March 8" textile factory, now full of patches to cover the torn spots and filled with the smell of sweat and gunpowder. Oh, how I remember that warm and salty smell. I also remember the day we popped out of a small underground shelter, holding a M26 grenade and lying in the midst of the tall grass, with faces blackened by gunpowder. After coming up here, I saw the film A Day in Hanoi, which made me remember you even more intensely, as if I were seeing you, getting closer to you. Oh, the girl who opens the window and gazes up at the sky (in the film) made me curious—I asked around later, and learned that she was Dân's younger sister! And by now, I also remember the doctor who came to work in Quảng Ngãi![2]

Through all the intense years of the war, I have never found such feeling, such friendship, such camaraderie, as I experienced when living with Trần Văn Thủy. I say this with the utmost sincerity, my dear friend!

Will you be returning to the South? Now that you're gone, I have realized how the "Hanoian" quickly adapted to the hardship and ferocity of life in this arch of firepower. That quality itself had left a deep impression on me. Those days of bitterness and hardship had brought us together and made us strongly attached to each other.

Dear Thủy, my wife was still in prison and she must have thought of you quietly, and that is very easy to understand. I've noticed many times that she has written letters to you, very sincere letters that in some places have a sisterly air. Perhaps for that reason, she has written but not sent them. While remembering you, I often sing songs that you often sang. How is your illness these days? Has the film you made been sent abroad to be developed yet? Are you satisfied with it?

To this day, I still dream of A Day in Hanoi—nothing would make me happier than for you to show me around the streets of the city, though I would be "a bewildered golden deer treading on the withered yellow leaves."[3] Oh Thủy, I've been carried away . . .

10

The Trans-Siberian Express

And so, thanks to the protection and assistance of Mr. Đoàn, and thanks to the interest of a number of elder, responsible officials, *The People of My Homeland* was produced and won the Silver Dove Award at the Leipzig International Film Festival in 1970. The film went on to be viewed in many places, including the war zone; and then it won the Silver Lotus Award in a Vietnamese national film festival.

From that time on, I felt that everyone looked at me with eyes that were more friendly and kindly disposed toward me than before. I was kept in the North, partly because of my poor physical condition, which would have made it hard for me to survive in the war zone, and also because the film school needed somebody with experience filming in combat conditions to be the principal lecturer in the next training class for cinema photographers to be sent to the South. Given my own experience in filming the war, I tried to help the students visualize and adapt to the harsh future that awaited them.

Around the middle of the year 1972, the director of the school, Mr. Trần Đức Hinh, let me know that the school board intended to give me further training as a film director by sending me to a course of study in the Soviet Union. I was very glad, but also undecided as to whether I should go or stay. I had been far from my family for more than ten years, including five years in the Northwest, and five years in the South. My parents were old, and my younger siblings still had no certain future. My wife had just given birth a few months previously to our first son, Trần Nhật Thăng. We lived from hand to mouth, and had to go out to evacuation points day in and day out.[1]

But the upshot was that I had to go—go so as to find a way forward in my life, and to find a way to rescue my family, as my wife observed to me when we parted at Lập Thạch in Vĩnh Phú.[2]

Now as I look back on those days, I cannot but express gratitude to my family and my wife, who gritted their teeth and accepted every hardship in the years that followed so that I could feel at ease about going away again for a few years. My father was even quite encouraged at the news, not because I had accomplished anything, but perhaps because this somewhat lessened his obsession with "backgroundology."

Due to the American bombing raids going on that year, students going to the Soviet Union had to assemble at Đại Từ in Thái Nguyên. Most of them were new public high school graduates, but there were also some older students who had gone on missions like I had, and others as well. Ca Lê Thuần was made chief of the group, while I was made deputy chief.

While waiting for the train and dodging American bombs at Đồng Đăng (a town near the Chinese border), the chief and his deputy (me) went out to drink on the sly and, having gotten drunk, went staggering around on the pebbly riverbank, exchanging ribald jokes and pledging to preserve our memories of that day forever.

Whoever has gone on the train journey from Hanoi to Beijing to Ulan Bator and then to Moscow will never be able to forget that ten-day, nine-night journey. Nowadays, going by airplane is certainly more convenient, but if you want to appreciate the surroundings as you travel, then the train trip is best. This journey introduced us to many different scenes, cities, villages, fields, rivers, complexions, and languages. One impression I'll never forget was of Lake Baikal, as our train ran along its banks. It seemed as huge and endless as an ocean. On a map, Lake Baikal looks like a grain of rice, but the train had to travel half a day before it could pass one sharp end of that grain of rice. Everyone craned their necks so as to gaze out the windows and feel the boundlessness of creation.

Then there were the rows of poplars—no, forests of poplars to be precise, one following on another in endless succession . . .

In 1972 and 1973, I studied Russian, together with the other international students at Lomonosov Moscow State University. That was the first time I had seen such an enormous university. In the summer of 1973, I went to the Pan-Soviet Government Institute of Cinematography (or

Всесоюзный Государственный Институт Кинематографии, abbreviated as ВГИК or, in English, VGIK) to take my qualifying examinations according to school regulations. There, to my extreme astonishment and joy, I again met Roman Karmen, whom I had first met in 1970 at the Leipzig film festival.

He was sitting in an elegant armchair in the middle of a room, surrounded by professors and department chiefs. I sat across from him, and sitting with me, ready to help me out if I ran into language problems, was Mr. Nguyễn Mạnh Lân, a close friend of mine who had gone to Moscow three or four years earlier and was fluent in Russian.

Karmen looked at me, laughed, and narrowed his eyes.

"Ooh-la-la! Дравствуй студент-лауреат [Welcome to the prize-winning student]!"

He asked me if I had gotten married and had children yet. And how did I think the war in Vietnam would develop? Were Mr. Mai Lộc and Mr. Phạm Văn Khoa in good health? Karmen was full of memories from 1953 and '54, when he did some filming in Vietnam. As he chatted expansively, he got carried away, and what he said had nothing to do with a formal interview. The other professors sitting nearby looked impatient, but Karmen paid no attention to them.

"What year in the curriculum would you like to study?" he asked.

I quickly answered, "I'd like to learn from you, sir, and start from the first year like everyone else."

"Then from now on, you can regard yourself as a first-year student."

There was some whispering. One professor raised his voice: "Wait a minute; we mustn't proceed so quickly and simply."

Karmen turned around and shrugged his shoulders. "This young man won a prize at an international film festival three years ago, in 1970, where I was among the judges. If you gentlemen could see that film, you would have the same opinion that I have. He filmed many scenes at the risk of his life. As far as I'm concerned, the fact that he is alive and sitting with us today is in itself a miracle."

Thus it came about that I would not have to take any qualifying examinations. My life has at times been blessed with luck, as it had eight years previously, when I entered the film school in Vietnam without having to take a qualifying exam. A young fellow who was "ethnic," but not a Lò, a Nông, or a Ma, had gone down to the lowlands to study at the Hanoi cinematography school without taking an entrance examination, and now a "country fellow from Hanoi" went all the way to the Soviet Union, and again, without taking any examination, was accepted in the university in the land that had produced all those "Soviet wide-screen color films" that had been shown in every corner of Vietnam!

From the first through the fourth year, we studied all aspects of the theory and practice of making films. The fifth year was reserved for making a (well-funded) "graduation film." In that year, the students were almost totally dispersed, and everyone was concerned with preparing for the examinations, and writing theses, so very few came to the lectures as scheduled. Professor Karmen, too, rarely came to class, because he had his own work to attend to and was traveling everywhere in the world.

Finally, I said to him, "Professor, I'd like to go back to Vietnam early."

"Why not remain here, so you can continue working on your advanced degree?"

"No sir!"

I felt that, having studied all aspects of the profession, my job was now to go out and make good films. My purpose in studying was to pursue a profession, not to gain an advanced degree.

"Professor, please give me permission to defend my graduation early. If I remain here for another year, too much time will be lost."

"All right. Use the film *The Place Where We Lived* [Там Где Мы Жили] as your graduation film, okay?"

That was a film that I had made at the end of my second year, a documentary about the life and work of the international students on the construction site for the Baikal-Amur railway line in Siberia. As soon as that film was produced, it won the Red Carnation Award—that is, the highest prize offered in the VGIK film festival—and was entered in a competition in Poland, where it was shown in many places. I used that film to defend my graduation, and received a "red diploma" before I returned to Vietnam one year earlier than scheduled. Thus I was in Russia only from 1972 to 1977.

Later, that film turned into a "classic"; it was shown every year to all of the first-year student directors. The Vietnamese students were very proud of that success. But actually it was only a normal film, a "добрый фильм" ("a not-bad film," good enough to watch); the teachers and students spoke well of it just to encourage me.

That I got an opportunity to learn from Roman Karmen was a great stroke of luck for me. During my years of study with him, I was the recipient of many favors, of which the foremost was that he trusted me and didn't demand too much from me. On March 3, 1976, he was awarded a major prize by the Soviet government. When he came to class after that, he brought along a copy of the paper *Soviet Culture* (*Советская Культура*), which carried this news along with his photograph. The students excitedly congratulated him, and each one of them wanted their teacher to give them the paper with a handwritten inscription. He said, "There are seventeen of you, and I have only one copy of this paper. I can give it to one person only." Narrowing his eyes, he gazed around the room at his students from Uzbekistan, the Sudan, Palestine, Kyrgyzhistan, Poland . . .

His gaze stopped when it fell on me, and he said, "Among us all, Thủy comes from the greatest distance—so let's agree to let Thủy keep this paper as a souvenir when he returns to Vietnam." He opened a black marker pen and wrote across the page next to his photograph, "To Trần Văn Thủy, my younger brother from Vietnam."

When I went to visit him at his dacha, he talked with me about Điện Biên Phủ, and about the book *Light in the Jungles* (*Свет в джунглях*) that he had written after leaving Vietnam. I think it's a pity that when you mention his name in Vietnam, many people are aware only of the film *Vietnam on the Road to Victory*—in the Vietnamese edition, with the narrative and the sound track written by Nguyễn Đình Thi (in the Russian edition, the narrative was written by Karmen, and the film was titled simply *Vietnam*). Few people know of this excellent book, and even the film Karmen made is hardly known at all to the younger generation in Vietnam.

The dachas of Karmen and the poets Konstantin Simonov and Yevgeny Yevtushenko lay next to each other in a suburb north of Moscow. We students used to gather there, and sometimes had opportunities to converse with famous personages of that era. Mr. Simonov never in his life had any knowledge of filmmaking, but after the publication of his collection of poems *Pain That Belongs to No One in Particular,* which spoke of Vietnamese children in the midst of war, and after the director Marian Babak made a film with the same title, Simonov was regarded as its chief writer.

In making such films, there are "behind the scenes tales" and professional tales. Film theoreticians and instructors all teach that a film's script mustn't be written until the images have been edited in postproduction. But in this case, the commentaries and poems for the film came first; then Marian Babak went to Vietnam to gather images to put in afterward. The conceptual framework of documentary filmmaking can be broken as long as two criteria are met: truthfulness and excellence. For this reason, when I make documentary films, I often have written the narrative first, though when editing the images I sometimes have to make further adjustments.

During my time in the Soviet Union, I got to study a wide array of subjects related to cinema and social science. My knowledge was greatly broadened. However, one drawback was that I was almost at a loss every time my Russian friends would discuss the political turmoil in their country in my presence. They often said to each other, "He doesn't understand a thing."

And I must truthfully confess that though I lived right in the capital of the Soviet Union, I had no deep understanding of Soviet society at that time; I saw only the tips of floating icebergs. I knew nothing of Solzhenitsyn, Pasternak, or Sakharov; I knew nothing of Trotsky, et cetera. When I watched Soviet movies, I always believed that the Red Army would win and that the White Army would lose.

Both the Cinema Institute (VGIK) and the dormitory where we foreign students lived were close to the National Economics Exhibition, called VDNH (ВДНХ) in Russian for short. For a time, a slogan was hung there in bronze letters as tall as a person that said, "The Communist Party of the Soviet Union solemnly pledges to the present generation that We will live according to the principles of communism."

The fact is that at that time, we Vietnamese from the North all loved Russia and the Russians enormously but had little understanding of what Russian and Soviet intellectuals were thinking. It was only later on that I gradually came to understand that they didn't approve of many concepts held by the authorities, and that they were dissatisfied with the regime.

At the time, though, the fact that I was now being given a chance to go overseas and study in a place like this was indeed a huge favor from the heavens.

On receiving my diploma late in 1977, I boarded a train and returned to my country. I had the good luck to be the only student in my class to graduate in the presence of our dear teacher. My classmates graduated in August, September, and October of 1978. By that time, Roman was no longer with us. He was born in November 1906 and died in May 1978 at the age of seventy-two. In his hometown of Odessa there is a street that bears the name Roman Karmen.

I remember also, during that graduation ceremony in Moscow, that my teacher asked me, "What will you do when you get back to your country—what topics are you concerned about?"

Politely, I said, "Sir, Vietnam is now at peace; there will never again be war—no enemy will dare touch our country again, as our party chief Lê Duẩn has said. Therefore, the topics that concern me are human destiny and the building of a better society."

But just when I got back to Vietnam, troubles were erupting along the Sino-Vietnamese border, followed by the "Nạn Kiều" event (Chinese nationals leaving Vietnam), and then by a bloody war with China that devastated most of the six border provinces. To discuss this war would require much paper and ink, much time, and much honesty. How could we have tolerated the Chinese People's Liberation Army troops pouring into our territory wearing Vietnamese army uniforms, burning houses and butchering local people before the shocked eyes of the horrified inhabitants? At that time, all of the film companies from the North to the South, including the Army Film Studio, the Feature Film Studio, and, of course, our Documentary Film Studio rushed to send crews to the border region to make films on this topic.

Having just returned, I followed current events from March 1978 on, when Mr. Xuân Thủy (former chief negotiator for the Paris Peace Accords) went on the air to answer questions posed by foreign reporters concerning the border problems with China. I had a hunch that war would certainly break out. Once, talking with Mr. Lý Thái Bảo, director of the Documentary Film Studio at that time, I commented to him, half in jest, as follows, "Now that war is about to break out at any time, if you chaps keep making films about the 'Nạn kiều' problem, the 'Bắc Luân' Bridge incident, or other nonsense stories, we'll all be sent to perdition . . ."[3]

Mr. Lý Thái Bảo nodded in silence. A few days later he met me again and said, "I've discussed this with the board of directors and the council of artists—everyone agreed with you but had no idea how to make sense of this and keep pace with events."

Then he chuckled, "Okay, since you were the one who made the point, you should make your own film—that's the best option."

I was startled. The regular practice in the profession when you join a filmmaking company is to go through a period of internship, assisting your senior directors in making a few films; only after two or three years are you considered ready to be an independent director.

But since Mr. Lý Thái Bảo had given me this assignment, I had no choice but to start at once making my first film for the studio. I searched around for documents to read, wrote a film script, and went up to the border to investigate the actual situation. I directed the film, organized the shooting, and wrote the narrative. Phạm Quảng Phúc, my younger brother-in-law, was the principal cameraman.

The name of the film was *Betrayal* (*Phản Bội*). The film made a big splash and won a golden award for "best director" in a national film festival in 1980. It was a 35-millimeter film, the longest in the history of the Documentary Film Studio of Vietnam at ninety minutes.

Documentary films are often difficult to make and difficult to watch, but *Betrayal* was as attractive as a good feature film, full of witty narrative and dramatic images. This attracted much attention, both within Vietnam and in other countries, such as Sweden, and at film festivals in Tashkent and Leipzig. In particular, Walter Heynowski and Gerhard Scheumann (two sharp-minded German filmmakers who directed *Pilots in Pajamas*)[4] set a high value on this film. Perhaps that's why in my film career, I have had no opportunity to enjoy the privilege of *cặp tráp* (to play a supporting role), assisting other senior directors. I have neither suffered nor enjoyed the influence of anyone. I did whatever came to my mind that seemed good.

These days people no longer show this film and don't want to mention it either, for sensitive reasons, both legitimate and illegitimate, within the political arena. If I had a chance to redo the film *Betrayal,* I would restructure it and rewrite the narrative. And the new title might be "The Sorrow of a Small and Weak Nation."

II
PEACE

Preface

"I looked out the window at the city streets and saw long lines of people waiting to buy food rations, and homeless people hanging around forlornly with nothing to do in the parks and sidewalks."
—From *Hanoi in Whose Eyes* (1982)

The official response to Trần Văn Thủy's postwar films followed a consistent pattern: they were deemed subversive and initially and often persistently banned by the government agency charged with censoring art, literature, and film. They were banned for the very reason that they had a powerful impact on those who were able to view them: they spoke to truths about people's lives in postwar Vietnam that everyone knew but that were not to be spoken aloud—let alone seen on a screen. When the Vietnamese edition of this memoir was published in 2012, it became wildly popular for that same reason: Trần Văn Thủy was telling truths that were widely recognized but not shared before in public discourse.

Thủy's first film after the war was *Hanoi in Whose Eyes*. Charged with creating a film to promote tourism to the city, Thủy instead made a documentary that when premiered in 1982 was met with much enthusiasm and then suddenly banned. The film showed a series of significant historic sites in Hanoi, and the script discussed how some of the enlightened kings had ruled and how some of the wise officials and intellectuals had conducted themselves in Vietnam's dynastic past. The party cadres responsible for banning the film saw all of this as a veiled criticism of the current regime, and were convinced that, in making it, Trần Văn Thủy was acting as an agent for some hidden malign political force.

This tension between what Thủy saw as his artistic duty to be original and truthful and the repressive policies that forbade any perceived criticism of the Communist Party or the state marked the rest of Thủy's career, and also reflected a societal tension between the policy of censorship and the freedom of expression sought by many Vietnamese artists, filmmakers, and writers that came to a head in the 1980s. In 1983, then prime minister Phạm Văn Đồng had a private viewing of the film and ordered that it immediately be "unbanned" and shown across the country. A few months later, the film was once again banned. Then again unbanned. Chapter 11 challenges any view that Vietnamese politics are monolithic, revealing as it does the clashes within and between the country's power structure and the artistic community. In that chapter and the next, Thủy recounts how in 1986 the policy of *đổi mới* renovation was initiated, which essentially moved Vietnam into a free market economy, while also urging more freedom of expression, importuning artists: "Don't bend your pen; you must write what you think." Even so, by this time, Thủy had finished what would become one of his most famous films, *The Story of Kindness,* but with the renewed banning of *Hanoi in Whose Eyes* and in spite of *đổi mới,* had no hope that it would be distributed or seen. In chapter 12, Thủy recounts the political maneuvering that finally allowed the film to be shown—and its subsequent popularity.

The Story of Kindness (related in chapters 13 and 14) was much more direct in its criticism of the directions Vietnamese society was taking. In Thủy's words, "Documentary films at that time were supposed to 'boost' the image of the regime and its programs. This film, while resolutely apolitical in tone, nevertheless made it plain throughout that the Communist regime was in many ways failing to live up to its own lofty rhetoric, and that there were many deficiencies in the fabric of Vietnamese social life." With its scenes of "bicycle repairmen who were former colonels with distinguished war records," former mathematics teachers forced to make a living as vegetable vendors, and Catholic nuns compassionately caring for lepers, the film touched a raw nerve in viewers: the people's government was not taking care of the people. The film was made even as Thủy was continually tailed and harassed by the police, and when finished, it was at first supported by the Communist Party general secretary and shown all over Vietnam—and then it slowly disappeared. But with its very personalized look at social inequality, corruption, and the gap between official rhetoric and reality, the film quickly struck a chord in the public—and its subject matter also fascinated Eastern Bloc, Cuban, and Japanese film festival delegates in Vietnam. It was 1988, and "the East Germans in particular felt that the film reflected problems that were of urgent importance in their own country," Thủy writes—so much so that the film was smuggled out of Vietnam to be shown in East Germany by that country's cultural attaché. A year later, the Berlin Wall fell.

This part ends with a film Trần Văn Thủy made in 1998 that reveals one of the other great themes threaded through his work: the need to commemorate war in a way that may lead to peace. *The Sound of a Violin at Mỹ Lai* (chapter 16) focuses on the Mỹ Lai massacre—the March 16, 1968, slaughter of over five hundred unarmed men, women, and children in that village by an American company from the Americal Division. The film's subject may seem a strange choice to speak to reconciliation. Thủy was not sure what his central narrative would be until he met an American veteran, Mike Boehm, who every year goes to Mỹ Lai and plays his violin at the graves of the slaughtered. The film presents Mike's story, and also includes interviews with two other Americans: the surviving members of the helicopter crew that had attempted to stop their fellow soldiers from killing the villagers and rescued Vietnamese who were about to be slaughtered. The two had now been invited to return to Mỹ Lai for the thirtieth anniversary of the massacre, and Thủy filmed the Americans meeting some of the people they rescued. By concentrating on the actions of those Americans who epitomized the best rather than the worst of what human beings are capable, Thủy, even in the most terrible circumstances, finds a potential for goodness in people that embodies the possibility of reconciliation.

—W. K.

11

Hanoi in Whose Eyes

For some time after the resounding success of the film *Betrayal,* I felt stymied as to what to do next; I feared to make a false step. The topics the leadership instructed us to cover were the routine ones: developing the economy, building cooperatives, educating people about political doctrine, promoting confidence in the party, and so forth.

Every month I continued to receive my meager salary and sit around idle. After doing nothing for some time, I began to feel embarrassed and bored. It went on like that throughout 1981. At the end of the year, when we did performance assessments, I fell into the "poor" category. But how can one always find a significant and interesting topic for a film? These things depend on being alert as to what life presents you, and having the instincts to know it.

At the beginning of 1982, I decided to ask the studio director for an assignment to make a film, so as to fulfill the duty of a person on the government payroll, and get a "good" performance assessment at the end of the year. Any sort of film would do, and any theme would be okay; good or bad didn't matter as long as I "fulfilled my duty."

This was how the saga of *Hanoi in Whose Eyes* all began; it was absolutely not part of any "plot designed by an evil force," as was later stated in a political indictment; nor was the author of this film a "fearless and learned man," as I was later praised.

Mr. Lưu Xuân Thư, the director of our studio, was a good-hearted person who understood my feelings. One day he was walking past the administration office where I was sitting and waved a stack of paper in the air like a salesman.

"Here's 'The Five City Gates of Hanoi!' It's a script for a tourism film! Whoever wants to do it, please be my guest!"

I stepped out and snatched the stack of paper from his hand. The script, written by Đào Trọng Khánh, had been approved by the studio for production. On the first page, Mr. Trương Huy, the chief of the editing division (newly transferred to the studio from his former position as chief of academic affairs at the film school), had written some comments regarding its content: "This is a film to promote tourism; the key materials are drawn from the writings of Mr. Hoàng Đạo Thúy."[1]

After reading the script, I looked out the window at the city streets and saw long lines of people waiting to buy food rations, and homeless people with nothing to do hanging around forlornly in the parks and on the sidewalks. Scenes in the city at that time (1982) were full of decay and misery. Pagodas and other historic sites, the old streets with good food and rare items, city folk with refined manners . . . nothing remained of Mr. Hoàng Đạo Thúy's dream of the good old days that could be used to promote tourism. I strongly felt that to make a five- or six-reel color film at no small expense, just so that it could be shown a few times and then cast away in a corner for storage, would really be indecent.

Looking at the world around me, the words of a poem by Nguyễn Trãi (a great strategic thinker who help found the Lê dynasty) kept repeating in my mind:

> *A cold sheet flung across my shoulders,*
> *I can't sleep at night; my heart is filled with care*
> *for the common folk I see surrounding me.*

The poem suggested the direction I needed to go. After all of the suffering of the war, my people were still poor, still in want, and their lives were still very hard. It would be meaningless and extravagant to make a film about our ancestors that would cost half a million *đồng* without bringing any benefit to anyone. The stories of our great ancestors are passed down for centuries, but the lives and deaths of our poor people are measured in days or even hours.

It is of course this line of thinking that kept landing me in trouble. When sitting around over a cup of tea with my friends, I often compare myself to an old jalopy with no brakes . . .

For the next several months, I wandered about the city temples and pagodas, the Huy Văn Palace (though to call that small house a "palace" is a mockery); the Bộc Pagoda; the Quán Thánh Temple; the shrines devoted to Nguyễn Trãi, Chu Văn An, and Ngô Thời Nhậm; the Temple of Literature; the grave of Đoàn Thị Điểm; and the places associated with Bà Huyện Thanh Quán and Hồ Xuân Hương.[2] I spent a whole month turning the pages of books in the National Library, the Hanoi Public Library, and the Liberal Arts Library, so as to become familiar with the work of such researchers as Mr. Nguyễn Vĩnh Phúc and Mr. Trần Huy Bá.[3]

Sometimes, as if awakening suddenly from a trance, I would ask myself, "What am I doing? I have forgotten entirely that the business now facing me is to make a film, not to engage in all this reading!" But everything I managed to collect and study regarding the legends of our ancestors obsessed me, swept me away. Living day and night with those stories, my whole soul was overtaken by them. I was stunned and humbled to discover that until that time I had never understood Hanoi at all. I felt myself a thousand times at fault before these ancestors, because I had never been conscious of the magnitude of their accomplishments, or the nature of the great hopes they placed on their descendants.

But, in any case, I had already agreed to undertake this project. Given the same budget, the same energy, the same time frame, and the same topic (Hanoi), I would try to make a film different in content and in spirit. *The Five City Gates of Hanoi* would have been a film to promote tourism. *Hanoi in Whose Eyes* would deal with a conceptual Hanoi, with how to rule and run the nation.

Before shooting the film, I devoted some time to making a careful "prescription," using pen and paper to make notes concerning the issues. In other words, I made a checklist of problems and illnesses in the current society that would require treatment. I underlined these issues by making a bullet point next to each, so that when I quoted legends from past history to illustrate the points, I could throw in anything that might make people relate to the current situation, startle them from slumber, or make them more thoughtful.

In one scene, for example, I filmed a site dedicated to emperor Lê Thánh Tông. Because he had experienced hardship in his youth and had suffered many injustices, or perhaps due to the goodness of his heart, in 1491 the emperor ordered the construction of the Quảng Văn Temple (now the South Gate Garden, vườn hoa Cửa Nam), inside of which he placed the Đăng Văn Drum. If anyone was suffering injustice and had nowhere else to seek redress, he could come and strike the drum three times, at which officials would come out to receive the complaint for the king to judge. In discussing the former feudal era, one historian made the following comment: "If a Đăng Văn drum had been placed here during the Hậu Trần (later Trần) dynasty, or in the Lê Mạt (later Lê) dynasty, people in the area would surely have been deafened."

It was a sentiment people could easily apply to modern times, and indeed, later, when I was interrogated about the film by the authorities, they asked me accusingly why I didn't use the term "feudal era" in the script, instead of "former feudal era": "Did you mean to say that the present era is feudal?" And "Which Lê did you mean when you referred to the Lê Mạt (later Lê) dynasty?"[4]

In another scene that included a shot of the statue of the emperor Quảng Trung, the film recounted how according to one legend, at the end of the Lê dynasty the emperor—then a general, known by the name Nguyễn Huệ—went to see king Lê Cảnh Hưng after destroying the Trịnh lords. The old king had long since lost his power, and only a remnant of his civil and military officials remained in his court, so when Nguyễn Huệ strode up to the throne wearing his sword, everyone present turned pale with alarm.

Only one mandarin, Phương Đình Pháp, dared to step forth. In polite but measured tones he said, "General, according to the laws of the state, it is forbidden to wear a weapon when approaching the throne. Please remove your sword!" Nguyễn Huệ glared at him, but Pháp retained his poise. Then, suddenly thinking that this was indeed correct, Nguyễn Huệ calmly turned his sword over to Pháp.

In the film the following words are spoken with solemn deliberation and accompanied by an echo for emphasis: "In the eyes of Quảng Trung at that time, *'A nation can only survive long, and a society can only be prosperous, when common people dare to speak their minds to their superiors, and when those in power know enough to listen to their subordinates speak of right and wrong.'*"

The narration continues: *"Perhaps that is why, starting from the year Bính Ngọ (1846), when every surviving vestige of Quảng Trung's reign had been destroyed and burned out of vengeance by the Nguyễn dynasty, the people still continued to build statues of Quảng Trung that they could worship. The words 'This statue of Quảng Trung was built in the year Bính Ngọ' were discreetly carved behind the base of the statue. Perhaps that is why the symbolic word displayed over the head of the statue for worship was not 'Dũng' (Courage), not 'Vũ' (Martial Strength), not 'Uy' (Authority), and not 'Linh' (Supernatural Power), but rather 'Tâm' (Heart)."*

The film then segues to the Museum of History, focusing on the statue of the emperor Lê Lợi, but more significantly on the words of one of his retainers, Nguyễn Trãi. Lê Lợi, who had driven out the Chinese invaders, had famously said, "I'm a commoner wearing simple hempen clothing and farming the land. I am now being forced to raise troops to fight the aggressors, but I have no intention of becoming a king or a lord myself"—a sentiment that did not last after his victory. Suspicious of Nguyễn Trãi, the emperor had him arrested, stripped of all official positions, and thrown into prison, even after the retainer had spent ten years "lying on brambles and tasting gall . . ." (sharing all hardships and dangers fighting against the Chinese invaders) with his ruler.[5] In spite of this, Nguyễn Trãi still advised Lê Lợi "to love and care for the people, so that in the neighborhoods and villages there will be no more sounds of hatred and sorrow. Herein lies the basis of the nation's health: loving the people and performing humane and virtuous deeds. Do not, because of personal favor, give rewards in a thoughtless manner, and do not, due to anger, administer thoughtless punishments. Do not love money and possessions, and so fall into extravagant habits. Only in this way can the nation be stable, secure, and long-lasting."

These and many more examples of the ancient virtues and wisdom of the elders, embodied in the ancient shrines and statues I filmed around Hanoi, the ancient admonitions that were being ignored in the country where I lived, were included in the film. As Nguyễn Trãi also said, "Whether a nation enjoys victory or suffers defeat, and whether it flourishes or goes down to destruction, is a matter closely bound up with the happiness or misery of its people."

And as Abu Talib (a popular poet from Dagestan) once wrote, "If you fire at the past with a pistol, the future will shoot back with a cannon."

At the end of *Hanoi in Whose Eyes* there are shots of the statues in the

Tây Phương Pagoda, the narrator asking, "Oh silent statues, what do you all have to say to later generations?"

Such is the content of the film. But from the moment it was born, it came under bruising attacks beyond imagination and its release into the world was forbidden.

In 1983, 1984, and 1985, we were living in poverty, without even, as the saying goes, "enough rice to eat and enough clothes to wear." My wife told me I was crazy, and my friends said the same, but, more than anything else, it was the intellectual loneliness that made me miserable and depressed.

I was never terrified, but remained calm and confident in the things I believed and the things I was doing. Whenever subjected to questioning about the film, I would state the following to security agencies and responsible authorities:

"The script for *The Five City Gates of Hanoi* was simply a pretext for me to get started, a means of getting some people to work with me, to get equipment and film stock. It had nothing to do with the basic spirit of *Hanoi in Whose Eyes*.

The content of *Hanoi in Whose Eyes,* that is, the actual script that I used in making the film, was written by me alone. I produced it myself, and I take all responsibility for it. When the film was mounted, I gave it its title. I cannot put the blame for my troubles on anyone else, and still less can I fabricate a lie that someone else urged me to do what I did."

As the pressure from the authorities increased, day after day I went to the places where I had shot this film to meditate, light incense, and praying silently as follows: "All you distinguished ancestors: have I committed any sins? The film speaks only of your great wisdom; what reason can there be for its rejection?"

I "appealed" to the people in power: "Please just tell me which parts are not right, which parts are incorrect, so we can fix them."

When the studio board of directors "respectfully transmitted" this wish of mine to those holding the reins of power, they agreed to the idea of fixing the film; but when asked "What parts need to be fixed?" one of them gave the curt reply, "This film is so wrong that it can't be fixed."

One of the members of my film crew was Lưu Hà, the chief cameraman, a son of Mr. Lưu Xuân Thư. This was the first film he had worked on in the Stage and Cinema School. I urged Hà to suggest to the school's board of directors that the film be shown at the Children's Palace under the rubric of "introducing a new work." The Children's Palace was at that time the best place in Hanoi to show films; it had five hundred seats for spectators, a white screen, and strong lighting. The list of invitees, aside from the teachers and students at the Stage and Cinema School, would include scholars, researchers, and leaders from many departments, bureaus, and institutes.

Thank God, the plan was accepted! The spectators were packed in tightly, filling all the seats. While watching the film, they yelled and clapped their approval, making a din in the theater.

After the showing, the studio director asked me, "What's your intention now?"

"The production of this film was due not only to my own efforts but also to those of the film crew and the whole studio. If the film proves interesting and is praised, then it is to everyone's credit, but if the film 'has problems,' all the strokes of the whip should land on me alone."

He answered sincerely, "You're right. But how are we going to fix the film now?"

"How you fix it is your own business. Uncle Hồ has taught us that we must know how to "listen to the masses." At the very least, you should show it to the people in the studio, in the Cinema Department, in other film studios, and in literary and artistic associations, so that they can contribute their opinions."

After seeing the film, many people exclaimed, in astonishment, "Why must a film like this be banned?" Everyone, without exception, praised the film's content, including all of the officials and researchers at the Institute of Philosophy, the Institute of History, the Institute of Literature, and the Institute of Chinese and Nôm (Southern Demotic) Texts.[6] But there was still an unwritten order from somewhere: "This film cannot be shown under any circumstances!"

This was in the middle of 1983.

I ran out of hope.

Suddenly one day, Mr. Nguyễn Việt Dũng, deputy chairman of the Office of the Government (formerly the Council of Ministers), called the studio, demanding that the film *Hanoi in Whose Eyes* be shown there. The studio director answered, "There's an order from the leadership that this film must not be shown."

On October 15, 1983, the Office of the Government called again, yet the request was again refused on the pretext that "the film is being edited in order to revise it." But on the other end of the line Mr. Dũng said, "We will decide whether the film can be shown or not. This is an instruction from prime minister Phạm Văn Đồng!"

And so a plan was made to show the film *Hanoi in Whose Eyes* to prime minister Phạm Văn Đồng at 3:00 p.m. on October 18, 1983. I suggested that I be allowed to come along, but director Bùi Đình Hạc refused: "No way. To go there, you have to pass through the 'red gate.' They'll be checking names off there!"

"Anh Hạc! Let me come along—I want to hear with my own ears what Mr. Đồng has to say!"

But Mr. Hạc didn't agree.

Before his departure for the showing, I snuck into the little white Lada (a Russian-made car) of the director and sat in the back seat, next to five canisters of film.

When Mr. Hạc saw me sitting there, he had to accept the situation. When we got to the gate, the guard in his watch post called out, "Whose vehicle is this?"

"It's the car from the film studio, coming to show a film to the PM!"

The barrier was raised, and the same voice called out, "Enter!"

I told Mr. Hạc, "See, no papers were demanded, and there was no checking of name lists!"

I carried the five canisters of film in my arms into the guest room. About thirty minutes later, the prime minister stepped into the room. He spoke at once, with obvious irritation: "Why is it so difficult for me to see a film? If it's too difficult, I won't trouble you anymore."

Who could imagine such a thing! The prime minister had had to wait nearly half a month to see the film from the time of his first request!

When the film was over and the lights came on, Mr. Đồng continued to sit silently, his head bent slightly forward, with his hand resting on his forehead. The other people present were also silent. You could hear the soft sound of the ceiling fans overhead.

A short while later, he turned to me and asked, "Who has seen this film, and what has been said about it?"

To be polite, I let Mr. Hạc explain it. Mr. Hạc said, "Sir, those responsible have concluded that this film has problems, that it uses the past to criticize the present. This film doesn't help the party solve current difficulties, but instead shows nostalgia for the feudal past, and spreads malicious ideas among the people and party members of a pessimistic, suspicious, and negative nature."

Mr. Hạc also said, "They've concluded that the author of this film was an artist, but not a revolutionary artist."

"Who said this?"

"Sir, comrades Hoàng Tùng, Hà Xuân Trường, and Văn Phác."

Having heard this much, Mr. Đồng was very annoyed, and grumbled, "Who gave you all permission to act as the final judges?"

He remained sunk in thought for a long time, then said, "I don't think this affair is as important as you make it out to be. My first comment is: Since you all are brothers and sisters in art, then you should know how to love and protect each other. If you don't protect each other, who else will do it? My second comment is: Mr. Dũng must put a note of this on the record and send it to the office of the party secretariat: 'Organize public showings of this film for the people to see; the more widely, the better, and the more often, the better! Show it at once! If anything wrong is found, it can be fixed!'"

Before we left, he spoke to me earnestly in private, saying that if I encountered anything bad, I should use every means to contact him directly.

I don't know whether or not it was due to his annoyance at the fate of this film or at my situation, but in the opening ceremonies of the Second National Cinema Conference held in the Children's Palace just two days after he viewed *Hanoi in Whose Eyes,* prime minister Phạm Văn Đồng arrived very early and made a speech that lasted more than an hour before more than five hundred cinema artists who had come from the entire country.

He spoke very deeply, very forcefully, and very extensively about how the arts should be managed, saying, "You must not force our artists to crawl through the eye of a needle, adhering to stereotypes and preset molds."

Indeed, many people who were present at that ceremony still preserve in their memories the indelible impression that was made when he turned in the direction of the conference chairing committee and said, "I beseech you all! I beg of you all! That when you censor films, you should try to be as tolerant as I am!" The whole assembly hall instantly exploded with the clamorous noise of applause. Everyone there knew what he was talking about. From that point on, the film began to be shown in some organizations and clubs, and the event was reported by a number of newspapers.

But, to our surprise, only a few months after prime minister Phạm Văn Đồng intervened, *Hanoi in Whose Eyes* disappeared again from the radar screen.

We knew only that it could not be shown, that it was banned, and that the ban was being enforced.

No one could give any explanation as to why and how this came about. An order to ban a work could sometimes be a formal written decision made at a conference to be circulated internally, or it could merely be some casual remark or phone call, and often no date was set to lift the ban.

At this time, I was also summoned to show *Hanoi in Whose Eyes* to two senior leaders, Mr. Lê Đức Thọ (in his Nghi Tàm villa by the West Lake), and Mr. Trường Chinh (in the office of the party central committee), who both discussed it with me afterward. These meetings had many memorable aspects; if it should prove convenient, I may talk about them on some other occasion. But the only concrete result worth mentioning here is that the film was still banned and couldn't be shown.

Then, several years later, when the film was shown publicly and won a prize, people invited Mr. Trường Chinh to watch it again. This time he was jovial, open, and had words of praise for us. But I don't dare repeat those words of praise, because I don't feel we actually deserved them.

12
Untie the Bonds of Writers and Artists

I should perhaps go back a bit, to mention some details concerning the making of *Hanoi in Whose Eyes.*

From the time the montage was complete and until I began to add the sound track, I still didn't know what name to give the film; I just knew that the title had to include the word "Hanoi." I was totally baffled by this problem. Then, through some mysterious blessing conferred on me by Heaven and Earth, I one day picked up a copy of the paper *Nhân Dân* (The People)—a completely unconscious action, because I never read that publication—and started turning the pages. Page three had an article by a contemporary American writer (I completely forget his name) concerning Ernest Hemingway. I read it attentively because I like Hemingway and, moreover, when studying in Russia, I had joined with some Cuban friends in making a film about Hemingway.

After finishing the article, I found that it hadn't left me with anything resembling Hemingway in my mind—I was irked. But when I looked again at the article's title, I saw that the fellow who wrote it had, as it were, fished up a prize: the title was "Hemingway in My Eyes."

How could you argue with that? The view he presented was indeed "in his eyes." But, like a flash of lightning, a thought occurred to me: this fellow has given me a most effective title . . .

I read the words in my head out loud, syllable by syllable: "Hà Nội Trong Mắt Ai." "Ha-noi-in-whose-eyes." Hanoi in Whose Eyes? Hanoi in the eyes of the artist Bùi Xuân Phái; Hanoi in the eyes of the guitarist Văn Vượng; Hanoi in the eyes of Lý Thái Tổ when he wrote "The

Proclamation on Moving the Capital"; Hanoi in the eyes of the Greek poet Ludemis; and on and on through the eyes of all of the personages who have gazed at Hanoi and thought about the city. In fact, Hanoi could be something different in anyone's eyes.

The prize I had snagged was without a doubt greater than the reporter's. I had stolen an idea, to be sure, but that idea was a treasure! And I should add something about the word *ai* (who, whose). The word has many meanings; it is not just a pronoun applied to people, like *qui, wer,* кто ... in other languages, but can also make one think of sorrow, resentment, tragedy ...

These days, when I respond to questions posed by interviewers, or questions asked me after I give talks, I say what I actually feel deep in my bones: that I'm not at all enthusiastic about recalling the period when I made the film *Hanoi in Whose Eyes,* nor do I want to watch the film again and recount the sad old stories of honor and disgrace that developed afterward.

There are many reasons for this:

- Everyone in Vietnam knows the stories relating to this film; to go on repeating them would become tiresome.
- Thirty years have passed already—when I look back at this film, I feel embarrassed from the standpoint of art, technique, and method—it leaves no impression worth mentioning; it consists simply of unadorned scenes joined together, which are guided along by words full of implications.
- The film was shot using 35-millimeter ORWO color film; the colors are faded and streaky; there are no copies left that meet good technical standards.
- The conclusion of the film was revised in a foolish manner; back then, when I could have been arrested at any moment, I had to add a scene at the end showing Ba Đình Square on a day when a celebration was going on. The appearance of that scene in the movie was totally against my wishes.
- And, above all, when I made *Hanoi in Whose Eyes* thirty years ago, society, though it had many things wrong with it, was not as depraved as it has now become.

I wish to add that this film became famous not because it showed great intellect or talent but because it generated controversy that went on for a long time. People jostled each other and stood in line to buy tickets because it was banned—it had been placed on the chopping board, had been classified as politically problematic, as antiparty. It sought to educate those in power, and it called upon people to take action. In short, it became famous due to the excessive suspiciousness and diligence of a number of people who were then in power.

And so, a number of years later, on December 15, 1986, the Sixth National Congress of the Vietnamese Communist Party opened, and Mr. Nguyễn Văn Linh was elected general secretary. This was an immensely important party congress; it inaugurated policy of renovation (đổi mới) and promulgated a number of new slogans:

"Look straight at the truth, reflect the truth, and evaluate things according to the truth."

"Untie the bonds of writers and artists."

"Let writers and artists save themselves before they are saved by Heaven."

"Don't bend your pen; you must write what you think."

Many scholars thought that these slogans were very revolutionary in the context of Vietnam at that time, but in the context of humanity taken as a whole, they were as old as the hills. How ironic—that just speaking the truth should be regarded as "revolutionary!" And it was a mere beginning; heaven only knew how long it would last.

The renovation policy would require a revision of all of the problem areas of Vietnamese society, including social science, literature, and the arts (factors not considered of great weight compared with internal and external matters, and with the problem of developing the economy).

One resolution that was immensely important for artists and intellectuals at that time was Resolution 05 of the Central Committee of the Vietnamese Communist Party with regard to the leadership and administration of culture and art. The content of this resolution concerned the reformulation and reorganization of procedures used to administer the arts.

All resolutions up to that point had merely specified what people must do, or what party members must do; there had never been a resolution saying what the party leadership must do to correct itself. Trần Độ was at that time the right-hand man of general secretary Nguyễn Văn Linh. He was the one who drafted that resolution.

In May 1987, Mr. Nguyễn Văn Linh saw the film *Hanoi in Whose Eyes* with his own eyes. In view of the rumors concerning the film that had flown about for so long, he was utterly taken aback when he saw it.

He turned to us, and in all sincerity asked, "Is this really all the film amounts to, gentlemen?"

"Yes, there's nothing more to the film than this."

"If that's all it amounts to, then why was it prohibited? Or is it because my knowledge is so limited that I can't understand it?"

I was deeply moved by these simple words and was haunted by them for a long time thereafter. After that, he had a showing organized for *Hanoi in Whose Eyes* in the Nguyễn Cảnh Chân Meeting Hall (located in the compound of the Communist Party Central Committee), and invited people in high positions, literary and artistic leaders, and chiefs of literary and artistic associations to come and cast votes approving or disapproving of the film.

The viewers all cast approving votes, which meant that the film would be shown to the general public.

On September 26, 1987, the office of the Communist Party Central Committee issued a directive requesting that the Department of Culture, the Department of Propaganda and Training, and the Ministry of Culture organize public showings of the film *Hanoi in Whose Eyes*.

On October 7 and 8, 1987, Mr. Nguyễn Văn Linh organized a great conference with more than two hundred writers, artists, and intellectuals at the Nguyễn Cảnh Chân Meeting Hall. In his opening remarks, he said, "Comrades, I have invited you all here today so that you may bare your feelings and allow others to hear all of your concerns, all of your troubled thoughts concerning our cultural and artistic policies and measures, so that we may work better with each other. I have come here to listen, not to speak."

He then sat down and began to listen to everyone speak. Back then there were still such major figures as Nguyễn Khắc Viện, Cù Huy Cận, and Nguyễn Đình Thi . . . all the prominent writers, researchers, and intellectuals of the North were there.

On the first day of the conference, a bell rang announcing a break, and everyone went out to the courtyard. Lưu Quảng Vũ came up to me and said, "Mr. Nguyễn Văn Linh told me to call you over for a little talk."

I went out to meet him and stood in a group photograph that included Nguyễn Văn Linh, Trần Độ, Lưu Quảng Vũ, and Nguyễn Văn Hạnh. Mr. Nguyễn Văn Linh said to me, "Now I've come to understand why they banned that film."

One could see from this how deeply this matter obsessed him—it had been back in May 1987 when he saw *Hanoi in Whose Eyes!* He said, "I suggest that you make a sequel, a "Part 2."

When I heard him say this, I knew at once what I must do. At that time, *The Story of Kindness* had been finished, but it was just sitting there, because *Hanoi in Whose Eyes* was still banned. There was no way to promote the film or get it approved by the board of censors so it could be distributed and shown. It was a pipe dream. But now an opportunity had come!

As soon as the conference was over, I returned to the studio and met with the designer Trịnh Quảng Vũ, asking him to add the words "Part 2" underneath the title "The Story of Kindness," indicating that this was part two of *Hanoi in Whose Eyes,* made at the instruction of the general secretary. I was very conscious that this was not the right thing to do with regard to Mr. Nguyễn Văn Linh, but circumstances left me with no choice but to behave in this way. It seemed to me that holding the reins of power and directing the weighty affairs of the nation was the business of our superiors, and that how to make films was our own business. Thus, thanks to the path opened up by Mr. Linh, *The Story of Kindness* came into the world, survived, and found its way into every corner of the globe.

Coauthor Lê Thanh Dũng (*left*) with Trần Văn Thủy.

Trần Văn Thủy (*far left*), age twelve, with his family.

Going south on the Hồ Chí Minh (Trường Sơn) Trails, 1965.
Trần Văn Thủy is the last in the column.

Trần Văn Thủy during the war.

Wayne Karlin in the photo he gave to Trần Văn Thủy.

Trần Văn Thủy at Lake Baikal in the Soviet Union.

Filming *The Story of Kindness*.

Mike Boehm in *The Sound of a Violin at Mỹ Lai*.

Trần Văn Thủy with NYU students at the bridge he filmed being dynamited during the war.

Trần Văn Thủy demonstrating how to enter a Việt Cộng tunnel, 2004.

Trần Văn Thủy, 2013.

13

The Story of Kindness

It was while being watched by the police, and while dealing with troubles related to the saga of *Hanoi in Whose Eyes,* that I got into still deeper hot water by making *The Story of Kindness,* a film that was far more direct and outspoken, not delicately suggestive like *Hanoi in Whose Eyes.* This film faced no less hardship and trouble than its elder brother. Born later, it was more nimble and adroit, but suffered even greater torment.

Documentary films at that time were supposed to "boost" the image of the regime and its programs. This film, while resolutely mundane and apolitical in tone, nevertheless made it plain throughout that the regime was in many ways failing to live up to its own lofty rhetoric, and that there were many deficiencies in the fabric of Vietnamese social life. The story of this film's creation is full of mysteries and tales worth pondering.

It all began when a very close colleague of mine, Mr. Đồng Xuân Thuyết, fell ill with cancer. We decided to turn on our film cameras.

One year later, he passed away, and one year after that was the first anniversary of his death, which made it necessary to wait about two years before the film was complete. When we filmed Đồng Xuân Thuyết, many people in the studio objected, saying that there was nothing special about him, that he was a person who had made no special contribution, had received no special honors, and that he was not a party member. But it was clear that he was suffering a fate common to us all, so we began filming him. Đồng Xuân Thuyết was a person loved and valued by everyone, not because he had great gifts, unusual wealth, or any special status, but because of his loyal and sincere way of living.

There was a time during his illness when a friend named Lò Minh had him drink the gall bladder juice of bears, and he got healthier. Thuyết roared up on his motorcycle to my house on Hàng Bún Street and shouted "Thủy! I'm not going to die! Your film's spoiled!" I went down and greeted him, thinking, *If this film project doesn't work, I'll make another one, but if Heaven takes pity on a good friend like him, nothing could be better!* A few months later, however, Thuyết passed away in Thủy Nguyên, Hải Phòng, his hometown. Before dying, he howled like a madman every night. Yes, we followed this personage for two years, starting and ending the film with Thuyết.

And then I heard stories about people with leprosy being neglected and scorned, and stories about bicycle repairmen who were former colonels with distinguished war records.

In my entire professional life, I have never made any film around such a vague idea as the film that came to be called *The Story of Kindness*. Mr. Hồ Trí Phổ drafted a script titled "On Human Suffering" to submit to the studio directors. It was only a sketchy outline concerned with love and misfortune, doctors and patients, lepers and nuns—it was written in a very noncommittal manner, so that our directors would feel reassured that we were making an ordinary, mediocre film.

As for the real script, we didn't actually have one; it took shape only gradually in our heads, as we carried on. This had nothing to do with any talent or skill of mine; I would urge all film students to never on any account work in this manner. Working with film (not video or digital) means that you have to deal with vehicles and machinery, including sound equipment. Nevertheless, we kept dragging this cumbersome stuff around on the road with no clear plan in our heads, nor any defined list of personages to put in the film. It was bizarre; no one at all makes films like that. The fact we were able to finish it was perhaps due to some supernatural force pushing us on to the final result.

We felt, for example, that the film had to have a cyclo driver in it, together with his feelings and family circumstances. We went searching for a cyclo man at Hàng Cỏ Central Station. Among all of the drivers waiting for customers, there was a tall, handsome young fellow wearing a torn pair of jeans. Our crew commented that this fellow looked a bit *cà chớn* (anomalous), as his appearance was not that of a typical cyclo man. We approached him and asked, "Excuse me, are you available to take a customer?"

"Yes sir, I'm waiting for a customer right now."

"So are you a professional cyclo driver, or are you . . . ?"

"I'm doing it for real, to seek a living and feed my children and family, sir."

"Then could you allow us to film you working for a while?"

At that time, our intention was quite simple; we would shoot him along the road in front of Reunification Park (near the station), taking close-ups, middle-distance shots, and wide-view shots showing the entire setting, without any idea how to make sense out of those scenes. But when we got to the park gate, it was raining hard, so we decided to step into a café and have something to drink while we waited for the rain to clear up. We asked each other polite questions to make conversation: "What's your name?" "What did you do during the war years?" Only then did the young man relate to us that he had been a security officer for the party committee of the 5th Zone (from Đà Nẵng south to Phan Thiết in Central Vietnam), where I had been as well. At that time, his wife was also there working as a doctor. When the war ended, he became a security officer in the Four-Party Joint Military Commission. I was astounded and thought to myself, "Here's a poor fellow *ất ơ* [hanging around] on the street whom we met by chance—he seemed just like anyone else, but when we happened to ask him some casual questions, he turned out to be a veteran with such a meritorious background! This was no longer a joke. I said, "Well, go ahead, finish your drinks and go home. Tonight let's think about what to shoot and what to write—if we start shooting right away, we'll have no idea what to shoot."

That was the way we made the film—we would go places, searching, shooting scenes, making it up as we went along, with no preconceived plan whatsoever. When I decided to invite Lê Văn Long to be my principal cameraman, we were again waiting for the weather to clear up, so I asked him a casual question to start a conversation: "Where is your home village?"

"My home village is in Thường Tín. You doubtless have no idea that when I go back to my village, I'm quite a big shot. My village is poor—everyone there tends ducks, grows rice, cultivates potatoes, and does miscellaneous work. Only I work as a cameraman."

Only later when I visited him at home, did he tell me the following story:

"Once in my childhood, when I went out duck herding, I was overcome with exhaustion, so I crept into a thatched hut and slept—then the ducks broke into some paddy fields and ate some rice seeds belonging to the cooperative. The elders in the village committee made a note of this duck incident in my *lý lịch* [personal record], and the result was that I was unable afterward to get into any university. Whenever I took an entrance exam, I would be rejected because of my record. Later on, just by chance, I got admitted to a film school (then a secondary vocational school). So I suddenly turned into a cameraman and became the most prestigious fellow in the village."

On my return to the studio, I went at once to the personnel office and asked the people there to show me Long's *lý lịch*. Sure enough, the notation Long referred to was right there in the record! However amusing Long's story might appear, it gave me great pain, because at that time, *chủ nghĩa lý lịch,* or "resumé madness" (the practice of making everything depend on a man's personal record) was still immensely heavy and pervasive. This was a problem affecting not just Long alone, but the whole society. "Resumé madness" held the nation in a vice, and polarized people's souls.

Why should such a trivial detail shock people? Because it touched on some issues in that era that had torn the country apart, with bizarre consequences.

Later on, Long related to me how in his school days at Tô Hiệu High School in Thường Tín, his mathematics teacher was Lê Văn Chiêu—an excellent teacher who had to abandon his profession and become a vegetable vender. This was not a story that concerned Lê Văn Chiêu alone, but rather the mistreatment of intellectuals that went on in the entire society.

Taking us to a market at the end of Bạch Mai Street, Long pointed to a man selling vegetables and said, "There! That's my teacher!" After that, I sent Long to teacher Lê Văn Chiêu's home to ask for permission to film him.

Teacher Chiêu said, "All right—whenever you want to film me, let me know beforehand. After I come home from the market, I'll wash up, change my clothes, make tea, and talk with you, so you can film me."

Nothing we said could persuade him to let us film him at the market. The scenes that appear in the film seem simple, but they were complicated to make, because they had to be shot by a hidden camera without his permission.

Whatever I perceive to be necessary and useful to a film, I'll always find some means to accomplish. I said to Long, "The day after tomorrow, we'll shoot at the market, but you must stay at home, without coming to the scene, okay?"

I asked a different cameraman, Nguyễn Trung Hiếu, to film the teacher. I told Hiếu that he was to pretend that he was shooting scenery for a tourist film. He was to stand with his back to Mr. Chiêu in a posture that would allow him to turn 360 degrees. That was how all of the segments taken by stealth were shot. Later, when the film came out and rumors about these scenes reached the ears of Mr. Chiêu, he made his way to the Polytechnic University, where he bought a ticket and watched the film. After that he couldn't sleep for several nights. He had Long come to see him and said, "I was very displeased because people told me that you had filmed me. I didn't want to cast aspersions on the regime. But now, thinking it over, I see that you've said nothing wrong."

Up until 1985, there had never been any film, performance, or newspaper in Vietnam that dealt fairly with people of the Christian faith—in other words, that spoke of the active determination with which they often offer up their intelligence, their energy, their emotion, and even their lives to save and serve humanity. Nearly all of them that I met in the course of making this film were decent people, who knew how to love and trust other human beings, and who were honest and trustworthy, telling no lies. That was the case when I observed, and was deeply moved by, the devotion with which the nuns cared for the lepers in the Quy Hoà Leprosarium.

In those years, the camps where lepers were cared for were medical institutions dependent on charitable contributions. Most of the government cadres who came to work in those places did so unwillingly. Fortunately, the former director of the Quy Hòa Leprosarium when I was filming *The Story of Kindness* is still alive; his name is Trần Hữu Ngoạn, and his home is right by Chợ Bưởi (Bưởi Market), near where I live. He was like a saint, kind to the point of oddity. He was the embodiment of a person endowed with *tử tế*, decency. It was thanks to him that we were allowed to enter the Quy Hòa Leprosarium to film scenes and witness the actual lives of the Catholic sisters who worked there. The sisters lived in rooms that had nothing in them but a bed eighty centimeters wide and 1.8 meters long, and a nun's habit hanging from a nail on the wall.

And their presence there was illegal! Without residence permits, they went by stealth from various churches to charity-supported camps so that they could serve people with leprosy! They had to sneak around because they had no permission to do what they were doing.

When he was prime minister of Vietnam, Mr. Phan Văn Khải once observed to a group of religious leaders that social ills were fewer within religious communities than elsewhere. There were fewer problems with drug addiction, theft, muggings, or fraud because in those places people knew enough to fear these things, even though their fear was based on vague ideas, without any clear explanations. A society consisting entirely of people with no religion, people who neither fear nor believe in anything, is an extremely dangerous society.

His observations might be right, since many things have unfortunately gone wrong in our society and people continue to suffer.

While working on the film, I fell sick and had to enter the Bạch Mai Hospital for observation and treatment. I wrote quite a bit during the ten days I stayed there, awaiting the results of blood tests and X-rays, and finished a version of the script that I was pretty well satisfied with. I asked to check out of the hospital, because I felt I had recovered.

The doctor laughed and said, "You're still in the observation phase—you haven't taken any medicine or received any treatment!"

But the fact was that having written the script, I felt much better. My medical record back then had been registered in the Việt-Xô Hospital, a hospital reserved for high-ranking cadres. Conditions there were better; each room had at most only three or four beds, and the patients were attentively taken care of. It wasn't noisy and messy like the Bạch Mai Hospital, which at the time catered to *thập loại chúng sinh* (all sorts of riffraff). The room where I lay was as wide as a public theater and had several dozen beds. Venders went throughout the ward shouting, "Who wants sticky rice? Who wants a drink?"

That was precisely my reason for writing the script in the Bạch Mai Hospital.[1] Only by staying right there could I really understand that in this life no one is so foolish as to throw away their comfort, affluence, and status in order to live the life of an ordinary person.

In the final part of the film, I wrote, "It has taken us a very long time to learn that to understand the suffering of others is not an easy thing at all. It's only through living other people's lives, sharing their sorrows and joys, that we're able to discover, understand, contemplate, and do a few things correctly. But like us, very few if any would be so crazy as to reject a more comfortable and powerful life in order to live the life of common people. Herein lies the paradox. Despite all of our efforts and pains, what we the filmmakers have finally learned is but a drop of water, and what we still don't know is an ocean."

There is a scene in the film at that point that shows us (the filmmakers) sitting in a car, chewing gum and smoking, while the common people struggle miserably along the road, some pushing ox carts, and others carrying shoulder loads. Those images accompany the words above.

Many people, including the American academics Dean Wilson and Michael Renov,[2] have observed that we filmmakers turned ourselves into objects of ridicule in this film. This starts right at the film's outset, when the brick maker we had come to film chases us away, and we say in response, "Yes! Our profession is indeed cowardly and insignificant. It is cowardly because, though we have many thoughts, we dare not speak out; and it is insignificant because no one needs what we make."

The voice-over in *The Story of Kindness* as well as in *Hanoi in Whose Eyes* was done by Mr. Trần Đức at the Vietnamese television studios. At that time, he was robust, with a voice quality that was well adapted for delivering emotional and inspirational effects.

When we finished making the film, we put it aside and didn't show it to anyone whatsoever; and it was necessary to fabricate excuses for this concealment, so as to delay the time when the film would be handed over to the studio directors in the usual procedure.

14

Kindness Repressed

And so it was not until the end of 1987 that *The Story of Kindness* was screened publicly.

It was said by all that this was done by the instruction of the party general secretary, so not a single censorship board dared raise an objection. And immediately after that, the film was shown widely from the South to the North; and it became the turn of *Hanoi in Whose Eyes* to follow in the new film's wake—it was also shown as a double feature. This was the first time in the history of Vietnamese cinema that tickets were sold to viewers to see documentary films. In March 1988, at a national film festival in Đà Nẵng, *Hanoi in Whose Eyes* won a special Golden Award, including awards for the film script, the directing, and the camerawork.

But then *The Story of Kindness* began to be silently buried.

The film became known abroad through an article by Mathias Weile, a correspondent from the ADN (Allgemeiner Deutscher Nachrichtendienst, the East German news agency) stationed in Hanoi, which was printed in all of the newspapers of East Germany and then spread to other countries. When members of the international delegations came to Vietnam to attend the March 1988 film festival in Đà Nẵng, almost all of them knew that there was such a film, and when they looked at the festival program, they saw *The Story of Kindness* printed there, but in the end it was not available to be viewed.

Among the international delegates was Santiago Anvares, a director from Cuba with a worldwide reputation. He had made thirteen or fourteen films either dealing with Vietnam during the war or providing portraits of Hồ Chí Minh and was regarded as a very close and reliable friend of Vietnam. Anvares observed, "It is very strange that though the program lists *The Story of Kindness,* we have not gotten to see it. By rights all of the cinematic venues in Đà Nẵng ought to be showing this film, so that the people can see it, but there isn't a single place where it is being shown. We therefore need to see this film."

But the organizing committee continued to ignore the matter and responded to inquiries in a vague, evasive manner. Mr. Anvares continued to demand to see the film, and was supported by delegates from Poland, Russia, Japan, and East Germany.

The fact that *The Story of Kindness* appeared in the program did not give me the right to demand it should be shown. To show it or not was up to the organizing committee, but they were following orders from above to avoid and ignore the matter. Even though Mr. Nguyễn Văn Linh had turned on the green light in October 1987, so that by March 1988 *The Story of Kindness* had been shown throughout the country, the authorities didn't want to show it anymore—and they *especially* didn't want the film to appear in any festival having many international delegations.

In fact, many of the delegations wanted the film for their own countries' film festivals. Two representatives of the Leipzig International Film Festival were even more insistent, saying straight out that "the Leipzig film festival has been the gateway to the world for all of the documentary films from Vietnam during the war. We have given our support to the countless prizes bestowed on films from the South and the North of Vietnam, so as to promote and publicize images of the Vietnamese struggle, the war of liberation in Vietnam. What reason could there be for refusing us permission to see, even once, a film that, according to our information, has been shown for several months in Vietnam? This is extremely unreasonable."

In the end, the prestige of Mr. Anvares and the strenuous entreaties of many international delegations forced the organizing committee to agree to show the film. But it was only to be shown privately to delegation members, not to the general public!

That decision unleashed a torrent of reaction. Many international delegates said, "This is what needs to be seen; only this is important. If this film is not shown, then what's the point of going to this festival?"

But the film committee did their utmost to keep the film and their efforts to kill it secret, so that they would not suffer any repercussions.

In particularly, a man and a woman from East Germany representing the Leipzig film festival were stopped by the police when they tried to make contact with locals.

I had no rights whatsoever in this matter. The authorities issued a very bizarre order stipulating that the film was not to leave the country, even though the government had made several dozen copies of the film and had sent them around to all of the cities and provinces in the country to be shown publically. At the same time, they didn't allow me to meet or communicate with any delegations. I was continuously tailed by the police. This was a time when any dealings with foreigners or foreign organizations were very strictly regulated and government decisions about such matters didn't have to be carefully thought through; it wasn't necessary to convene meetings, or reach conclusions through discussion. Orders from above could consist merely of a phone call made by some powerful official.

The international delegations were very upset. The East German delegation angrily demanded that some way be found to send the film to Leipzig. Why were they so eager? At first I thought it was because they felt that there was something distinctive about the film, or that it had something they would be able to identify or empathize with. Only two years later (when the Berlin Wall fell) did I come to understand the true reason. The East Germans in particular felt that the film reflected problems that were of urgent importance in their *own* country.[1]

At that time, the representatives of the Leipzig film festival asked the organizing committee to let me go out to a site on the bank of the Hàn River and meet an East German female delegate for a photo session.[2] As I mentioned, the film committee didn't want me to have contact with any foreign representatives, but on discussing the matter among themselves, they reasoned that I was familiar only with Russian, because I had studied in Russia, and that I knew a bit of French as well, while the German delegates spoke only German. With this language limitation, I wouldn't be able to make any plans or conspiracies with them, so they allowed me to go to the riverbank for photographs with the German woman.

But now I must tell the truth: the police trailing me and the organizing committee had no idea that this woman was a Russian and, not only that, had been a classmate of mine in Russia. She had been a student in the Pan-National Film Academy's Production Economics Department—and after graduation she married an East German who had also been a classmate of mine.

After marriage, she had followed her husband to Germany. The couple was working in the Cinema Department of the Leipzig film festival organizing committee, and she had gone from there to Vietnam as a representative of that festival. Everyone thought she was German.

When we met on the riverbank, she told me how moved she had been by the film and how she wished our mutual mentor Roman Karmen were alive to see what his former pupil had created. "The long and short of it is that all of us in the delegation have agreed that this film must by all means be shown in Leipzig."

"That's wonderful, I'm very grateful to you," I answered.

But, knowing I would never get permission from the people who had wanted the film censored to ship it abroad, I wondered how, first, I could get hold of a "virgin"—that is, unprojected—film suitable for an international festival, and secondly, the difficulties I'd face to clandestinely ship five reels of 35-millimeter film, each reel three hundred meters long and weighing 2.3 kilograms, together with their steel canisters. After placing those five canisters in an additional steel box, the whole would weigh about twenty kilograms.

"Look," my friend said, "obviously I can't help you with getting a copy—all I can say is please do whatever you can to get it into your hands. As for getting it shipped, get in touch with Rugerd, the cultural attaché of the East German Embassy in Hanoi. He'll be able to help you."

I told her I couldn't promise anything, but that I would do everything I could.

I had a million questions in my head. Where could I get a copy of the film? How was I going to communicate with Rugerd, so as to get the film shipped? Sooner or later people would find out that I was the chief culprit in this operation. And on top of that, it was by no means certain that the film would win a prize—a news report about the festival said that "256 films from 40 different countries would be shown. 256 films, one Golden Award, and two Silver Awards." What was the probability of getting an award?

Winning or not winning an award had nothing to do with any desire for fame on my part—the problem was far more serious: if the film didn't win a prize, then I would go to prison; if it did, it would not look good for the Vietnamese authorities to have me arrested. That was almost an absolute certainty. Under my feet yawned an abyss.

In March 1988, at the conclusion of the Đà Nẵng Film Festival, I joined some friends in a long tour through Vietnam, through the entire central region, and then back into Saigon. During that trip, I was constantly preoccupied with the problem of seeking a way to obtain a copy of the film. But I returned to Hanoi empty-handed.

In the middle of the same year, I returned to the South. Whatever you may say about them, the people of the South are risk takers and fun lovers—they're not timid, and they're very honest and frank. In accordance with the orders of the party general secretary, *The Story of Kindness* and *Hanoi in Whose Eyes* had been shown throughout the country, so copies of these films lay in the film repositories of all of the provinces. On one occasion, I was touched to see the effect of my films on audiences, through a little "story of kindness" that occurred to me and boosted my morale during this tense period. I went into the South this time by train. Unable to buy a ticket at the station, I boarded the train and asked the conductor to sell me one. But then, having bought the ticket, there was no place either to sit or to lie down. So some people cleaned out a toilet compartment and placed a plank there for me to pass the night. The compartment was so cramped that when I rested my legs on the open window, my feet got smashed by small branches of trees growing along the railway, and if I retracted my feet, I would soon get tired and stiff. The sour smell of the dining car pervaded the whole place, and the door could neither be securely shut nor entirely opened, so it swung back and forth, making the light from outside shine on and off in my eyes. Around two o'clock in the morning, a stranger stopped outside and fixed his gaze on me curled up in the cramped compartment.

"Are you anh Thủy?" he asked.

I was startled. People who have been trailed by the police are hypersensitive. *How can he know who I am?* I thought to myself.

"Um, why are you asking?" I asked.

I dared neither to confirm nor to deny it, because I didn't know who this man really was. Then he continued, "So, it's you, right? Last week you came and talked at the Railway Club, showed films and chatted with the audience. I was also there that day. The Railway Department chiefs are on this train for an inspection. But why are you lying so badly in such an uncomfortable spot? Let me go and report to them."

In a moment, some of them came rushing to see me, and soon I was taken to an upper compartment, where I was provided with amenities and special care.

When the train arrived in Saigon, these gentlemen introduced me to the local railway authorities, saying, "Take anh Thủy to the guesthouse of the department, and see that he gets good food and good rest while he's here, and then give him a ride back—he's an honored guest of the department."

During that time in the South, I was finally able to get a clean copy of the film, thanks to a friend willing to take risks to help me. It was a copy of the finest quality that had not been shown even once. Even now, I cannot reveal the identity of that person.

It was only when the film was finally in my hands did I start to think about how to get it to Leipzig. To this day, none of the colleagues who worked on the film with me know how the film "escaped across the border," and Lê Văn Long, the cameraman, even guessed that I borrowed the film from some Vietnamese living overseas.

The police followed my every step and monitored all of my relations with others. No one dared do anything as risky as what I planned. Back then, you had to have clearance documents even to carry a cassette out of the country.

I wasn't seeking anything for myself, not profit or fame or money. The key thing was that I felt that this was necessary and would benefit my country. I have never made a film to please my superiors, or to show that my political thinking is in line with official policy, or to win a prize, or to make a name for myself. I absolutely do not think of these things—and I say this before the altar to my ancestors. However I act, I act as Heaven directs me to act.

Back then I lived at 52 Hàng Bún Street. My house was always under surveillance by the police, who did their watching in two groups, one on Hàng Bún Street, and the other on Yên Ninh Lane. I went to a telephone I didn't ordinarily use and dialed Rugerd's number. I didn't know German, but Rugerd was fortunately fluent in Vietnamese.

"Is it Rugerd? How are you doing?"

"Anh Thủy! I'm doing fine!"

"It's been too long since I've seen you. Let's go out for a coffee."

During that period, merely going somewhere with a foreigner was in itself taking a risk. We sat in an empty place on Bà Triệu Street and drank coffee. It was a café run by the artist Ngọc Linh, who also worked in the cinema industry. As we sat and chatted, I examined the surroundings. Seeing nobody was watching us, I told him I'd obtained a copy of the film. He was immediately excited.

"As to what's to be done next, the Leipzig festival people told me that this will be decided by you."

He nodded, and assured me that in our next meeting, he would tell me exactly what must be done.

We met in the same coffee shop a few days later. We sat, drank coffee, and talked about whatever came into our heads, all the while looking up and down to spot if anyone was tailing us. Finally Rugerd said, "Listen carefully! At 3:00 p.m. this Sunday on Bạch Thảo Street, a white car with a diplomatic number plate will be parked along the right side of the road. The trunk will be open. I'll be standing on the sidewalk smoking, with my back to the car. Do whatever is necessary to throw the film into the trunk without anyone seeing you. Then disappear—leave the rest to me."

It was like a detective story. I drove my Honda motorbike and set out from Hàng Bún Street. The film casket was behind me, unsecured. I went past the red gate of the Presidential Palace. Bách Thảo Street was very empty on Sunday at 3:00 p.m. In the distance was a white car with an open trunk parked by the side of the road, and a man standing and smoking on the sidewalk with his back to the car.

When I was still fifteen to twenty meters away, I saw a few people coming in the opposite direction from Ngọc Hà Street, and immediately revved my motor and sped past the white car. When I reached the Ngọc Hà intersection, I turned around, drove back, surveyed the scene again, and saw no one was there. I drove at an even speed, my right hand on the gas control, and with my left hand—I'm left-handed—threw the heavy metal container holding the film into the trunk.

To this day, I have no idea how the film was shipped to East Germany.

In the meantime, our officials in charge of cultural and artistic affairs were still engaged in ceaseless discussion concerning the issue of delivering or not delivering the film to the festival. Many supported the idea of delivering the film.

On August 24, 1988, a meeting took place at 49 Phan Đình Phùng Street in which Mr. Nguyễn Văn Hạnh (the deputy director of the Department of Culture and Art; Mr. Trần Độ was director) and Mr. Văn Phác (minister of culture) took part. For some reason, I too was present at the meeting. Mr. Nguyễn Văn Hạnh wrote something on a scrap of paper, then pushed it over to Mr. Văn Phác. Mr. Văn Phác wrote a few words on it, then pushed it back to Mr. Hạnh. Mr. Hạnh read it, then pushed it over to me, saying, "That's it, now it's okay for you to go; you can put your mind at rest."

I quickly read the scrap of paper: "anh Văn Phác, I earnestly suggest that you allow the film *The Story of Kindness* to be sent to the film festival in the Democratic Republic of Germany."

And then the words: "This matter has been approved."

According to the rules of etiquette, I should have thanked him and returned the scrap of paper to him after reading it, but instead I folded it and put it in my pocket, for protection later.

Later on, during the many occasions when I was detained and interrogated concerning this matter, I had to produce this scrap of paper. It had on it their handwritten evidence, not just typewritten words.

In spite of this "approval," I was relieved that Rugerd had gotten the film to Germany, since in the end I wasn't allowed to take a copy with me. The officials in charge kept discussing whether or not they should permit the film to be shipped abroad, as well as whether or not they should "edit" it first. This procrastination went on and on, almost until November 1988, when I was finally told I could go . . . but under no circumstances could I show my film.

15
Kindness Abroad

In those days, going to foreign countries was extremely difficult. Even trips undertaken purely for government business or for professional reasons were not as simple as they have now become. There were many occasions when a film festival or a conference would invite somebody, and the leadership would send somebody else, who had no connection with the business at hand, in that person's stead. It was due to this that the letter of invitation from the Leipzig festival sent to Trần Văn Thủy explicitly stated that this invitation was for the person specified only, and could not be applied to anyone else.

The Germans were well aware of my situation. They knew that the shipment of *The Story of Kindness* to Leipzig was a very risky business, as two of their representatives had already witnessed the petty harassment concerning whether or not to show the film at the Đà Nẵng festival in March 1988. A point worth noting is that though the Leipzig festival would not take place until the end of November 1988, the letter of invitation was dated October 6, 1988. They understood the bureaucratic decision-making processes in this country pretty well.

Close to departure, I was "invited" to yet another meeting in which the leadership would present their decisions to me. The meeting included a deputy director of the Cinema Department and Cao Nghị, a deputy director in charge of finance. In addition, there were some people in charge of foreign relations, security, and some others as well. Mr. Bùi Đinh Hạc, representing the leadership, said, "We have received the invitation from the Leipzig film festival, and the leadership has decided to allow anh Thủy to go. To ensure that the mission is done in a good and responsible manner, Mr. Cao Nghị shall act as chief of the delegation. Mr. Cao Nghị will have the responsibility to oversee and direct the mission. In other words, both of you can go; but the film absolutely cannot go there. If anything should happen, and if *The Story of Kindness* shows up in Leipzig and is shown at the festival, then the two of you, and especially Mr. Cao Nghị, will bear the responsibility for this."

In that era, people going abroad were often given such precise warnings.

When Mr. Bùi Đình Hạc had finished speaking, I asked, "Have you finished?"

He said, "Those are all of the points I need to communicate."

I asked, "Are the things you have said simply the thoughts of friends and colleagues offered to me before I leave, or are they orders from the leadership?"

Mr. Hạc said, "These are orders from the leadership. You must not allow *The Story of Kindness* to be shown in Leipzig!"

I also responded in a frank manner, "anh Hạc, if you're worried that this may happen, then you'd better take necessary formalities to keep me here—because my nature is different from others in that after I've crossed the border, I won't be able to remember a thing, and anything may happen."

Maybe they thought I was just boasting. I made an additional remark: "It is now Saturday morning. You still have the afternoon to arrange to keep me here. If Sunday passes, and nothing happens, then on Monday morning, Mr. Cao Nghị and I will go to the airport as planned, and we will then fly out of the country. After that I don't know what will happen."

So it was that on Monday morning, I went with Mr. Cao Nghị to the airport, and we flew to Moscow, and then to Berlin. From Berlin we went more than three hundred kilometers by car to Leipzig, a city in the southeastern part of Germany. When we got there, we were led directly to the executive committee of the festival, where we did the paperwork, received our badges, programs, money, and introduction letters to the Astoria Hotel for check-in. The Astoria was an old hotel, the finest in Leipzig at that time.

About half an hour after we moved into our room, a knock came at the door. Before I could even ask who it was, the doorknob turned, the door opened, and a person appeared, who introduced himself: "I'm a security man from the Vietnamese embassy in Berlin, and I've been sent here on special assignment by the ambassador to meet the two of you to find out and confirm whether the film *The Story of Kindness* is available here or not, because we've got an order from home that this film must not appear in the festival."

I told him that I was just a delegation member, and that the person in charge was Mr. Cao Nghị. But he continued to wrangle about the same subject: "Did you people bring anything with you? The ambassador is waiting on the other end of the line in Berlin."

Mr. Cao Nghị was sincere and gentle by nature, and moreover he suffered from a heart condition. I had to think about protecting him, and feared that some mishap might befall him. I felt sorry for him—I felt that I was in some way being unkind to him because he was a decent man who had been forced into this awkward situation. He knew nothing about the real situation, and kept trying to explain: "Don't you know how difficult that would be! The film canister is so big; it's not something so small like a matchbox that could easily be hidden. We went through the customs with all the proper paperwork. As for the film, only the government has it; how could you ask such a question?"

The security man said, "The program has the film listed for showing on the 27th of November at 8:30 p.m. at the Capital Theater."

Mr. Cao Nghị said, "Then go to the executive committee of the festival and ask them about it. We just got here, and have only just now moved into this room. We were told to stay here, so this is where we'll stay! We haven't even had time to wash or eat anything!"

My wife's younger brother, Nguyễn Tiến Dũng, was just then sitting in the inner room. When he saw how tense the situation was, his face turned pale with alarm. When I entered the inner room to get some papers, Dũng said to me in a low voice, "anh Thủy, you've got to step back—you have to think of your wife and your children! If you take one more step forward, there will be no way to go back home!"

I drew close to his ear: "There's an abyss behind me—I can't step back even one millimeter!"

I had to act in this manner because I didn't want to be bullied into submission. If I had been cowardly and allowed myself to be censored, so that no one in other countries could see the film, it would have been like being buried alive.

Among the 256 films to be shown, what were the chances that my film would win a prize? If it didn't win a prize, I would have to live in exile, washing dishes in some restaurant for the rest of my days.

That was what I most feared—having to live abroad, to live far from my homeland, far from the graves of my ancestors. I was accustomed to the smell of incense and smoke, the smell of straw and rice stubble.

The security man kept going over the same points with Mr. Cao Nghị at length until he went to speak with the festival executive committee. I don't know how he spoke with them; perhaps he tried to make himself sound authoritative—in any case, the executive committee's reply was, "We can speak only with the Vietnamese Ministry of Culture."

Throughout our days in Leipzig, from November 20 to 27, I couldn't eat or sleep, and grew thinner and thinner as I waited for *The Story of Kindness* to be shown.

I never sought fame or honors; I longed only to do something useful. I imagined that when foreigners saw that film, they would be moved, and feel affection for Vietnam. They wouldn't think that it was a film by Trần Văn Thủy, but rather that it was a Vietnamese film.

The people in charge of cinema in Vietnam had at their disposal a way of raising Vietnam's status in the world, but they didn't know how to do it; instead they regarded me as a criminal. As for my mother, she kept weeping as I got involved in one problem after another: "My son! Why do you make yourself so miserable! Phúc isn't like that at all!"

Phúc was her son-in-law, the husband of my younger sister. He made films that were cheerful and positive, so that he could bring home chicken and duck eggs as by-products. He made films about science, so everywhere he went, people would bestow gifts on him. This delighted my mother, who would say, "See—if you make films, you have to make them the way Phúc does. When I see you making gloomy films, as if you were dealing in counterfeit money, I get so worried that I can't sleep, son."

Such were my circumstances. I did have one possible path of retreat open to me in case I was to be arrested. Before going to Germany, I had received an invitation from the Vietnamese Association in France, and had received a signed decision from Mr. Trần Độ allowing me to go there. I had gone to the French Embassy and obtained a visa. If the worst happened, I could remain in France.

On the afternoon of the 27th, I asked my younger brother-in-law Dũng to take care of Mr. Cao Nghị. "Take him to your dormitory. See that he gets a good meal and is able to rest. He should drink wine only. After that, find some pretext to have him pass the night there; don't let him go back to the hotel or to the movie theater."

Dũng did just as I instructed him. He invited Mr. Nghị to drink some light wine, then spoke to him in a very friendly manner: "So, my brother, it's late already, and it's started snowing. Stay with me tonight, then tomorrow when I go to work I'll take you back to the hotel."

While Dũng was doing this, I went out to the Capital Theater. Every seat had been taken, and many people were standing. They packed the theater wall to wall.

As they watched the film, the spectators applauded three times, and when it was over, all of the members of the audience gave me a standing ovation as I climbed uneasily to the stage.

"This is great fun," I said. "I'm very grateful, but please excuse me, I've got to attend to a little task."

I hurried upstairs to get my stuff, which had been packed up in readiness, and left a slip of paper with a message on it that I had written in advance: *"Dear anh Cao Nghị, I have to go to Berlin for a few days to buy a ticket for the trip to Paris. Please remain where you are and eat carefully to safeguard your health. Dũng will take care of everything for you. As for all that concerns the film and the prize, please let me decide."*

I had to write these things because I was afraid that Mr. Nghị might intervene with the executive committee about this and that. I placed the slip of paper at the head of his bed, then took all of my things and disappeared at once from Leipzig.

The Leipzig train station is regarded as one of the major train stations in Europe, but at that time, it was as dark and cold as a grave. I took a train to West Germany. If I had remained in Leipzig that night, I would surely have been seized.

During this Leipzig-to-Paris journey, West German customs officials boarded the train to check the passengers' papers as soon as the train reached the West German border. I didn't have a West German visa! Only then did I learn that on reaching the Frankfurt am Main station, it was necessary to get out and change to a different train. But to step down to the train station floor was to set foot in West Germany—you must have a visa. *If they make me get out at this station and take me into custody, the game is over,* I thought.

They questioned me again and again in German, French, and even Russian, but from the beginning to the end, I said only the following brief phrases in English: "I am a film director—Hanoi—International Film Festival Leipzig—Paris." Pretending that I didn't know Russian, I just repeated these phrases over and over. The train had to remain stationary for half an hour due to my situation.

Several West German frontier soldiers kept questioning me, but when they saw that I just kept repeating myself, they grew disgusted—how could they converse with a fellow who just said the same thing ten times over? They finally threw my passport into the corner where I was sitting, waved their hands, and went away.

I was totally worn out. In my hands was a cloth sack with few changes of clothing and a cake of steamed rice that my brother-in-law had wrapped for me the previous night. There were also a few pieces of stewed pork and some pickled cucumbers, not separately packed. The sour juice of the cucumbers had seeped into the rice, so it was hard to swallow.

When the train reached Frankfurt am Main, the shops were dazzlingly illuminated. As part of West Germany, Frankfurt am Main was part of a capitalist country—this was the first time I had been to one. I changed trains at that station, and after that arrived at the German-French border. By then I was exhausted. My rice tasted like rotten dregs left in a cooking pot and I couldn't swallow it. I went into a restroom cubicle to wash my face and drink some water to ease my thirst. A French border guard thought I was some kind of stowaway and started violently kicking the door. I stepped out, my face haggard, and with ragged clothes, as if I had just crept out of a pile of garbage.

The border guard questioned me haughtily, assuming that I was a criminal trying to slip past the border.

I said, "Je suis Trần Văn Thủy, réalisateur. Je suis invité ici par le responsable. Attendez-moi un peu, je viens là-bas pour prendre mon passport." (I am Trần Văn Thủy, a film director. I have been invited here by those responsible. Please wait a moment while I return to my seat and get my passport.)

When he had finished examining my papers, the border guard made a classic formal gesture—he bowed nearly double at the waist and joined his arms to make a circle, and, indicating the exit, said, "S'il vous plaît, monsieur."

The name of the station at the border was very easy to remember: "La Fontaine," the author of the line *"The cicada sadly hums . . ."*[1] Then the train came to Paris. I had been invited for the 1st of December, but I had somehow made my way there by the 28th of November!

Public phones in France were more complicated and had more buttons than the ones in our country. I didn't know which buttons to push, and I hadn't even a penny in my pocket. I kept looking closely at other people as they used the phones, to observe what they did. On seeing a benevolent-looking old lady, I held out the phone number for her to see, so that she could help me. She gave me a few coins, but I told her I didn't know how to make a call, so she dialed the number for me and handed me the receiver. On the other end of the line was a woman's voice speaking Vietnamese.

"Hello."

"Miss, may I ask if you are from the Vietnamese Association in France?"

"Yes, what can I do for you, sir?"

Only then did I thank the old woman who had helped me, and only when she left did I say, "Miss, please speak with me very clearly—if you hang up, I'll be stranded here. I'm Trần Văn Thủy. You all sent me an invitation, but it was for December 1st, and today is only the 28th of November. Can you help me make contact with anh Trần Hải Hạc, anh Nguyễn Ngọc Giao, or anh Bạch Thái Quốc, so they can come pick me up?"

"No problem, you can rest easy. Where are you standing? What station are you at?"

"I have no idea what station it is; I just know that it's the station you get to when coming from West Germany."

"What location are you standing in?"

"I'm standing inside the station."

"Look and see what the number is of the rail line that you're next to."

"Number 13."

"Stay right where you are, okay? Don't go anywhere else."

Only later on, after going to France many times, did I learn that the station is called De l'Est (East Station). When people call and make arrangements to meet or greet each other in Paris, it is generally necessary to do so several days ahead of time. To call in the middle of the night and tell someone that you've arrived is next to impossible.

But, forty minutes later, anh Trần Hải Hạc ran straight to where I was standing at rail line 13. He was wearing a loose, white-lined denim jacket, the lower flaps of which flew along in the air as he ran! The first thing I said to him was, "Anh Hạc, is my early arrival causing you any trouble?"

"No, no, no; no trouble at all. We're very happy you've come; it's no trouble at all!"

Since then, during my many trips to Paris over the years, I have usually stayed at Trần Hải Hạc's house at Place d'Italie in Arrondissement (District) 13.

Through him I have had the good fortune to make the acquaintance of many friends, and he and I have grown very close. The people in his circle are very sincere, very attached to the Vietnamese homeland, and share wholeheartedly the joys and sorrows of their compatriots at home. Nevertheless, it would not be appropriate to talk about them here, for many reasons.

In 1946, when Hồ Chí Minh went to France for the Fontainebleau Conference, he was photographed holding in his arms a one-year-old Vietnamese child living in France. That child was Trần Hải Hạc.

After the 1989 *tâm thư* (letter from the heart) incident,[2] Trần Hải Hạc's name, and those of many other people in the Vietnamese Association in France, were blacklisted. When these people went back to Vietnam, they were followed by the police; and they sometimes found it hard to return to Vietnam, or were refused entry altogether.

A few days after my arrival, the Vietnamese Association in France assigned Ms. Thanh Thiện the task of taking me to get "outfitted." She wrote me a check for several thousand francs to buy me new sets of inner and outer clothing—she even asked me to take off my shoes, to see if my socks were torn.

So I became a fashion plate. And for what purpose? So that Trần Văn Thủy could go on a speaking tour and converse with audiences in many parts of France.

But the thing that made me almost crazy with anxiety then was of course the results of the Leipzig International Film Festival. I read newspapers all day long, and came across different publications. The longest article about me and *The Story of Kindness* was by Elizabeth D. in *Liberation*. *Le Monde Diplomatique* ran an article by the famous journalist Jacques Decornoy, and then there were notices in *Le Peuple du Monde*, *Le Figaro*, and many others. On reading *Le Monde Diplomatique* and then *Liberation*, I saw that they had printed the results of the Leipzig festival. I saw that *The Story of Kindness* appeared among the titles of the prize-winning films. I was in an inner room at the time; anh Trần Hải Hạc was sitting in his study on the other side of the kitchen.

"Ha-hah!" I shouted. "I'll be able to go back to Vietnam now!"

Up to this time, I had been perpetually consumed by the question of my return home—how could I do it without getting into trouble?

Just recently, in December 2012, my brother-in-law Dũng and his wife went back to Hanoi to visit the family. I asked him about what had happened in Leipzig at that time, and Dũng still kept a good memory about Mr. Cao Nghị. He recounted some more details:

On the night of November 30, 1988, at the conclusion of the festival, the awards ceremony took place in the Capitol Theater. When the executive committee announced that *The Story of Kindness* had won the Silver Dove Award, the spectators, nearly a thousand of them, burst into applause. The Vietnamese delegation was invited to come on stage to receive the prize.

Dũng said to Mr. Cao Nghị, "Come on, you go up and receive the prize!"

Mr. Cao Nghị demurred: "The director's disappeared. I'm not going up there for anything. If I accept the prize, it will be my death warrant when I return!"

When Dũng reached this point in his story, I suddenly felt bitter. I wonder if, in the history of world cinema, there has ever been any case where the author of a prize-winning film at an international festival has had to undergo such a bizarre and miserable experience.

At that urgent juncture, it became necessary for Dũng to accept the prize on behalf of the Vietnamese delegation. Fortunately, he was a tall and good-looking young man who had lived in Germany for a long time and consequently spoke German like a native.

Even up to this very moment, nearly thirty years after the event, I still have no idea what the prize looks like, or where it now exists.

Anyway, I remained in Paris for three months, until March 31, 1989.

Mr. Cao Nghị returned home wretched, anticipating the worst. He submitted a detailed report and a critical review to the Ministry of Culture and the Police Department, where he was repeatedly dragged over the coals. Now, every time I think of this event, I have a feeling of guilt, a feeling that I failed to do right by him. But I have no regrets whatsoever with regard to any other aspect of the matter. The problem lay not with Mr. Cao Nghị nor with me, but elsewhere. Mr. Nghị was made wretched, and I too "skinned my shins and elbows" many times, and was aware that many others were also suffering for no reason at all. Did they deserve all that? And what has this wretched country gained by acting like that again and again? Well, let everyone judge this for themselves.

Recently I made a phone call to Mr. Cao Nghị. He lives in Saigon these days. When I touched on the former events in Leipzig, all he said was, "You were very courageous and did many useful things." As for the severe interrogations he had had to endure afterward, he mentioned them only in passing, but everyone knows how harshly he was treated.

My German colleagues, on the other hand, were very kind to me. In the following year, 1989, they invited me to join their panel of judges in what would be the last film festival held there before the government of the Democratic Republic of Germany was overthrown.

I was in France at the time, so I didn't have to seek anyone's permission, or make a report to anyone. From Paris I flew directly to Berlin and then to Leipzig. The films submitted for consideration that year were very fine, especially the film *Parade* from Poland. I gave the film a full ten points, and later on it was in fact given the Golden Dove Award.

I returned to Paris and Western Europe, remaining there until the beginning of July 1990. That was when a series of momentous historic events occurred. The Berlin Wall came down. The socialist governments of the Eastern block countries disintegrated, and the Soviet Union also fell apart . . .

16

A Violin at Mỹ Lai

The approach of the thirtieth anniversary of the Mỹ Lai Massacre—the murder of nearly five hundred Vietnamese villagers, all unarmed men, women, and children, by American soldiers—stirred many memories of the victims, and I felt that I had to make a documentary film about that event.

But that was about all I had in my mind. I didn't have an outline or a script.

Nevertheless, Nguyễn Văn Nhân, the director of our film studio, and Lê Mạnh Thích, the deputy director, agreed with the idea and gave me all that was necessary to make the film; they believed that as long as my team did it, the film would be okay.

From the newspaper *Lao Động* (Labor), I learned that two Americans named Hugh Thompson and Larry Colburn with a direct relationship to the event were coming to Vietnam and would go to Mỹ Lai. Thompson, an army helicopter pilot, and Colburn, his gunner, along with crew chief Glenn Andreotta (later killed in action) had tried to stop the massacre by training their guns on their fellow soldiers who wanted to go on killing civilians, and had rescued some of the threatened villagers. Just as I was thinking this over, my son Thăng came to me and said, "It looks like those two Americans are staying at a place on Hàng Bạc Street."

A casual piece of news—but hard-pressed as I was, I made my way to Hàng Bạc Street. "Here you are, check out this guest house," my son said.

"Sir, are there some Americans staying in your guesthouse?" I asked the owner.

"Yes, some."

"Please call one of them down so I can meet him for a minute, okay?"

"Who do you want to meet? What's his name?"

"Any of them will do."

(What a bizarre answer!)

So a big lumbering American, neither Thompson nor Colburn, came down and the two of us exchanged a few words. In a voice as cavernous as if it came from the depths of hell, the American said that he would also be going to Mỹ Lai. That was all there was to it. He gave me the telephone number of a Vietnamese friend of his named Phan Văn Đỗ (later on anh Đỗ made many contributions to the making of the film).

On returning home, I phoned anh Đỗ and invited him to my house to have dinner with me that evening together with some of my filmmaking associates.

The trays of food were laid out, making a fine display, but the agreed-on time came and no one appeared. The phone rang. *Something must have gone wrong,* I thought to myself.

"Anh Thủy, is it okay to ask another person to come along?"

"Bring as many as you like—just come and enjoy yourself."

A short while later, anh Đỗ appeared at the gates to my house, which had been thrown open, and next to him was the lumbering American whom I had met in the morning. It was as if arranged by fate.

"Hi, I'm Mike Boehm."

Beer flowed freely, and "my boss" Hằng (my wife) gaily offered everyone all the delicacies of Hanoi. The guests chatted as naturally as if they had been old friends.

Then, slowly, Mike recounted that he had had nothing to do with the Mỹ Lai affair—when it occurred he was in Bình Dương working for an army unit that was not involved in fighting. Nevertheless, since the Mỹ Lai Massacre had occurred and stunned the world, Mike felt as if Vietnam were a piece of his own flesh and that the massacre had changed his life. Everywhere he went, and at all moments, his thoughts were painfully involved with Vietnam.

"Do you have a family yet?"

"Oh, I had a girlfriend—a wonderful girl, and I loved her very much. Every year I would go to Vietnam to visit Mỹ Lai on these occasions, and each time she would see me off at the airport. Once, before I got on the plane, she said to me, 'Mike, please answer me very clearly. If you had to choose between me and Vietnam, which would you choose?' I was taken by surprise; she repeated her question. I said, 'I love Vietnam and I love you. Don't force me to make such a choice.' But she still insisted. After a long and painful silence, I said, 'If you insist on forcing me to choose one, then it must be Vietnam.' We both wept, and then she turned her back on me and slowly exited."

Having heard the story up to that point, everyone grew silent, and no one wanted to eat or drink anymore.

Moments later I said, "If you go on living like this, it will be too sad; you must cheer up! You must do something fun to give you the happiness you need to live, such as sports or music . . . the war's been over for a long time."

"I do have something—I play the violin."

"Oh, that's wonderful—let me find you one to play on!"

"I have one already. Wherever I go, I take it with me. Every year I go to Mỹ Lai and stand with the violin in front of the graves and play it for the departed to hear. I only play two tunes, 'Prayer' and 'Ashokan Farewell' [a violin piece made famous in the Ken Burns documentary about the Civil War]."

I instantly leapt up, throwing my hands to the sky, and exclaimed, "I've got the film now!"

And so we went together to Mỹ Lai.

I wanted to make this film very badly. The massacre had been horrible beyond all imagining. I knew that at the time and in the future, humankind would continue to do such horrible things; the wanton slaughter will not cease. An animal that regards itself as the highest of all the animals did something that no lower animal could ever do: perpetrate a massacre. There must be an awakening. Aside from the consideration that the thirtieth anniversary of the event was approaching, I was also preoccupied with many questions concerning it.

I was incapable of imagining that there were no causative factors leading to the massacre. At the very least, the village must have directly or indirectly inflicted continuous losses or presented lurking dangers for the American unit involved (I regret that this idea could not be given due expression in the film).[1] I was also obsessed by a series of questions about some of the participants. A child, Đỗ Ba, who had been rescued from death by the Americans, was later imprisoned for theft: Had what happened to him then led him into a criminal life? The helicopter crew chief who had pulled that child from the ditch full of massacred bodies was killed later in the war: How was it such a good man had to die? What led Mike Boehm, a veteran who had no part in the massacre, to take it so much to heart that it saddened the rest of his life? In the end, to my great regret, I could not explore those questions in the film.

And the final reason I wanted so much to make this documentary was that the Cinema Department officials back then tried to keep me from doing the film—they thought that the subject "had nothing new in it" and they would not give their approval. I wanted to demonstrate to those people that they were wrong; that the subject of wartime atrocities and the pain related to them could never be old.

It seemed that all would go smoothly until a barrier as huge as a mountain loomed in front of us. The American television network CBS had signed a contract with the provincial government giving CBS News the exclusive right to cover the key parts of the commemoration ceremony. And they had deployed a sizable army of television crews to "flood" the scene.

Having sufficient talent to make an excellent film is in fact not enough.

You still have to know how to focus your camera on the necessary objects when you are prevented from doing so, and once you've got the film, you have to know how to get it to viewers when you are prohibited from doing so. Such techniques might be called witchcraft. They can't be learned at a school.

At first CBS News would not agree to let us join them in filming the visit of Hugh Thompson and Larry Colburn to Ms. Nhung and Ms. Nhành (thirty years before, these two ladies, together with many people of the village, were rescued by these two men and Glenn Andreotta, and taken by helicopter from the scene of the massacre).

Flying over the village on the day of the killings, Thompson noticed that although he had seen no enemy resistance, there were piles of dead bodies everywhere. When he landed to investigate, he saw a group of frightened women and children in a bunker, and wanted to take them to safety. Getting out of the helicopter, he saw an American lieutenant moving with his men toward that group, stopped the officer, and asked him how he, Thompson, could get the people out. "With a hand grenade," the lieutenant said, an answer that infuriated Thompson. He ordered Colburn and Andreotta to train their machine guns on the GIs and fire on them if they tried to kill the people in the bunker. Later he said, "I don't know how I would have felt, shooting at American soldiers, but that day they were the enemy." He called down several larger helicopters that evacuated the people. Years later, talking to another American, he said calmly, "It was what anybody should have done." In the end, his allegiance to his humanity was greater than any other loyalty, though for Thompson he felt he was also defending the honor of his country. Later, flying over the ditch where hundreds of people had been shot, he landed again, and Andreotta, covered by Colburn, waded into the bodies, looking for survivors. He found one child, a boy later identified as Đỗ Ba, still alive, and brought him back to the helicopter, and they flew the child to a hospital in Quảng Ngai. Thompson would say, with tears in his eyes, "I had a son at home that same age."

My film crew and I went to Quảng Ngãi, came to the village, and interviewed the two ladies before the CBS crews appeared on the scene. We filmed them recounting how they had been rescued and expressing their desire to meet the humane and courageous Americans who had saved them. It was very moving. Because of this, the continuation had to be filmed as well: the two ladies and the people of the village meeting and welcoming the Americans. We had to do it no matter what the difficulties might be.

After negotiations with CBS people with which Mike assisted, the company agreed to let us do this, and moreover had us organize the scene for filming. It was an easy, natural, and meaningful task for me to lay out the scene, because I'm Vietnamese, and I too felt immense esteem for the courageous Americans involved.

I stood behind the camera when Thompson and Colburn walked onto the meeting ground; Ms. Nhung and Ms. Nhành came out, and the two groups embraced each other, sobbing. Ms. Nhung kept holding and stroking Thompson's arm, not letting go, and Colburn's eyes brimmed with tears. I wept. That image of the survivor comforting the man who helped rescue her is one of the most powerful in the film, more powerful even than the words spoken. And I kept the camera running a long time, using up film stock (when we shoot 35-millimeter film, we normally follow a very high ratio, using two thirds of the shot film for the documentary, while foreign film crews often follow a low ratio, using only about a tenth of what they've shot).

And another powerful image is that of the big, bearlike Mike Boehm playing his American Civil War lament near the graves of the dead, as if bringing them the peace he denied himself.

And so *The Sound of a Violin at Mỹ Lai* won the Best Documentary Award at the forty-third Asia-Pacific Film Festival held in Bangkok in 1999.

After that, arrangements were made to show the film in the solemn atmosphere of the National Movie Center in Hanoi. The auditorium held five hundred seats, half of which were for Vietnamese spectators, and the other half for Americans and other foreigners invited to the event. The American ambassador Pete Peterson, a former prisoner of war himself, watched the film with five hundred Vietnamese and American spectators, and afterward came to the stage and made a moving speech. Mike was there also, and when he spoke, his eyes swam with tears—he is by nature a highly emotional person.

Our film studio presented Mike with an enormous canister holding the entire movie on 35-millimeter celluloid film. Mike took the film back to the United States and, driving hundreds of miles in his run-down car, showed the film everywhere he could find a venue.

When later I went to Madison, Wisconsin, to visit Mike, he asked me to go for a ride in that same car. Before we took off, he went into town and loaded water bottles, bread, and canned meat into the car. The shops he went to were all street stalls where he could obtain the goods free from his friends—he didn't have a cent in his pocket!

Mike drove me to his hometown close to freezing Canada. He went all the way to a place where, as a child, he had drilled a hole in the ice of a river to fish. At the time, he said, he was just over ten. Somehow, he lost his footing and fell into the hole—he still doesn't remember how he got out of the freezing water. Such accidents are often fatal, because the current underneath the ice carries you off, so that you can no longer find the hole and go up again . . . and in addition the water is freezing cold, your eyes can see nothing, and your limbs lose feeling and the power of movement.

Mike also brought me out to a dam where, as a child, he would go to sleep through the night because he had been scolded by his father.

Mike lived by himself in a dark, run-down apartment bare of decoration except for a document on the wall in Vietnamese that testified that he was a member of "The Women's Association of Quảng Ngãi." He loved Vietnam deeply, but there seemed to be nothing about his own country he liked. When he saw me taking a picture of the town hall in Madison, a beautiful building reminiscent of the capitol building in Washington, DC, he told me that there was no point taking that picture—the people inside the building were all ugly characters, not worth my admiration. When I bought an American flag as a souvenir, Mike was also displeased: "Those fifty stars are not fifty states but fifty monopolies that are tearing the United States apart!"

Mike kept living in a random, ascetic manner, saving his pennies so that he could have money to go to Vietnam and engage in charitable activities.

Recalling these things, I feel sorry for Mike, and wish that he could forget about the past and live for himself. To be so sad and disillusioned for such a long time was enough . . .

The *Sound of a Violin at Mỹ Lai* was finished, and, as I have said, won a big prize, but there were still some related points of interest that didn't appear in the film itself, as is often the case.

Our film crew had undertaken a project without having received any decision from the Cinema Department—could that be why the department didn't censor it? We had made the film on a "proceed before asking permission" (fait accompli) basis, and when the department was invited to watch it, they refused!

Nguyễn Văn Nhân, the director of the film studio, sent a direct invitation to Nguyễn Khoa Điềm, the minister of culture, to see the film— simply to see it, censoring it or not was another matter. At first Mr. Điềm thought it was only a film script; when he learned that it was a completed film, he came down to see it alone with his driver on a Sunday afternoon.

When he had finished watching the film, his eyes were red. He said, "The people of Quảng Ngãi thank you, gentlemen, and the souls of all those unlucky victims thank you."

He instructed the Cinema Department to watch the film, make many copies of it, distribute it for public viewing, and send it out to film festivals across the world.

Yet, only one week later, when the Cinema Department officials came down to watch the film, and when they subsequently heard that the executive board of the forty-third Asia-Pacific Film Festival in Thailand had announced that the film had won the Best Documentary Prize, the department's director general was overjoyed, while the deputy director general, perhaps because the film had been made without official permission, remained distant and reserved.

When we finished making the film in Quảng Ngãi, the members of my team felt provisionally satisfied with the work they had done. I say "provisionally" because the film could have been better, and would have gone further, if we had been given permission to develop the topic as we originally planned.

There were at least three episodes in the film that we had to omit, as follows:

Episode 1: Thirty years after the massacre (in 1998), on the occasion of the memorial service, the Americans who returned to the scene wanted to find the child, Đỗ Ba, who was rescued from a pile of corpses, to see what the boy's life was like now, but the young fellow was in prison for theft. This was certainly a joke of fate, if not a matter for shame. If this detail had been related in the film, it would have made even the most insensitive viewers see how much the word "liberation" had been insulted. All of us in the film crew, and the journalists writers who were there, tried hard to find some way for Đỗ Ba to be let out of prison, so he could meet his benefactors, but this proved to be impossible; our hands were tied. It was a bitter disappointment.

Episode 2: I had also hoped to relate the fates of other participants. As mentioned, the crew chief, Glenn Andreotta, had crawled into the pile of corpses and dragged Đỗ Ba out, covered from head to foot with blood, and then the crew carried him by helicopter to the Quảng Ngãi hospital.

A few weeks after the boy's rescue, Andreotta was serving as a door gunner on another helicopter when he was shot and killed just before the helicopter was shot down. Andreotta was the eldest son in a middle-class family. War is like that.

The pilot, Hugh Thompson, the man who couldn't be deterred from aiming his gun at a group of American soldiers and was prepared to fire at them if they continued slaughtering innocent people, died in the United States only a few years after the memorial service.

When the helicopter gunner, Lawrence Colburn, returned to the United States after the war, he went into a period of personal decline and disgust with life, in which he became addicted to drugs, a state from which he couldn't extricate himself.

With these details, viewers could have had a deeper experience and could have reflected more deeply on the meaning of the word "war."

Episode 3: Another important detail that had to be omitted was a description of the life and destiny of Mike Boehm, the person who plays the violin at Mỹ Lai in the film. From the time the war ended until today, he has lived alone, has received no pension, and has refused to acknowledge that anything American could possess any value.

He wasn't guilty of any misdeed and was not connected in any way with the massacre at Mỹ Lai. Therefore there was no need for him to seek "absolution" or to "engage in repentance," as some have imagined. Mike simply did what he did each year to satisfy his own feelings and to soothe the pain with which the war had afflicted him as a human being.

From despising the war, Mike went on to despise, and hold himself aloof from, all of America—from the president to Congress to the flag. People willing to carry their ideas to such an extreme are usually seen only in countries like the United States.

A film that remained faithful to the rich human details in the destinies of the personages portrayed in it would surely have gone further and been better . . . We were all very aware of this, but our limited film stock, budget, and time didn't allow this, especially given the pressure from the Cinema Department and the "film censorship system." They didn't want to accept this film. If I had been more committed, I'm sure that all of my colleagues in the film crew would have supported me, but I was leery of the trouble and the collateral damage that might accrue to the directors of the film studio who had wholeheartedly trusted and supported me.

As for me, I'm still sorry that I wasn't able to completely carry out my intentions and express all of my feelings in the film.

Most of the people of Mỹ Lai, and the family members of those who were massacred, still have emotions of shock and terror when they speak of this event, though it has receded far into the past. It was the greatest nightmare of their lives, and it unfolded in only four hours on the morning of March 16, 1968. It was a wound that can't heal. It still seems to them, as they recount it, like an unimaginable nightmare, especially when they consider that the army unit involved came from such a civilized place as America.

The people of Mỹ Lai also often mention the rescue operation of Thompson and his flight crew that day, and especially how year after year, on March 16, Mike comes with his violin to stand by the graves and play the melodies "Prayer" and "Ashokan Farewell" . . .

The number of people rescued was around twenty, not many compared with the 509 elderly men, children, and woman killed in cold blood. But that number, twenty, is not a bit small as a measure of the moral decision of those Americans who stood against something they knew was wrong without regard for the consequences to themselves.

What I will always remember, what I can't forget, is that during the years when I went to several dozen American universities to show the film, many students, teachers, and war veterans, having seen the film, would ask me, "So the Vietnamese have no hate?" I don't know how to frame an accurate reply to this. The fact is that we Vietnamese often hate, and sometimes nurture this hatred for a very long time, especially when the offenders are fellow Vietnamese. But with regard to Americans and America, I beg to state that this hatred has long been a thing of the past—if there is hatred now, it is directed against other people, other countries.

The worst misfortune for the Vietnamese is that they must always have someone to hate.

III
TO THE ENDS OF ALL THE SEAS

Preface

"Reconciliation [between the Vietnamese] is much more difficult to achieve than that between the Vietnamese and the Americans."
—Trần Văn Thủy

From gaining its independence from France in 1954 to April of 1975, Vietnam suffered two simultaneous wars: a civil war of Vietnamese against Vietnamese and a war with the Americans supporting one side of that conflict. As much as Trần Văn Thủy views his films as a reminder to his countrymen of their duty to make their country a place worthy of the best aspects of its own history and of the sacrifices of the war, his art is also driven by the need to heal the terrible wounds that war rendered between them, the pain he witnessed with his own eyes and through the lens of his camera. In this section, Thủy recounts his work—as a reluctant writer, as an unofficial emissary, and as a filmmaker—encouraging reconciliation between former enemies whom he still sees as fellow countrymen.

In 2002, Thủy was invited to the United States by the William Joiner Center at the University of Massachusetts, Boston. One of the aims of the center, which was created by American veterans, was to bring veterans who had become writers and artists, from all sides of the conflict, together. Under the auspices of Joiner, Thủy traveled throughout the United States, speaking to students and veterans. The trip resulted in a book titled *If You Go to the Ends of All the Seas* (published in the United States, in Vietnamese), which, like his films, aroused controversy, accusations, and threats—but this time by a number of people in the overseas

Vietnamese community in the United States, as well as the authorities in Vietnam. To understand the intense emotion aroused by the book, one has to understand the die-hard feeling of hatred and bitterness born from that long civil war.

There is perhaps no war as bitter as a civil war. Many of the Vietnamese who had come to the United States (at different times) were not only from the losing side of that war, but also after its end suffered imprisonment and humiliation in Vietnam and immense hardship when they left, fleeing in small, overpacked boats, thousands dying at sea. They had lost their country, and for many years the idea of any contact or interaction with their former foes was unthinkable, on both sides. Việt Kiều (overseas Vietnamese) who promoted the idea of reconciliation or even simply traveled to Vietnam had been attacked, ostracized, and even murdered. At the same time, expressing anything positive about the Việt Kiều was also anathema in Vietnam.

When Thủy completed a draft of his book, he showed it to the writer Nguyên Ngọc, who stayed up reading it for three nights and then "with eyes red from putting in late hours, he placed his hands on the stacked manuscript and, looking into my eyes said, 'Thủy! This is badly needed and useful!' A friend of mine standing nearby who had overheard us offered nothing in the way of praise or commentary but simply said in a deliberate manner, 'If this manuscript is published, you won't be able to go home! If you go home, you can never get it published. There's never been any fellow who published anything like that over here who dared show his face in Vietnam again.' After only a few seconds of silence, I said very clearly to Mr. Nguyên Ngọc, 'If you feel that this manuscript is badly needed and useful, I'll publish it immediately—and then I'll return to Vietnam!'"

In this country, Thủy was attacked by overseas Vietnamese for being a "Communist lackey" and a "cultural guerilla" while at the same time many members of the same community took him under their wing and treated him with a kindness and a hospitality that overwhelmed him. In Vietnam, the book received (in Thủy's words) a "scathing criticism" by the authorities, but pirated copies soon became available on the streets, and a Saigon publisher printed a copy, in spite of the risks. The edition of this memoir published in Vietnam contained large excerpts from *To the*

Ends of All the Seas and so gave many more people there an opportunity to read what had been printed only in a limited edition. In this American edition, we have included only Thủy's account of a letter from a childhood friend, Nguyễn Hữu Đính, who fought on the other Vietnamese side of the war and was later imprisoned in a reeducation camp. The letter poignantly recounts in the fate of one man what became the fate of many who were on the losing side of that war; the tale of how Thủy found again his friend, who became an enemy, and then a friend again, encapsulates the fratricidal tragedy of the war.

—W.K.

17
A Letter

After I came to America and connected with the overseas Vietnamese community, I couldn't avoid being bothered by the words I had uttered so earnestly at my Auntie Nhuận's graveside in earlier days: "*If you go to the ends of all the seas, going on and on without stopping, you will at last return to your own homeland, to your native village.*" I don't know if there was ever a period or a circumstance in the turbulent history of our nation that led to such a deep polarization of human souls that millions of people abandoned their own homelands and risked their own lives in the open seas. But I know with utter clarity that a good many Vietnamese, being away from their homeland, have *"continued past all the oceans and all the continents, going on and on without stopping,"* but in the end have been unable to *"return to their homelands, to their native villages."*

I have in my possession a letter, which, when I read it to my wife and children, would elicit this response: "Father, this could be the script for a wonderful feature film." I've never paid much attention to films that tell fictional stories with actors playing roles, focusing instead only on real events in people's lives—but the letter in my hands was a real-life story, a real story of a friend who had once been my childhood classmate.

Let me be a bit discursive, and say that in the 1953–54 school year, we joined the seventh-grade B3 class in the Nguyễn Khuyến School, which in former times had been the Nam Định Thành Chung School. It seems that in every person's life, one's school days leave the deepest and liveliest imprints. I remember that in our class, there were many people who sang beautifully, such as Lưu Linh, Đào Thúy Lan, and Nguyễn

Thị Phương Khanh. I miss so much those lovely songs, such as "Chiều" (Dusk), "Thiên Thai" (The Other World), "Sơn Nữ Ca" (Song of the Mountain Girl), "Thu" (Autumn), and "Đêm Đông" (Winter Night).

In class I sat next to a close friend, a good student, quiet and reserved by nature, named Nguyễn Hữu Đính. His family traded rice. His home was large and roomy, built in a traditional style but with a balcony where the shop sign "Linh Lợi" (written with curvilinear strokes) was displayed. The address was 41 Bến Thóc (Rice Pier) Street, and in front of the house stood a large phoenix flower tree.[1]

Đính's story is related to that of another friend of ours in the same class, whose family name I can't recall, but whose given name was Viễn. Viễn's home was in the country, where he and his family lived in poverty. Viễn was only an average student, but at the age of thirteen he had read and virtually memorized all of the Chinese novels that were available at the time, such as *Tales of the Táng Dynasty* (*Shuō Táng Yǎnyì*), *The Eastern Campaign of Jié Rénguì* (*Jié Rénguì Dōng Zhēng*), *The Western Campaign of Jié Rénguì* (*Jié Rénguì Xī Zhēng*), *Journey to the West* (*Xī Yóu Jì*), *Romance of the Three Kingdoms* (*Sānguó Zhì Yǎnyì*), *Outlaws of the Water Margin* (*Shuǐhǔ Zhuàn*), and *Dream of the Red Chamber* (*Hóng Lóu Mèng*).

My own home wasn't especially roomy, but my parents always sought to please the friends of their children, so Viễn lived in my home. In those years, not so much because "the price of rice was high" but because he cared for his friend, Đính often took rice on the sly from home to give me as a contribution to support Viễn. When he gave me a packet of rice at home or when school let out, he wouldn't say much, aside from a brief admonition: "Mind you—don't let Viễn know and feel sad."

And then, after 1954, my circle of friends broke up—some went to the south, and some returned to the countryside or moved to a different province. One night, when he ought to have been in bed already, Đính knocked on the door of my house. As always, he was quiet, and finally after some hesitancy said, "Hey Thủy, my family is leaving. Let's not forget each other, okay? I'll write you."

After that night, we didn't meet again. Đính went to the South with his family, and left me a six-by-nine-inch sepia photograph that showed him in profile, with light falling on his slightly upturned face. Back then communication between North and South was limited to postcards printed for that purpose on which people could write a couple of lines concerning their health. And after a couple of exchanges of that nature, Đính and I lost touch with each other entirely, so that our friendship existed only in our memories.

Then came the terrible years of warfare. I took a training course for cameramen and then was transferred to the South to film the war. So for three years I dragged myself here and there amid bombs and bullets, a movie camera in my hands. I had many close brushes with death in which I would vaguely imagine my friend of former times, now on the other side, pointing a gun at me. Thank God that never occurred.

When I visited Saigon in 1978, and again in 1981, I made efforts to find my friend but could learn nothing about him anywhere. And in later years, on the many occasions when I went to other countries to attend film festivals or professional conferences, no matter where or what the occasion was, I would make further efforts to learn about him. Every time I was interviewed by the press or on TV, I would always remember to run through a set of phrases, such as: *"In the 1953–54 school year, my friends and I joined the seventh-grade B3 class in the Nguyễn Khuyến School in Nam Định . . ."* to see if I could get any word concerning my friend. But I never heard a thing.

I returned to Nam Định many times, and went back to Đính's old house, putting out feelers in the neighborhood, but no one knew a thing. The house had changed owners three or four times. The situation was like the one in the story of Từ Thức returning to his home village. And so I thought that was the end of the matter—my friend was no doubt dead; I could not expect too much from Heaven.

But then, due not to skill but to sheer luck, a person was able to help me discover a relative of Đính's still living in Saigon. I hurriedly wrote a letter to that person, and received an answer only a few days later:

Hồ Chí Minh City, November 11, 2000.

Dear Mr. Trần Văn Thủy:
I have had the honor, sir, to receive your letter, and would like to introduce myself to you: I am Nguyễn Hữu Thái, the younger brother of Nguyễn Hữu Đính. My brother and I lived in the rice shop "Linh Lợi" at 49 Bến Thóc Street in Nam Định during the years 1950–54.

Back in those days, my brother Đính was close friends with you and

Mr. Son. The three of you would often go to watch movies at the Văn Hóa Theater on Paul Bert Street, and at the Majestic on Hàng Thao.

I was truly moved by your letter. It was profound in content, and you were very passionate and sincere in the way you described your feelings concerning the turbulence and pain endured by the Vietnamese throughout their lives, together with your fond recollections of the loveable streets of Nam Định in days gone by: the flowers and vegetation, the riverbanks, the old streets and sidewalks, and all of the friends of those beautiful days that are now so distant.

I still clearly remember the night when you and Đính bade farewell to each other—you gave my brother a book of wonderful written reminiscences that he still carefully preserves. And on that night my brother wept when he returned to our house.

My brother Đính is still living in Montreal. I know for a fact that he will be overjoyed to meet the dear friend of his childhood once again.

I wish to share the joy of this amazingly lucky reunion and to respectfully convey to you my brother's address.

Nguyễn Hữu Thái

I sent a letter from Hanoi to my friend in Canada and shortly afterward received an answer from him. The full transcript of his letter, written by hand, sixteen pages long, is as follows:

Montreal, Dec. 7, 2000

Dear Thủy,

I just received a letter from my younger brother in Vietnam, in which was enclosed your letter and address. I was truly overjoyed and astonished!

And so, I have found again the close friend of my early days after forty-five years of lost contact!

After going to the South, I would sometimes look in the album you gave me. Looking at your picture, I would remember the days when our houses were near each other, and we would go to one or the other to talk. And I also would remember your elder sister Muội—we would often use her name to write letters teasing the musician Hoàng Giác.

After going to the South, I made many other friends, especially when I grew older and began my adult life, but these friendships weren't the same as the one I had with you, a friendship both naive and pure.

Once in France I sat and watched **The Story of Kindness**, and, seeing that the filmmaker was Trần Văn Thủy, I said to my wife, "Perhaps this filmmaker is my old friend."

I watched the film many times; I liked it very much, because it was very deep, and spoke of things that everyone seeks and hopes for. And I thought to myself, "In times like these, to speak in this way for everyone to hear takes guts; in fact, one can only say that it is courageous."

One day, when I went to the Asian market in the thirteenth district (arrondissement) in Paris, I met a student who had just come there from Vietnam, and I asked him about the film director Trần Văn Thủy. He told me that Trần Văn Thủy was still very young. When I heard this, I thought that the filmmaker could not be the Thủy that I knew, because by then you and I were both already over fifty—hardly young! And then I kept thinking about the phrase "Born in the North to die in the South"—with bombs raining down so fiercely how could you have remained alive?

Yet, you are still alive; you have sent me good news. Forty-five years have passed—nearly half a century—fearsome indeed. And I feel a bit sad when I reflect that I'm already sixty-three this year—I can live, at best, for another ten years. I have no idea if I will get to see you once more before closing my eyes forever. So I have this suggestion: if you have occasion to visit the United States or Canada on business, then stop by Montreal to see me; and if I have occasion to return to Vietnam, I'll go up to Hanoi to visit you.

From the time that I first came here until now, I have been back to Vietnam three times, but each time it was because my mother was seriously ill, and the last time for her funeral—so I didn't go anywhere for fun at all but remained the whole time in the environs of Saigon. My mother died in January 2000 at the age of ninety-one.

Now let me relate to you what happened in my life after we parted.

We left Nam Định early in a morning with a fine mist while it was still dark. My family of six people left in three groups of two. We brought along no baggage, just as if we were going to Hanoi to visit relatives. We left the lights on in our house, with all the mosquito nets still in place.

After staying in Hanoi for one day, we left the next day for Hải Phòng by train, still in three groups, as if we didn't know each other. On reaching Hải Phòng, we remained there for a week, and boarded a ship bound for the South.

In the South, I studied in the sixth, fifth, and fourth levels [đệ lục, đệ ngũ, đệ tứ] in the Nguyễn Trãi School in Saigon. Then I studied in the third, second, and first levels (đệ tam, đệ nhị, đệ nhất) in the Chu Văn An School, also in Saigon. Among our old classmates studying with me in Saigon were Lê Triều Vinh, Lâm Hữu Trãi, Trần Đình Chi, Nguyễn Thị Phương Khanh, and Nguyễn Thị Vinh.

Later on, Lê Triều Vinh graduated from college as a mathematics major, and became a professor of mathematics. Lâm Hữu Trãi graduated from the National Administration Institute and became a provincial de-

partment chief. Trần Đình Chi became a teacher. Nguyễn Thị Phương Khanh became a nurse, and Nguyễn Thị Vĩnh became a public servant.

As for Ms. Băng Tâm, our old English teacher, she continued as a teacher after coming to Saigon—but she killed herself in 1959 due to unhappy family circumstances.

After graduating high school, at second level, I enrolled in medical school. But in my second year there I developed inflammation of the lungs. My teacher at the medical school advised me to choose another branch of study, because medicine is a very arduous profession that requires you to remain awake throughout the night working in hospitals—he feared my health couldn't stand up to this. Back in 1961–62 there were no effective medicines as there are today, so many people with inflamed lungs succumbed to tuberculosis and died. I therefore listened to my teacher's advice and abandoned medicine—that was my first failure; I shall in due course recount the ones that followed.

My withdrawal from medical school made me wretched and downcast for a year. On one sad and listless day in the following year, I paid a visit to the law school to see a few friends. They encouraged me to study law, so I enrolled in the law school. In my third year there I read in the newspaper that an examination to select law clerks would soon be held, so I submitted my name and had the good luck to get a passing grade, after which I was selected for a position in Bến Tre Province.

After working in Bến Tre for two years, I had to enter military service. The war was escalating at that time, so young men all had to join the army. I studied at the Thủ Đức Officer Candidate School for nine months. Because I had certificates in administration and finance earned while studying at the law school, I was reassigned to the National Training Academy for Cadres in Vũng Tàu, and was put in charge of administration and finance. I worked there until 1970. In that year, I met my future wife, whom I married two years later, in 1972. By then I was thirty-five years old.

The reason I was so late in starting a family was that it had been my intention to remain a bachelor throughout my life. The reason for this was that I had grown up in a family in which my parents were in sharp conflict. This conflict was too severe to be resolved, but my parents didn't wish to live separately because they feared for the futures of their six children. So the two of them passed their days side by side, hardly conversing, as if they were two dim shades of the departed.

This state of affairs, which went on for decades, made me afraid of conjugal life. And in addition to this, when I worked as a clerk in the Bến Tre provincial court, the chief magistrate there put me in charge of separation and divorce files. Every week married couples would appear in court with children weeping because of their parents' separations. This made me even more disillusioned with marriage.

And so I made my decision to remain a bachelor. I studied cooking, bread making, and tailoring, with the idea of doing all of the tasks that women do, so that I would never need a woman to help me. My mother ran a large store in Saigon's District 4. She had many friends, and among them were many matchmakers. My three younger sisters were students in the Trưng Vương School, so their friends often came to my house, but I ignored everyone.

On one occasion my mother called me into her room and said, "You're grown up now—you must get married, so I can be at peace." My reply was, "I've decided to remain a bachelor, mother!" I saw her expression darken at this, as she lowered her head and slowly shed tears. I felt keen regret. To this day, I still feel keen regret.

And so a struggle began deep in my heart, and when I reached the age of thirty-five, my friend, I had to accept defeat and submit to the laws of nature! Let me tell you the whole story! When I was working at the National Training Academy for Cadres in Vũng Tàu, I got sick and had to go to the hospital. On weekends the wives, children, and loved ones of the friends on either side of me at the hospital would come swarming in to visit them; but as for me, my father and mother were busy with their store, and my younger sisters were too busy with their studies to come visit, so I just lay in my bed, abandoned and alone. It was too sad!

When I took a ferryboat back to Saigon after getting well, I noticed a husband and wife with a little child sitting on a bench in front. Throughout the trip from Vũng Tàu to Saigon, the couple and their child played and joked together in a very happy manner. This began to shake my resolve to be a bachelor.

One day I was preparing to go on a business trip with the director of my academy. While I was sitting in his living room, waiting for him to appear so we could set off together, the daughter of the director came into the room and asked, "Where are you going?"

"I'm going to Saigon on business with your father."

"You'll be visiting your wife, right?"

"No, I don't have a wife."

"Are you telling the truth?"

"Yes!"

"Then I'll introduce you to a good friend of mine."

The daughter of the director (her name was Lệ Tâm) fixed a time on the Sunday of the following week for us to meet at the Pink Cloud Café on the Front Beach in Vũng Tàu, so that she could introduce her friend Hồng to me.

But then that week I had to go to Saigon on business, and got so involved in it that I forgot all about the appointment. On Monday, when I returned to work in my office, Tâm phoned and scolded me severely: "You *made me and my friend wait for a whole hour on the Front Beach in Vũng Tàu—you never showed up."*

I apologized and asked her to make an appointment for the next week. But when the date came, I was restricted to quarters and couldn't go out. Some friends invited me to drink with them, and I forgot to phone the director's daughter, so the two young women again waited for an hour. And I got scolded again. I asked to arrange a third meeting and promised that this time I would appear punctually.

When I arrived at the agreed-on place, Tâm introduced her friend Hồng to me. She was of partly French parentage, had been born in Nam Định, was quite attractive, and seemed good-natured. I say "good-natured" because I had twice made her "climb a tree" (i.e., stood her up), and expected to be scolded, but that didn't happen. She was cheerful and pleasant, as if nothing at all had happened. "This girl," I thought to myself, "is attractive and good-natured. She would make a good wife." So I decided to marry Hồng. It was an easy, spur-of-the-moment decision, just like my previous decision to enter the law school.

Two years later, the wedding ceremony took place on December 24, 1972. And on April 11, 1973, Hồng presented me with our first child: Hồng Ngọc. Hồng was a teacher in Vũng Tàu at the time, and my salary was also sufficient to live on, so the two of us lived easily in material as well as spiritual terms.

Then the upheaval of April 30, 1975, occurred. We knew before then that the government of the South would collapse. I had arranged to have my wife and child go to Saigon, and I myself went to Saigon on the first of April. The reason I gave was that I wanted to receive further professional training, but actually I had reserved an airplane ticket to take us all to France. Around April 10, 1975, my wife asked to go back to Vũng Tàu to settle some financial accounts. I told my wife to stay only one or two days there and return immediately to Saigon, but she didn't listen to my advice, and lingered for several days. When she started back, fighting had erupted everywhere, the roads were blocked, and she could no longer get back to Saigon. When the date of the flight arrived, I couldn't bring myself to go alone, leaving my wife and child behind. My wife at that time was five months pregnant with our second child.

And so I decided to stay. When the revolutionary tank brigade entered the city, we saw quite a few soldiers of the old regime run into alleys and kill themselves. Sometimes it was just a single soldier, and sometimes a group of two or more—they would bring their heads close together before pulling the pin of a hand grenade.

And I too went out of my senses, fearing imprisonment, so the thought of suicide began to preoccupy me. On the afternoon of April 30, 1975, I went to see some friends who dealt in medicine, and told them (falsely) that I had insomnia and needed sleeping pills. I managed to collect forty pills (twenty pills were sufficient to induce a fatal coma). I decided to commit suicide on the night of May 1, 1975. I wrote a long letter to my wife explaining my reasons for taking this step.

When you're about to die, my friend, you enter a very strange state. As you look at your surroundings, and at the people walking up and down the street, you have the impression that all of this belongs to another world, and is no longer a part of your own world. And another strange thing is that each time you bring the sleeping pills to your mouth, images of your wife and children appear before your eyes. And then you hear, as if in the distance, the sound of your child crying. And then you remember how, each day, when you returned from work, your child would run up and happily embrace your legs. So I asked myself, "Why are you departing this life? Why are you abandoning your responsibilities? Why are you putting all of the heavy burdens of life on Hồng's shoulders?"

When my reflections had reached this point, I sat up, tore the letter to pieces, and threw it into the toilet, together with the forty sleeping pills, then pulled the chain to flush them all away—this was the first of my failed suicide attempts.

On May 12, 1975, I presented myself for reeducation. Here, I ask not to recount all of my experiences in "reeducation" camps; suffice it to say that I passed through four such camps: Hóc Môn, Long Khánh, Phú Quốc Island, and Hàm Tân. Once on Phú Quốc Island I grew sad to the point of despair; and so for the second time I tried to commit suicide. I still remember that it was a night dimly lit by the moon. Around midnight I disengaged the drawstring from my hammock and carried it stealthily toward the latrine. Next to the latrine, along a fence, was an unfinished building, the steel frame of which had just been erected. I had walked past this structure many times in the afternoon. My intention that night was to climb a ladder there, tie one end of the drawstring cord around my neck, and attach the other end to the steel framework.

But it seems that matters of life and death are predetermined by fate. On that night, having carried the cord by stealth past the latrine, I came to the foot of the ladder and began climbing it, mumbling a few Buddhist prayers. But when I was halfway up the ladder, a security guard standing on a watch post next to the fence shouted, "Hey you! What are you doing?"

I hastily slid down the ladder, returned to the place where I slept, and then as before thought dreamily of my wife and child. The next morning, I planned to cut the drawstring to pieces, but I didn't have a knife, so I coiled it up, did the same with the other drawstring, and threw them into the latrine ditch.

After three years in reeducation camps I was allowed to return home, the reason being that, though I belonged to the army, I had been assigned to a civil affairs unit, and had not been involved in any fighting. Furthermore, I had risen only to the rank of first lieutenant in the civil affairs unit; therefore, both my crimes and my rank were regarded as "light." I left reeducation camp in 1978. My father died in 1979.

After leaving the reeducation camps, I couldn't find work, so I began trying to escape Vietnam by boat. I made five unsuccessful attempts, and lost all of my money in the process, but fortunately escaped death on two of those occasions.

The first time I waited with others at the Back Beach in Vũng Tàu in some shrubbery for a small boat that would take us to a large boat. It was the middle of the night, and it was drizzling steadily. Everyone was kneeling on the sand, reciting prayers. The Buddhists were reciting sutras, and the Catholics were reciting supplications to God. My two children started crying loudly. This alarmed everyone present, and they told us to give the children some cough medicine to make them sleep. They each had a spoonful, but didn't sleep. They took second and third spoonfuls, but still didn't sleep. When they had drunk half the bottle, they didn't cry anymore, but started laughing unrestrainedly. Everyone was afraid the police would discover us, so they shooed us back home, and wouldn't allow us to go with them anymore. And so the four of us went back by stealth on footpaths so as to avoid police guard posts. The result was that we lost sixteen taels of gold.

The next day we heard that the small boat, which could only take about forty passengers, had been boarded by seventy people. No one yielded to anyone else—they just kept climbing aboard until there were seventy people on the boat. When the boat reached the open ocean, it was overturned by a great wave, and nearly everyone on it was killed—there were only a few survivors. Among those killed was my wife's younger brother Hùng. Hùng was a handsome young student, tall in stature, and known by everyone around Vũng Tàu to be a good swimmer. When the passengers came aboard, the lady in charge of the boat collected fees in gold from them and put it all into a backpack that she had Hùng wear on his shoulders. When the ship went down, some people greedy for the gold drowned Hùng by forcing him down in the water so they could get the bag. The boat owner and her three children were killed along with the passengers.

Now, Thủy, let me tell you how I escaped death a second time. This escape attempt was organized by my cousin's friend. Each person was to pay four taels of gold, but at the last minute the boat owner increased the fare to five taels. This made me angry, so I withdrew from the enterprise. The boat went out to sea as planned, but during the twenty years that have elapsed since then, no letter has ever been received from any of the passengers on that boat, among whom was the husband of my cousin.

She grew so distraught that she went insane. She now lives in the Ottawa insane asylum, about two hundred kilometers from my home.

So you see, Thủy, that I'm a lucky person—I encountered death four times, but each time the god of death spared me. After five unsuccessful attempts to escape by sea, in which I lost all of my money, I still was unable to find any work, so around the beginning of 1980 I decided to work as a cyclo driver in Saigon. There's no need to describe what that sort of life is like. I'll never forget the meals I ate on sidewalks consisting of a bowl of rice with a dried fish. The rain would run down from my hat into the bowl, turning the contents to soup. And I'll never forget the ragged clothes I wore, driving the cyclo. My passengers were sometimes old friends of mine, or sometimes former students or girlfriends.

During this cyclo-driving period, my wife applied for permission to go to France as a Eurasian requesting repatriation. And, thanks be to God, her application was accepted.

We left Saigon for France on August 19, 1983. I remember that when the plane went up from the runway that day, every one around us burst into tears. My wife sobbed, tightly hugging her children. And I too couldn't keep back my tears as I gazed through the window at the city beneath us, the place we had lived for more than twenty years with memories both joyful and sad.

In France, I found work in a chemical manufacturing company. The salary was enough to live on, but consumer prices were high, and there was widespread unemployment, which made it hard for students to find work after graduation, so we decided to immigrate to Canada in July of 1992. I still have a younger sister who works as a sidewalk vender on Bàn Cờ Street in Saigon. My older brother died in a reeducation camp.

Well, enough for now. This has become a long letter. I promise to continue the story in my next letter. I wish happiness and peace to you and all your family.

Your friend from former days,
Nguyễn Hữu Đính

When I came to Boston at the beginning of October of 2002, I at once called Đính, and my friend zoomed down from Montreal to see me. We embraced and gazed into each other's eyes. Yes, we were old now, old indeed. But my friend was still gentle and quiet as always. On the night of that rare reunion, awaited for nearly half a century, a VC soldier and an RSVN officer shared the same room and talked to each other into the small hours.

I couldn't sleep. Not exactly because memories of the school days I had spent with my friend came flooding back. Not exactly because Đính had twice tried to commit suicide in reeducation camps. And not exactly because I had had so many brushes with death in the war. But because I kept imagining a swap of destiny that could easily have occurred in our respective lives. I imagined that, back in 1954, if my parents had not been so bound to their ancestors' land, or had yielded to the persuasions of others and taken their children to live in the South, then it would have been hard indeed for me to avoid becoming a *ngụy* ("puppet" or RSVN) officer. And if the family of my friend had for some reason remained in the North, then my friend would certainly have become a VC soldier.

Neither of us felt the slightest need to avoid talking about politics, or felt the slightest hesitancy in resuming the innocent friendship of our school days. We were both, deep in our hearts, completely at peace, and I also recognized that this was a moment to be savored, an unlooked-for blessing in our fleeting lives.

In the small hours, Đính suddenly asked, "Hey, do you think that fellow Viễn is still alive?"

I remained silent, pretending I was asleep.

18

A Birth

When the book *If You Go to the Ends of All the Seas* appeared in Orange County in 2003, it immediately made waves. Many readers in the United States accepted the book; the difficulty, however, was that it had been written by someone from Vietnam. In that period, it wasn't easy for the popular news media among the Vietnamese community in the United States to show sympathy for the work of a person who lived in Vietnam under the "Communist totalitarian" regime. So the people who favored the book kept silent, while those eager to denounce and level charges against me had a ready-made forum from which to speak.

The situation of *If You Go to the Ends of All the Seas* in the United States at that time was similar to that of *Hanoi in Whose Eyes* in Vietnam during the early 1980s. The people who appreciated and supported the film in Vietnam—and the book in America—were numerous, but they had no power and no forum, while the people who denounced it and leveled charges against it were few, but they had the power, the forum, and even the machinery. But, as with the film, people were anxious to seek out and read the book, to give it to friends as a gift, and to send it to Vietnam not precisely because it was a good piece of work but because it had had the good fortune to be attacked and discussed, and hence was blown up into a great affair. Very soon, the first edition was sold out, and in 2004, Hoàng Khởi Phong had to get the book reprinted. The reprinting of a Vietnamese-language book in the United States is a rare event, for in the United States, the number of people who can read Vietnamese is slowly but steadily diminishing. Thus one can see the truth in the words of our elders in the past that "disasters conceal blessings."

I once had occasion to speak of this relationship of blessings to disasters with some American film directors at the Brooklyn Academy of Music, where a showing of my films had been arranged, with the presence of the Oscar-winning director Peter Davis. People asked me, "When you make films in Vietnam, do you have to submit them to government censorship?"

My reply was, "Your question seems to come from someone living on another planet—of course we do!"

"Why?"

"If you make films in Vietnam for public showings, then the authorities insist you must submit them to the censors. But it is thanks to the censorship, criticism, and noise created by government banning that I get to enjoy public attention, and become famous! So you see, ladies and gentlemen, that if I could make films the way I wanted to, as you do in the United States, I'd have no way of becoming famous. I feel very sorry for American film directors, who often have to spend a third of their budget for advertising so as to attract audiences. I don't lose so much as a penny on this; instead I rely totally on censorship, criticism, and banning to become well-known."

And so, my dear friends, you may rest assured that I feel entirely at ease with the criticism, attacks, and smear campaigns that have been directed against the book *If You Go to the Ends of All the Seas*. This is nothing, absolutely nothing, in comparison with other trials that I've had to live through in the practice of my profession. These have been far more terrible and bizarre. Those experiences, though true, seem to have been made up, and are as entertaining as the events in Chinese kung fu novels.

But, if anything, I feel sorry for my own people. Everyone knows that the United States has long had a concept referred to as the "melting pot." This has a great deal of meaning for all of the groups that have immigrated to the United States. In America, this mixing doesn't come about through some enforced process of assimilation but is based on the foundation of the acceptance of differences, so that different peoples can join in building a civilized and prosperous life. This, it appears, is the fundamental character, the essence, of a "melting pot." Does this, then, have any impact on the Vietnamese community with regard to the problems that we have referred to?

According to many researchers, past and present, the core nature of the Vietnamese is rife with problems. It is precisely due to this that Phan Chu Trinh regarded raising the intellectual level of the Vietnamese as the first order of business, and the scholar Nguyễn Văn Vĩnh wrote a column titled "Examining Our Faults" that appeared in his newspaper at the turn of the twentieth century.

So could it be that the origin of the problem is not only the political system of Vietnam (though naturally this is of the utmost importance) but, at its deepest level, the belligerent nature of the Vietnamese?

Among the people who went with me to participate in the William Joiner Center program were anh Huệ Chi, anh Hoàng Ngọc Hiến, and many intellectuals from different countries. Anh Huệ Chi, an intellectual of great integrity who was never a Communist Party member and who was always pained at the unreasonable things going on in our society, was also yelled at in the United States and denounced in a very abusive manner as a Communist operative and a "cultural guerilla." Anh Huệ Chi just smiled and concentrated on learning computer techniques, so that he now manages one of the most respected webpages in the country: "Bauxite Vietnam."

At that time, anh Hoàng Ngọc Hiến was also strongly attacked, but he only laughed and joked about it. We loved him and used to meet him very often at home, at the club, and at a seminar on Vietnamese-American literature. Witnessing the paradoxical situations and circumstances of the Vietnamese living inside and outside Vietnam, he often shook his head and said something everyone could appreciate, "Well, such are the Vietnamese!"

But what was the attitude of authorities within Vietnam with regard to the book? It was terribly amusing. Let me elaborate on this.

A few days after I had returned to Hanoi after leaving the United States, a friend of mine who had formerly gone with me to the war zone (he was a writer, and I was a filmmaker) came to visit me. He had no problem with *If You Go to the Ends of All the Seas* and was particularly interested in getting a copy for a friend, also from the war, who was now the head of the party's Department of Ideology and Culture. I was extremely hesitant, saying that it wasn't really a literary work, and that I wasn't actually a writer at all; it was just a sociological research paper with nothing interesting in it—it wouldn't be suitable to give him a copy. But my friend persisted in this request, and said that the person he referred to would meet me after he read it. He went away with the book, full of sincere intentions. Of course, I had no interest in waiting to see anybody. But later on, in early 2005, an unwelcome development occurred. A person who cared for me gave me a document with the title "Report on the Review of Ideological and Cultural Conditions in 2004." It bore a "top secret" seal and was signed by a person named Đào Duy Quát. Of course, in this "top secret" document that I had no choice but to read, there were many trivial stories that I had no interest in. But when I came to a section consisting of a scathing criticism of *If You Go to the Ends of All the Seas,* of course I had to take note.

Perhaps due to all of the criticism and all of the speculations of the "sidewalk news agency" (the grapevine) blowing up the importance of this book, quite a few copies of *If You Go to the Ends of All the Seas* secretly found their way into Vietnam. Many people passed photocopies of photocopies to each other, and even rented copies from book vendors along the streets. Mr. Nguyễn Đức Bình, the director of the Văn Nghệ publishing house, came up from Saigon to see me in Hanoi and discuss printing *If You Go to the Ends of All the Seas.* I happily thanked him for his interest and said that I wouldn't take a penny of copyright money. I had one condition, however. The publisher must print the entire text, one hundred percent, down to the last period and comma. Anh Bình said that if a word was too sensitive, he could replace it by a series of dots. I said that this should not be done, because it would put my friends in the United States at risk of being accused of "falling into a Communist trap." They were all people who had conversed with me, and helped me write the book. It was indeed not a simple matter.

Vietnamese people, starting from what period and for what reason I don't know, have expended immeasurable quantities of effort, time, money, and human life to attack each other.

It's truly a shame! A people afflicted with every sort of privation and difficulty will find it hard to get along even if they are united in love and loyalty to each other—so how can they improve their lot if they are only interested in attacking each other? Where can they find any leftover energy or calories to build up their society? Could it be that the business of "advertising your political stance" and getting lost in the "political labyrinth" (I meditate a good deal on the term "labyrinth" as used by

Nguyễn Mộng Giác)[1] remains the permanent predicament and karma of the Vietnamese? No political regime or group of intellectuals, it seems, has devoted adequate attention to this predicament. It is obvious that along with all of our fine traits, many outworn and injurious habits and faults of conduct still lurk within us.

After my visit to the United States, a book was even published with the title *Trần Văn Thủy A Story of Unkindness,* accusing me of being a tool of the Communist Party: "The [Communist] Party must be credited with building Trần Văn Thủy into the phenomenon that he now is. Don't say that I'm a suspicious person! Do me the favor of providing a single example of a courageous person who dares to tell the truth under the Vietnamese Communist regime who has not been crushed with the heaviest of punishments..."

Later on, a rumor arose that I wasn't any sort of film director at all but was just an agitprop cadre sent out to spread propaganda.

And yes, I had to protect myself from reprisals when I came back home as well. What a wretched life.

In talking about *If You Go to the Ends of All the Seas,* and about my Vietnamese and American friends, I must mention Diane Fox.

My friend Diane drove me up the coast of California, Oregon, and Washington in her own car.[2] This was only one of hundreds of trips that I've taken in the course of my travels, but it is nevertheless an unforgettable memory.

Both before and after that trip, I had the mindset of an observer. If you want to appreciate and absorb your surroundings, you shouldn't travel by plane but should rather "crawl" on the earth's surface. And you can easily imagine how tired of climbing up and down stairs leading to airplanes I must have grown, after having taken so many flights to more than thirty different universities across the United States for countless talks and film shows.

Diane had sought me out and first came to know me through the Web.[3] An anthropologist who spoke Vietnamese and was especially concerned with the effects of Agent Orange, she had been to Vietnam many times, had stayed there many months, and was closely acquainted with many Vietnamese researchers.

She also took time to translate, without remuneration, the script of our film *A Story from the Corner of a Park* so that it could be shown in the United States and other countries. The film is about the devastating effects of Agent Orange on the family of a veteran who, like so many, had been exposed to that poison.

I remember that before she left Vietnam to return to the United States, Diane gave me a sum of money to help a child living in poverty so that he could continue learning how to fix motorbikes for a living. She instructed me not to give him the whole sum at once, lest he spend it all.

In Hanoi, she formed similar relationships with many underprivileged children.

Now she was guiding this underprivileged man through a place I had always wanted to visit. In the world of film, the west coast of the United States is a place of power and mystery. This is reflected a great deal in novels, but Diane explained to me many details concerning the spectacular scenes whizzing by the windows of our car. It seemed that on that day, the ocean waves were bigger, the vault of the sky higher, the rocky cliffs more jagged, the forests taller—and the ten-lane highway seemed endless.

I began to think of the destiny that had pushed me along in my turbulent life as a filmmaker, with its precarious ups and downs, its moments of glory and ignominy, a destiny that had at last led me to see strange lands, lands connected with the ocean, with lakes, or in other words with "Thủy" (meaning water), the name bestowed on me by my parents, as one of the five basic elements of life in traditional Chinese cosmology.

During my period of study in Russia, I had had the opportunity to pay eight visits to Lake Baikal, the largest freshwater lake in the world; and once I had stayed there for several months to make a documentary film.

From the top of a hill in the Marseilles harbor I had gazed down at the Mediterranean; from the city of Sochi I had observed the Black Sea; from Hamburg, the Baltic; and from Saint Petersburg, the North Sea

I had seen the oceans from every direction. I had seen the eastern Atlantic from the city of Nantes, the western Atlantic from the feet of the Statue of Liberty and from Massachusetts. I had seen the eastern Pacific from Los Angeles and San Francisco, and the western Pacific from Japan. I had seen the southern Pacific from Sydney and Melbourne, the Caribbean Sea from Florida, and the Manche Sea from d'Auville. I had seen the sea surrounding England from Manchester and London, and the Adriatic Sea from Milan, Rome, and Venice.

I have also had occasion to take in the sight of Lake Tahoe, lying between California and Nevada, a beautiful and mysterious lake that seemed to belong to a world of fairy tales.

For the gifted, the powerful, and the wealthy, traveling around the world and seeing all of these sights is an ordinary affair, but for a humble fellow like me, who in early life had lived with primitive tribespeople who went about half naked and lived on tubers and beasts of the forest, and who for ten years, from age twenty to age thirty, had no hope more cherished than to be able to eat a decent meal and walk on a level road, this was truly like a pipedream. Many times in my life I had become a zombie-like creature, close to death . . . so I had truly never imagined that I would be able to gaze at high skies and wide vistas like this.

But these adventures were of great benefit to a documentary filmmaker.

When Diane and I got to Portland, it was dark already. We stayed there for two days. Each morning I went for a walk in the neighborhood to get some exercise, and noticed that Diane's house and others nearby all lay in wooded areas. As had been planned, for two days she took me to two universities there for interactions that included talks and film shows. The next day, we continued our journey until we reached Seattle, Washington.

The University of Washington was where Diane worked,[4] and was also the institution that had invited me, Wayne Karlin, and Trương Vũ to give presentations. Many interesting things occurred there.

I got to meet Ms. Rosemary Nguyễn, a Caucasian American woman who spoke Vietnamese like a native; her Vietnamese name was Thảo. Her husband was a man of Vietnamese ancestry named Nguyễn Hiếu. Rosemary astonished all of the Vietnamese she met with her thorough and deep familiarity with Vietnamese language and culture. When I was helped by my friends to publish *If You Go to the Ends of All the Seas*, she, together with Thái Tuyết Quân and Diane Fox, translated Wayne Karlin's contribution without asking for any compensation.

The dean of the University of Washington's Southeast Asian Studies Department in Seattle was a German man who spoke excellent Vietnamese and knew a great many humorous stories concerning Vietnam.

I took part in three discussion sessions at the university, one of them with Wayne Karlin, an American writer and Vietnam veteran, and Trương

Vũ, a "Việt Kiều" ARVN veteran who had come to America as a boat person and became a NASA scientist and author-editor, joining me. The two of them, along with the writer Lê Minh Khuê (herself a veteran of the youth volunteer brigade on the Hồ Chí Minh Trails), in Hanoi, had coedited a book of Vietnamese and American short stories about the aftermath of the war by authors who, like the editors, came from all sides of the conflict.[5] The book was an effort at reconciliation through literature, and I feel that the discussion we had left an especially strong impression among American teachers, students, and veterans.

Finally, my program with Diane in Seattle and on the West Coast came to a conclusion. We parted with reluctance.

My stay on the West Coast had been full of rich experiences. But there was one in particular, perhaps more moving and unexpected than any other during my visit to Seattle.

After one of the discussion sessions at the University of Washington, many members of the audience stayed around afterward to converse with the filmmaker (me). Among them were a young couple named Thanh and Kiệt, who invited me to their home, where they received me very warmly.

The rooms in their house were tidy and tastefully arranged. I cast my eyes around, looking at everything (a very ordinary thing to do among us Vietnamese, but not too polite in the West), and saw on the wall a handsomely framed photograph behind glass, right in the middle of which there sat an elderly, white-haired woman in formal dress, while behind her stood five youths dressed in suits and wearing round glasses. Their faces all looked alike, and they were close to one another in age, so it wasn't possible to tell who was older and who younger.

"So where is your father?" I asked Kiệt.

Kiệt pointed to a small black-and-white photo carefully hung next to the larger photo.

"This is my father!"

"Is he in good health?"

"My father is no longer alive."

"Oh, I'm sorry. Where did he die?" (again, a typically Vietnamese question).

Kiệt hesitated a few seconds and then said, "My father died in a reeducation camp."

I was stunned! The family of a man whose father had died in a

Communist prison was greeting a person from Communist Vietnam with such cordial warmth!

"It has been a great honor for us today that you accepted our invitation to visit us. But in a short while, I shall ask your permission to take Thanh to a hospital to give birth. She has been advised to go to the hospital soon! I'm sorry for this unexpected affair," Kiệt said politely.

Good grief! His pregnant wife was about to give birth, but she and her husband still invited me to visit them at their house. Such an unexpected episode was beyond the imagination even of an experienced filmmaker.

Two days later, after I had returned to Boston, I received an e-mail from Thanh and Kiệt saying that their baby was born, and was such-and-such a length and such-and-such a weight. Then they gave me three different names, and asked me to select one of them for their child!

I was immensely moved. How could life drive me into such unimaginably strange situations? And could I ever get over my own complex of being a VC?

Could it be that Diane intentionally designed this visit with its interactions at a number of West Coast universities because she wished to build a bridge of reconciliation between Vietnam and the United States? But surely she could never have known that there would be some Vietnamese spectators—like Thanh and Kiệt—who would invite me to their home and show me such astonishing generosity and respect.

This was an example of "reconciliation" among the Vietnamese, a reconciliation that is much more difficult to achieve than that between us and the Americans.

IV
THE
LABYRINTH

Preface

A culture that is not free is a dead culture. A culture that relies only on propaganda is also a dead culture. The more the authority of the leadership is increased, the more culture will be strangled, the poorer cultural values and the rarer fine artists will become.

—Trần Độ

In adapting this book from its original Vietnamese edition, with the encouragement and approval of Trần Văn Thủy and Lê Thanh Dũng, among other sins, I shifted the order of chapters and excerpts from chapters in order to shape the narrative into one more coherent to an American audience. The first chapter in this section originally appeared near the beginning of the book, in the section now labeled "War," as an anecdote Thủy told Dũng while recounting the difficulties he had being admitted to film school when he was a young man because his perceived bourgeoisie background threatened to keep him from membership in the Communist Party, and how those difficulties reminded him of an incident that took place many years later. I was advised to eliminate that story from the American version since it was both out of the chronological order of Thủy's life, and because it might seem trivial, its significance puzzling to American readers. Yet I feel it important to keep this little aside in the narrative because of the way it acts as a measure of how much of a sea change there has been in Vietnamese attitudes since the war, and what that change signifies to people of Trần Văn Thủy's wartime generation. Party membership—held by only about five percent of the population during those times—was, at least in the minds of true believers, the equivalent of being elevated to a holy order dedicated to independence, social justice, and economic equality, and, on a more practical basis, opened up rank and career possibilities that were blocked for nonparty members. Coming from a family considered to be too well-off or reactionary would preclude membership, and, as Thủy recounted, "From then [1962] until now—late 2012—no one at all in the rest of my family has been allowed to become a party member, including a dozen or so brothers, sisters, and in-laws, among whom several have worked for dozens of years in government. My younger sister applied to two schools, the Hanoi music school and the army music school. Though she obtained very high scores in the qualifying exams for both schools, she was not admitted to either, due to her 'improper background.'" If Thủy had not been accepted to the party himself, he would not have had his career as a filmmaker. His shock and depression about an incident recounted in chapter 19, during which he was cursed as an "old Communist," marks the depth of the changes in his society, but more, it stirs an old man's rage at the loss of youth, at the memory of lost ideals and unthinkable sacrifices, at the erasure of personal history.

Thủy's films from the 1990s on, though not recounted in detail in these final chapters, continued to turn a gimlet eye on his own society. In 1992, he made *A Spiritual World,* reflecting his deep belief in, and fascination with, spiritual culture, particularly the ways in which the dead are commemorated and connected to in Vietnam, and the way in which compassion and a sense of spiritual transcendence go together. The author worked on the film with the famous poet and singer Trịnh Công Sơn, whose songs of the cost of war and the common pain of Vietnamese are loved by people all over Vietnam. Thủy made another film, *There Was a Village,* soon after: it revealed how in one small, poor village Vietnamese traditions could knit people into a common, caring community—a contrast to the competitive drive and the chase for individual wealth that was eroding that ethic, something happening in Vietnam but also in Japan, which Thủy came to understand was the reason a Japanese TV station had commissioned him to make the film.

In the last chapters of the book, Thủy reflects also on the place of art and literature in Vietnamese culture: the ways in which writing, film, and art have been both celebrated and repressed, that repression itself a recognition of how much every regime in Vietnam has understood the dangerously transformative power of art, and how some of the great men and women of Vietnam—not only artists but also political and military leaders—understood how that power had always allowed the Vietnamese "to understand and cherish the spiritual and cultural threads that bind us together." He mentions in an anecdote his friendship with general Võ Nguyên Giáp—the leader of the armed forces in both the war against the French and the war against the Americans and the Republic of Vietnam—who asked for a secret, private showing of *Hanoi in Whose Eyes* and who put his arm around Thủy's shoulders afterward, and with lieutenant general Trần Độ, a deputy minister of culture and head of the party's Department of Culture and Arts during the heyday of reform in Vietnam (1986–89), who supported lifting restrictions on the arts, freeing writers, artists, and filmmakers to experiment with new forms and to explore social problems freely. But he also tells how Trần Độ fell out of favor in 1989 and was taken out of office by conservative elements in the party, afraid of the changes occurring in Eastern Europe and China. Thủy describes how at Trần Độ's funeral, people were forbidden to use the words "immense sorrow"—and Thủy's sadness at the continuing abuse and censorship of artists and writers, recounting how he has been affected by the years of being under constant surveillance, of being hauled in for interrogations, of having to fight to make films and then to not have them banned. He details those in high and low places, from prime ministers to policemen, who supported him, and those who harassed him, all the while questioning his patriotism.

The last chapter is a cry from the heart for people to understand that the way Thủy loves his country, and the way his films, by revealing both the flaws that need to be addressed and the strength and goodness that can be drawn from the country's history and culture that can serve as models to heal those flaws, are the truest ways to love one's country. An American reader of the translated manuscript told me that Thủy's statements about patriotism are redundant and somewhat bromidic, that his experiences speak for themselves in demonstrating his love of country. While this is true, it misses how Thủy assessed that his Vietnamese readership, bombarded with films and literature whose only purpose is to praise the status quo, is unfamiliar with the concept of art that points out social flaws in order to correct them. His Vietnamese readers needed, he felt, to hear a clear statement of—simply—how his critical art, and the work of those writers, musicians, and filmmakers he admires, is the highest form of patriotism. It is smugly arrogant to believe that this is not a statement that an American readership needs to hear as well. In that statement, in this book, in the body of his work, in his life, and in the lives of those he admires, Thủy continually answers the universal question of how a serious person, in spite of the temptations of comfort and wealth and the pressures of fear, may move through his life and his work with grace, integrity, and courage.

—W. K.

19

An Unpleasant Occurrence

Having told my story up to this point, I am reminded of an unpleasant occurrence . . .

In the year 2000, when I had just turned sixty, an annual conference of the journalists' association took place in the Hùng Vương Guesthouse in Hanoi. As documentary filmmakers, we were given journalist passes to attend the event. It was a long time ago, so I no longer remember exactly what the content of the conference was—only that there was lots of talking that went on and on, followed by lots of beer drinking.

On the last day of the conference, I drove my motorcycle to the guesthouse to attend the farewell party. From Hoàng Hoa Thám Street, I turned onto Ngọc Hà Street. About halfway down the sloping street, I ran into a traffic jam in which people and vehicles had come to a halt. I saw a hulking fellow who had parked his motorcycle and was coming up menacingly to a taxi that was parked crosswise in the street. This ruffian yanked the door of the taxi open, dragged the driver out of the vehicle, and began pummeling him on the face and nose. The taxi driver had the look of a timid country boy who had come to town to work. There were people crowded all around, but no one said a thing. At this juncture, I raised my voice and said, "Hey you two! If you have some disagreement, let the police and the laws take care of it—why do you have to hit people like that?"

To tell the truth, when the ruffian hit the young man, I felt as if the blows were falling on my son's face. Everyone these days knows that intervening in some affair going on in the streets or marketplace can involve you in no end of trouble, but this ruffian's behavior was too barbaric; I couldn't contain myself. I raised my voice to a shout: "Stop at once! You can't hit a person like that! I'm a journalist!"

The ruffian let go of the taxi driver, turned around, charged up to me, seized me by the collar, and said, "F— your mother, you old Communist!"

I was overcome with shock. Some old ladies standing nearby said, "Hey sir! Go away, go away!"

There was nothing I could do! This was not a place to talk about right or wrong. What more could be said? I had no choice but to swallow my rage and seek a path of escape. Riding my motorcycle on the road to the Hùng Vương Guesthouse nearby, I was like a man in a trance.

"How did that fellow know I was a Communist? Ah . . . I was a journalist, so I must be a party member, a Communist. But why did he curse me in such a profane manner? If I had never gone to the South, and had never become a party member, would that fellow's curses have been so presumptuous and unreasonable?"

But there are various kinds of party members. People even make fun of it, saying, "Though he's a party member, he's a good person!"

At the guesthouse, the first floor was flooded by bright lights, with food and drink spread out on the tables, and crowds of guests producing a roar of conversation and laughter. After parking my motorcycle, I entered the foyer in a daze. The first person I met was Khổng Minh Dụ, who was in charge of A25 (an agency responsible for cultural security) in the Ministry of Public Security. On seeing me, he said, "You look like a person who has lost his soul, why?"

I didn't say a thing. Though there were many people about, Mr. Dụ paid attention only to me, no doubt because my expression was so bizarre. Mr. Dụ pulled me to a far corner and the two of us sat down on some chairs next to the wall. He brought a glass of wine over and said, "Come on, drink it. What's made you so sad?"

I didn't know how to keep my private thoughts from showing in my expression, but at the same time I felt unwilling to say what was on my mind. What would be the point? And if I talked about it with a person like Khổng Minh Dụ, what would he think about it? But Dụ appeared very sincere: "Well, if something's bothering you, forget about it—let's sit with our friends and enjoy ourselves. Drink up!"

Only then did I say, "I just ran into something very unpleasant."

"Then go ahead and tell me about it."

"I don't know how this story will strike you, but let me tell you anyway."

I related the story as it had happened. Khổng Minh Dụ was thoughtful and sympathetic. This made me feel closer to him.

Mr. Dụ said, "I'll share an experience with you from which you'll see that there's nothing out of the ordinary in what you encountered. One day I was going to Hải Phòng with some high-ranking security officers. It had grown dark and rainy, and the road was blocked by bad traffic. Cars were at a standstill and horns were blowing noisily. An old farmer with a rake on his shoulder and a water buffalo behind him was threading his way through the traffic. On coming in front of our car, he struck the hood very heavily and started cursing Đỗ Mười at the top of his lungs." (Đỗ Mười was then the Communist Party general secretary).

His curses were fearfully vulgar. They were in fact so profane that they cannot be reproduced here. The public security officers sitting in the car had no choice but to endure the cursing—what else could they do? Scold the man? Arrest him?"

Mr. Dụ was lost in thought for a while, then said, "So, Mr. Thủy, we just have to keep our mouths shut!"

Mr. Dụ's story gave me some comfort. But that year was also the last year that I was a party member. After having worked on the government payroll until I retired at the age of sixty, I didn't really "retire" at all but kept on working hard as usual: I made films, wrote books, and participated in professional activities. There were countless film festivals and conferences to attend inside and outside the country, as well as some philanthropic work . . . Even now, I haven't stopped to rest. I very much want to rest, but it's not possible. Now, though, if I go out on the streets and hear youths shouting the curse "you old Communist!" during some disturbance, I'll be a bit relieved that they'll be cursing someone else, not me . . .

20

Immense Sorrow Is Forbidden

In the days when the director Lê Mạnh Thích was still alive, we often got together and traded stories about our profession. Once some younger filmmakers discovered that in all of the films of their esteemed elder Thích, there would always be a scene shot in the rain . . . and in all of the films of director A there would always be a scene with a setting or rising sun, while in the films of director B, there would always be a scene of flowers, leaves, and floating clouds. Then the younger folk made the discovery that in all of *my* films there would always be a scene with incense smoke and burial sites.

I was startled!

Indeed, in all of the twenty-odd films that I had made, whether good or bad, there were scenes with incense smoke and burial sites, all as if by pure coincidence.

In stories concerning life within the country, the incense smoke and burial sites would be associated with war victims, martyrs, people from general walks of life, friends, and distinguished people of former times.

No matter what country or city I came to, I would always seek out a cemetery. When I was in the United States, I paid repeated visits to the grave of Abraham Lincoln and to the cemeteries of Boston, where I resided. When I went to Westminster, California, there was a cemetery called The Eternal Gardens in front of Green Lantern Village, the apartment complex where Hoàng Khởi Phong lived. This was a place where many Vietnamese literary and artistic people were buried. I spent many hours there seeking out and murmuring the names of many people of artistic reputation, such as the writer Mai Thảo, the poet Nguyên Sa, the musician Phạm Đình Chương, the singer Ngọc Lan, the journalist Lê Đình Điểu, the playwright Vũ Hạ, the musician Trầm Tử Thiêng, the singer Thái Hằng, and many others.

But let me speak about the funeral of lieutenant general Trần Độ in our own country.

Trần Độ was a man who deeply understood how essential freedom of expression and the arts are to the spiritual health of our country. He was a deputy minister of culture and head of the party's Department of Culture and Arts during the heyday of reform in Vietnam (1986–89). As a talented and dedicated administrator, he supported reform policies and maintained close relations with artists and intellectuals.

He took intense delight in any sort of new thinking, and he loved the articles that appeared in the pages of *Văn Nghệ*[1] during the period when the writer Nguyên Ngọc was the editor in chief there. He loved *Trương Ba's Soul in the Butcher's Skin*[2] and *Hanoi in Whose Eyes*.

In Trần Độ's memoirs, we can read such passages as the following:

> *I have a special love and respect for writers, artists, and performers, because their labors are of a special type, and I always feel that they are a precious resource of the nation and that the talented ones in particular are a source of national pride...*
>
> *We can have a great many ministers and deputy ministers; and may have many prime ministers and deputy prime ministers, but we can only have one Xuân Diệu, one Nguyễn Tuân, one Chế Lan Viên, one Văn Cao, and Trần Văn Cẩn, one Nguyễn Sáng, and one Bùi Xuân Phái.*[3] *None of these individuals could be exchanged for anyone else. Due to these considerations, I usually regard artists with a high degree of tolerance and a deep respect for their professions. I don't subject their lifestyles to narrow scrutiny, and I am ready and willing to create the best conditions for them to maximize their abilities, so as to serve the people and serve the nation.*
>
> *A culture that is not free is a dead culture. A culture that relies only on propaganda is also a dead culture. The more the authority of the leadership is increased, the more culture will be strangled, the poorer cultural values and the rarer fine artists will become.*

I regard Trần Độ as a benefactor, and a person of feeling and principle. He rescued *Hanoi in Whose Eyes* and opened the way for *The Story of Kindness*.

When *The Story of Kindness* was first shown to officials in the Department of Culture and Arts, everyone went upstairs to drink tea and exchange opinions. They all looked apprehensive—the atmosphere was in fact completely devoid of comfort or enthusiasm. Mr. Trần Độ seemed to be somewhat at a loss.

So I asked, "Anh Độ! How do you feel about it, now that you've seen it?"

After a moment's hesitation, he said, "I feel quite confused. You gentlemen go ahead and give us your opinions first." Perhaps some will be disinclined to believe that he used the words "quite confused." But that is the absolute truth. It was as simple as the reaction of Mr. Nguyễn Văn Linh, who, after viewing *Hanoi in Whose Eyes,* said, "If that's all it amounts to, then why was it prohibited? Or maybe I failed to understand it because I'm a man of limited education?"

Some other people cautiously expressed a few opinions. Then Trần Độ turned to me and asked, "How about the sections portraying the Catholic sisters?"

I told them in detail about the dedication of those nuns and the privations they endured so that they could care for the lepers in the Quý Hoa Leprosarium—things that I had witnessed with my own eyes. He listened attentively and then, slowly and with emphasis said, "If that's the way it is, then it must be told the way it is."

In *The Story of Kindness,* there are many ideas and episodes that had their origin in the views expressed by Trần Độ to artists and intellectuals. With regard to the use of the word "people," for example, he had said, "It's so strange, comrades, there isn't any other place in the world where the word 'people' is used as much as it is in our own country—we have such phrases as 'people's artist,' 'people's journalist,' 'people's army,' 'people's court,' and 'people's committee,' but the people have no rights whatsoever. For example, when I joined the party central committee, I immediately felt I was powerful and wiser, and that people would show me greater respect." But then he said, "When I was in office, I always thought I knew everything; but now that I'm retired, I feel I don't understand a thing. Now when I read Buddhist sutras, I feel that they're splendid!"

In March 1989, when I returned to Vietnam from France, I went to see Mr. Trần Độ to report what had happened and to chat, but because I had just arrived home, I didn't dare mention that I had been invited to return to France a few months later.

Only when the day of departure drew near did I mention the matter to him and ask him to make a decision authorizing me to go. He said, "Why didn't you mention this right away the last time?"

"Why is that?"

"Because I've lost my position!"

Then, after thinking a few moments, he said, "But you must go! Let me summon Nghiêm Hà." Nghiêm Hà was very close to him, working as his trusted secretary. When he arrived, I don't know what Trần Độ said to him, but the next day I received an authorization to go to France signed by Trần Độ—he was already out of office to be sure, but the date on the authorization paper was backdated to a time when he still held his position.

That was Trần Độ!

Later on, I learned that Mr. Trần Độ had lost favor and his political position because his liberal and reformist views had grown to be at odds with the party's hard-line leadership, which had turned more conservative after 1989, in a negative reaction to turbulent changes in Eastern Europe and major protests going on in China.

The death of Trần Độ touched off strong emotions in the army and in the literary and artistic community, because he was a person of such pure humanity. People's feelings for him were entirely natural and devoid of pretense. They reflected a need for those around him to have someone to turn to whom they could trust, and in whom they could hope to find decent human qualities.

My wife and I brought a funeral wreath inscribed with the words "In immense sorrow for anh [Elder Brother] Trần Độ," and, on the line beneath, "em [Younger Sibling] Trần Văn Thủy."

The woman selling funeral wreaths went ahead of us, bearing the wreaths. When we passed through the gates leading to the place where the observances were to be held, we were stopped by a couple of guards. One fellow was passing a metal detector over the wreaths so as to detect explosives and the like. The other guard looked at the words on our wreath, and said in a rough voice, "Instructions have been issued that people are not permitted to have "immense sorrow"—so why does your wreath have the words "immense sorrow?"

Only then did I grow dimly aware that there was such a directive, and later on I learned that this was an unpopular decision. Even the wreath sent in by General Giáp was stopped at the entrance for this reason.

The fellow with the metal detector said to his companion, "Look—above it says "Elder Brother Trần Độ,," and below it says "Younger Sibling Trần Văn Thủy." The instructions say that family members are allowed to use the words "immense sorrow."

Before I had a chance to make any response, the two fellows waved us on in a rude manner, though we were both old enough to be their parents.

So it turned out we were related to Mr. Trần Độ and didn't know it! What a joke! Those young guards weren't aware that his real name at birth was Tạ Ngọc Phách—he had absolutely no relationship to my Trần family. I thought to myself, "When he took the alias Trần Độ many years ago in order to be take part in the revolution, did he foresee this ridiculous situation? Could anyone overhear him giggling in his coffin?"

And so we went in.

Inside the funeral memorial service hall, we saw that the words "immense sorrow" that one customarily sees permanently inscribed on the walls were covered with black cloth, over which a few words written on white paper had been hastily hung that read, "Funeral Service for Mr. Trần Độ."

The top leadership's decision to deny general Trần Độ due honor and civility at his funeral, including a ban on public display of feelings, was perceived as an extreme case of ill-treatment toward a popular general and official for his liberal and critical views. This provoked a strong public reaction, turning his funeral into a scandal, and polarizing army and party ranks.

I have known some of the great men and women of our time, and have come to see that one of the things that makes them great is their understanding of how art and literature have always allowed our people to understand and cherish the spiritual and cultural threads that bind us together. General Võ Nguyên Giáp was one of them.[4] On one occasion, after the banning of *Hanoi in Whose Eyes*, he asked for a private viewing of the film on the sly—with his family—at the documentary film studio. After the showing, just as people were sitting and drinking tea, the electricity was cut off, and the sky was more or less black outside. The general stood with me for a long time, and finally said, "You've lost a lot of sleep, haven't you?" Then he put his arm around me, patted my back, and said, "Life is the mother of truth . . ."

This is a saying very easy to understand and very easy for mindless or shallow people to trot out in a glib fashion. But only people who have passed through many experiences on the road of life are able to understand it deeply, and the more they experience, the deeper will be their understanding. In this case, the experience of the old general, after having passed through years of warfare, lay within that saying.[5]

Allow me to add that I do not take the slightest delight or pride in dropping such great names as Phạm Văn Đồng, Võ Nguyên Giáp, Nguyễn Văn Linh, Võ Văn Kiệt, and Trần Độ into this humble and insignificant account of my adventures. But I have no choice but to recount these matters because they are the truth.

I am grateful to these gentlemen because they were well-disposed toward me and because they rescued me from difficulties. It would not be too much to say that they protected me during the long years when *Hanoi in Whose Eyes* was in trouble, and when *The Story of Kindness* was banned.

As for all of the "secrets of the inner circles" and "great affairs of state," it is not for a humble fellow like me, however interested I might be, to make any comment or assessment. Let history be the judge of such things.

But I am sad! Above all, I am sad!

I am sad because these were precisely the people with power who could do earthshaking things—yet why is the country still afflicted with so many absurd and inhumane problems? I am sad because intellectuals and artists, people of dedication and ability, are still so wretched and upset—and what is still more painful is that the more dedicated and able they are, the more wretched and upset they will be!

Many times I have asked myself: "Why?"

It isn't hard to answer.

People who like to play games with words say that these things are due to "systemic faults." Fair enough! But if we really care for this country, really love this nation, we must wake up and call things by their true names; otherwise we will go on walking hand in hand under a road sign inscribed only with the word "Labyrinth."[6]

21

The Language of My Land

I love this land, and I want to make this land even more beautiful. I am consumed with the wish to make human life worthy of the sacrifices that have been made for it . . .

—Trần Văn Thủy

I once shared my deepest feelings with the director Đinh Anh Dũng on the subject of patriotism, a subject that is as old as the concept of nations and yet as new as every new day. I said that patriotism is part of human nature, and especially of the nature of Vietnamese.

I also spoke my mind about a further point: in this country you would have to light a torch and conduct a painstaking search to find a few people who don't love their nation (not counting corrupt officials and a few insane people). But one must note that each person expresses his love of country in his own way.

We may be unequal in rank, status, money, and power, but Heaven and our ancestors have bestowed on all of us an equal right to define how we love our country. This has been true since ancient times.

Take this excerpt from a letter written (in 1924) by the scholar Nguyễn Văn Vĩnh (1882–1936) to the scholar and revolutionary Huỳnh Thúc Kháng (1876–1947):

> *We crossed paths on the road, and each of us claims to be on the right path precisely because it is not yet known. But since, after all, since we are both going in search of the truth, it is not imperative that we have to take the same road.*[1]

Wonderful, isn't it? These people of former times can really inspire admiration!

So let me now risk stating the following: "I am a patriot!"

All the films that I have made, all the things I have written, all the lonely roads I have walked on, all the desperate situations I have endured have arisen simply because I love my country. Don't waste your time looking for some enemy force controlling my actions from behind—I am neither clever enough, nor stupid enough, to be involved in any such thing.

When people see anyone who differs from themselves, who thinks differently from themselves, or who wishes for anything different from what they themselves wish, they define him as an enemy. How have they behaved in life, how have they loved and hated, that they should have so many enemies?

There's nothing good about having so many enemies.

For many years on end, security personnel stood guard around my home, and on many occasions would arrest and interrogate me merely because they suspected that some political force was directing my activities (I kept a full record of who did the interrogating, how many times, on what dates, in what locations, how many nights passed, and what the content of the interrogations was).

They looked into all of my associations with people, and examined all of the names and phone numbers in my notebooks so as to interrogate me more carefully. They asked me about all of my relationships with Vietnamese intellectuals inside and outside the country, and even inquired about my relationship with Mr. Trần Độ—it was bizarre that they should go to such an extreme. They also asked me why I was invited to the French foreign ministry to talk with Mr. Blanche Maison before he came to Vietnam as an ambassador. They asked me why there was an organization in Paris called Friends of Trần Văn Thủy. These were of course all silly questions, but I gave clear, transparent, and polite responses to all of them. I felt that the way they spoke to me also expressed a degree of politeness and respect. Nevertheless, a fellow named Bảy once couldn't control his temper when interrogating me and, pointing his finger in my face, said, "You're a reactionary! You're in contact with saboteurs! You're transporting documents to foreign countries, and from other countries into Vietnam!"

I pulled apart the lapels of my shirt so as to expose my chest and, no longer able to maintain my calm, said, "Shoot me! If you know so much, just shoot me! What's the point of asking these questions?"

Though a public security officer, he didn't understand a basic legal tenet: that only a judge in a court of law has the right to conclude at the end of a trial that the accused is guilty.

The above event took place in the late afternoon on April 20, 1991, in a place that I later learned had once been the headquarters of the Saigon police.[2] Just as working hours drew to a close, a vehicle parked by the front gate. They told me to get into the car. Inside, aside from the driver, there was a very young security guard, about my son's age, and a blanket for the detainee. After a spell, we arrived at Camp Thủ Đức, a place surrounded by a high wall with barbed wire. I had to pass the night there.

The young security guard slept on a bed next to mine. I was very tired, but I was incapable of closing my eyes; the sounds of explosions from the war long ago kept recurring in my head.

The next day I was questioned again, and I gave the same answers as before. Aside from Bảy, the people questioning me included someone named Đồng, and Phong. All of the interrogations were recorded by a high-quality recording device in the next room.

After dark, a high-ranking official from the Ministry of Public Security, whose name was Thành or Thanh, came by, wearing a smart-looking white outfit. He had come to see me as a pre-release formality. He exchanged a few quiet words with me that I can no longer remember. I noticed that Bảy hovered around his superior officer with eager servility, trying to explain to him that I was not accused. He even bade me farewell with a pleasant smile!

But then a few days later, when I went back up to Hanoi, I had to report to A15 (the counter-espionage agency) at the Ministry of Public Security for continued questioning about all kinds of "earthshaking" matters (that is, things of no significance). These interrogations occurred on May 1, May 11, and May 13 of 1991, and were conducted by police officers Trần, Hạnh, Mâu, and Long.

Thus, even ten years after my memorable meeting with prime minister Phạm Văn Đồng concerning *Hanoi in Whose Eyes,* I was still having trouble with security organizations.

One afternoon in 1992, a visitor came to my house and introduced himself as Nguyễn Tiến Năng, the secretary to prime minister Phạm Văn Đồng. He said, "The prime minister would like you to come see him in order to discuss something." I was a bit bewildered, as I could not imagine how the prime minister still remembered me, or what he might wish to discuss.

I came for the appointment, and found the prime minister weaker, his eyesight much worse. He received me alone in his capacious guest room. He asked me about my work and my family.

I said that, thanks to Heaven's favors, everything was normal.

Then, coming to the point, he said, "What do you mean by 'normal'? I just got a letter from the scholar Hoàng Xuân Hãn in France complaining that Trần Văn Thủy isn't being treated decently at home, and asking me to look into it."

I said, "In general, things are normal except for two matters: The first is that security people have been asking me to report for interrogation a bit too much. The second is that the Ministry of Culture won't let me travel abroad, even though I've had a dozen invitations from France, and especially Japan, for purely professional working trips."

Looking somber, the prime minister said, "I no longer have any power or position—but I'll find out who is in charge of these matters and speak with them about it. If they're close to me, I may be able to influence them."

"If they're close to me, I may be able to influence them." Those words of the prime minister made me very sad. It was a pervasive sadness, hard to put into words.

Twenty years have passed since then—the police operatives who used to tail me and interrogate me in those days have surely all retired by now and become old men. As I reflect on this, it seems to me that every person has a profession and a job to do; I have mine, and they have theirs; if we should meet again now over a glass of wine and chat about our lives, there would surely be many amusing things to talk about.

But as I think more about it, I can't imagine how much taxpayers' money and how much time and effort on the part of these young men have been poured into surveillance and investigations to "break cases" of this sort. This is clearly ridiculous!

In hindsight, however, I find that I must thank all of those policemen, for if in those days they had gone a bit too far, then perhaps I would have been finished off, and would not be able to sit here today chatting about it. And this is not to mention the fact that among the security personnel with the power to make decisions, such as whether I should be arrested or not, there were some people who looked out for me. That is something that I have learned only recently.

And then, by coincidence, just a few months ago, I again met (former) Hanoi police chief Phạm Chuyên, a brigadier general, after a lapse of thirty years. Together with friends, he came to our montage rooms and watched the film we were working on: *Songs Resounding for a Thousand Years, Part III.*

I can say that Phạm Chuyên has been kindly disposed toward me, and that we even have a fond relationship. We chat with each other, go out for fun, visit each other's homes for a beer and a chat . . . We often refer to him with affection as Chánh Sở Cẩm (an old name for a police chief in the French era). He lives in a gallant and generous manner. What most impresses me is his special friendship and regard for general Nguyễn Cao Kỳ.[3] Phạm Chuyên also protected some intellectuals and artists when they got into trouble.

I remember that thirty years ago, in 1983, when *Hanoi in Whose Eyes* was in limbo, it was shown in order to get the comments of feature filmmakers. There were heated discussions, and I had no idea why Phạm Chuyên, then chief of police in Hanoi, was there as well. When the discussion drew to a conclusion, he came over and squeezed my hand tightly, saying, "I'm Phạm Chuyên. I can guarantee to you that, sooner or later, this film will be accepted and will come before the public."

I should relate as well that only recently my wife went to visit the family of an old friend and schoolmate named Phụng whose whole family worked in the police system. They were close to each other from childhood and lived in the same Hàng Bột Street neighborhood. In the course of a long conversation, they found that Huy, Phụng's son and a policeman, had in those days once been required to stand guard outside my old house at 52 Hàng Bún Street. He had no idea it was the house of his mother's close friend. As they recounted this old story, everyone present laughed until tears came. Phụng said to my wife, "If I had known he was watching your house, I would have told him to go inside, so he would be less miserable!"

I feel sorry for this boy and other such young fellows. Whether in the blazing sun, or in the drizzling windy cold, they had to stand there watching for something that they would never find, because it never existed. Now Huy and his brothers are already lieutenant colonels. Phụng has retired as a major, while her husband Tuyên obtained the rank of colonel before he passed away.

I had a sworn younger brother named Hoàng Trần Doãn, also in in the film business, who now teaches in the Stage and Film School. We were very close to each other when I was making *Hanoi in Whose Eyes*. But after that he suddenly vanished without a trace for nearly twenty years!

Then one day we met again at a conference about Vietnamese cinema attended also by director Việt Linh. Doãn told me the following story:

"The last night I left your house, it was drizzling outside. I had just jumped on my pushbike and pedaled a few dozen meters when a fellow in a raincoat came up to me and patted my shoulder: 'Hey! You're going in and out of Trần Văn Thủy's house too much!' I was scared and didn't dare go to your house anymore. Now, on meeting you again here, I feel very embarrassed."

I don't know how many people who came to my house "had the privilege" of being patted on the shoulder in this fashion, but there were surely quite a few people who avoided me out of fear or caution.

I remember that back in those days, the director Phạm Hà, an elder colleague of mine, was peddling a bicycle on Hoàng Hoa Thám Street down to Bách Thảo Garden from the documentary film studio while I was peddling up in the opposite direction. At the gate of the beer house, Hà caught sight of me and at once braked his bike, jumped down, and pushed it by hand, saying, "Oh Thủy! You haven't been arrested yet?"

It has been nearly thirty years since then, but I remember those words, and his bewildered look, as clearly as if they were printed on paper. I was all at sea; I hadn't the slightest idea how desperate my situation was! I went up to my place of work as usual, greeted everyone as usual, and merrily chatted and joked with them until my friend Lò Minh, an experienced person of few words, had to pull me over to a deserted corner and admonish me: "Why are you still so blithe? Are you devoid of fear?"

How strange! What should I have feared?

And then my studio had to make a detailed report, and submit my personal file for examination by the security agency, and had to halt preparations to receive the honorary title "heroic work unit." It was a wretchedly unfair business for the film studio directors, who hadn't the faintest idea what the dark design or the sinister enemy force might look like, or where they might be hiding.

Having told the story up to this point, I must add, for purposes of clarity, that the three men most eager to openly denounce *Hanoi in Whose Eyes* were Mr. Hoàng Tùng (1920–2010, in charge of propaganda and ideology), Mr. Văn Phác (1926–2012, minister of culture), and Mr. Hà Xuân Trường (1924–2006, head of the Department of Culture and Arts). To say that they were "open" in their denunciations is to imply that there were others who were not open. These gentlemen never gave me an opportunity to say anything to clear my name; they just watched the film, reached conclusions, affirmed what they thought, and issued directives . . . But in hindsight, I feel indebted to them for doing me a favor. If they had been smarter, they would have ignored the film, in a *mackeno* ("forget it") fashion.[4] If they hadn't made a great noise about it, then nobody, not even a ghost, would ever have paid attention to that half-baked film of mine. Instead, they were so stupid as to blow things out of proportion, using the opportunity to "show off their political stance," unaware that they were turning that poor fellow Thủy into a saint . . .

Nearly twenty years later, when the dust of this saga had settled down and I was making a film about professor Hoàng Minh Giám, I went with my film crew to interview Mr. Hà Xuân Trường in his home; this was also an opportunity to visit him. In his last years, he was not in good health. When we had finished shooting and were packing up our equipment, I went into his bedroom to bid farewell to him.

He was very embarrassed, and was trying, incoherently, to say something to exonerate himself: "In those times . . . in those times . . ." he began, but was unable to say what was in his mind. I politely wished him well, urged him to take care of his health, and then departed with my colleagues.

How absurd! My filmmaking career is but a grain of sand in the vast ocean of our changing society, so why should it be treated in such a solemn and complicated manner? What about great affairs of state? Why have we Vietnamese, from one generation to another, kept focusing all of our time and energy on wrestling with such nonsensical problems? And the most melancholy fact of all is that even now, we are still afflicted with the same calamity.

Just recently, we completed making part three of a film in several parts titled *Songs Resounding for a Thousand Years* to help celebrate the thousandth anniversary of the founding of Thăng Long (Hanoi). To introduce a number of love songs that had been strictly banned for many decades, I wrote the following:

"Prohibitions arising from different tastes and viewpoints brought much pain and misfortune to authors, and to their literary and artistic productions; and this continued for half a century—but, luckily, it has been no one's fault!"

And it was not just authors and their works that suffered misfortune, but people who appreciated them as well.

When the film was being turned over to the government, some found the above passage a bit hard to "swallow," but I stubbornly defended it. After all, I had said (ironically) in the passage that *luckily it has been no one's fault!*

When the film was turned over, this passage was still there, but several months later I learned that they had cut these words out prior to distribution (October 2012)—and no one had said a word to me about it. I was deeply afflicted, and couldn't eat or sleep normally for a month. To behave like that with each other is to be indecent to life itself.

And this was something that happened thirty years after the controversies surrounding *Hanoi in Whose Eyes*.

There had been no change, no progress, whatsoever.

Sad! So sad!

I suddenly remember that many years before, at the beginning of *The Story of Kindness,* the cameraman Đồng Xuân Thuyết, before passing away, read us a passage from the book *Rules for the Ages* by Đumbatze that he was holding in his hands:

> *A man's spirit is a hundred times heavier than the body, so heavy that one man alone cannot carry it. For that reason, we must try to help each other, while we are still alive, so that our spirits may become immortal. You help my spirit toward immortality, and I help another, who then helps yet another person, and so on without end.*[5]

I have a deep and earnest love for the land that gave me birth. This is precisely my starting point.

*I have loved the language of my land
From the time I first saw light,
Oh people . . .
My gentle mother with her distant lullabies . . .
Ah, ah, oh . . .
The lullaby of a thousand lives,
The language of my land,
Four thousand endless years of joy and sadness,
I laugh and weep with the changing fortunes of my land . . .*[6]

EPILOGUE

A Few Words to Thủy's Daughter

Lê Thanh Dũng: I remember one day, late at night, you [Thu Hương] and Đức drove your father Thủy and me to Nội Bài Airport to pick up Uncle Đính on his return from Canada—Nguyễn Hữu Đính, whom you read about in your father's book *If You Go to the Ends of All the Seas.* While waiting for the plane to arrive, you and I had a chance to talk about many things. That was the first time the two of us met, and I got to understand a few things about you—and I must say that I have very warm feelings toward you.

Thus it is very natural that when the thought of writing this book occurred to me, the first person I thought of was you—or perhaps one could say that my reason for writing it was so that you and your relatives and friends could read it. I hold you in great esteem, so instead of writing an introduction to this book about these little stories, I want to share a few thoughts with you.

Your elder brother is an artist who specializes in abstract paintings, right?

In the realm of art, three things were considered unwarrantably extravagant in our homeland: symphonic music, ballet, and abstract painting. In your father's time and mine, there were very few abstract things. Whatever wasn't white was black, whatever wasn't ours was the enemy's; political stances were clearly defined, social classes were strictly identified. Everything had to be concrete, concrete like the films your father made, and like the articles your father wrote.

But your father and many other people were often in bad repute, and were subjected to treatment that was very . . . abstract.

You know, your father's life was replete with bitter experiences—I know you love your father very much, but I also guess that you don't yet thoroughly understand him. The life of your father Thủy was full of things so bizarre as to be unbelievable—many loved him, yet many hated him for no reason—so the idea occurred to me that I should try writing a book about him. Your father welcomed this idea very hesitantly, and with a touch of the laziness that often comes to people in old age. Reliving all of those ironic, paradoxical, unsettled experiences with all of the confusions mixed up in the darkness and turbulence of a difficult filmmaking career—just thinking of this is enough to shock you, and to recount all of those things anew is like being subjected all over again to torture!

A loving, filial daughter like you must surely appreciate your father very much, but I still believe that there are many things about your father that you will learn only when you read this book, for your father seldom spoke to you in a comprehensive manner about the difficulties he faced in his profession; partly, perhaps, because he didn't want to trouble your heart with these things, and partly also because, in his eyes, you were always a little child.

But I must write the book, because it will surely be of use, especially now, when your father and his circle of associates are of such an age that friends within the group are keep getting scarcer and scarcer—"to sit and count on your fingers all those who have passed away takes a long time, but to sit and count those who remain can be done in a few moments." As Trịnh Công Sơn said, "Any affectionate hand grasp may turn out to be the last hand grasp."

As I write of the many ups and downs, the many tribulations, endured by your father, I envision you driving to a party in a stylish Mercedes on a high-speed highway. And I shall be very delighted if, at such a moment, you should think of your father in former days . . . for five years in the Northwest, your father had only two wishes: to eat a full meal, and to walk on a level road when going on a mission—because he was continuously hungry and, whenever he left his dwelling to go anywhere, had to descend and ascend mountain slopes, slopes such that his knees kept bumping his chin, and every trip was seventy or eighty kilometers! And during all of this, the sun was burning his flesh and skin, or a gale was blowing with drizzling rain . . .

And after that, before having had a chance to eat a square meal, or walk on a level road, he saw bombs over his head as he participated in the war in the South for another five years.

Yet your father trudged along, trudged along, and reached his destination, reached his goal, while many others failed to enjoy the same good fortune. Talent is one thing, and persistence another, but there is also the factor of fate.

Life must improve by degrees; every day we get a little happier, a little more prosperous. But we must enjoy prosperity not only of things, but of the spirit as well. In these terms, you are prosperous, and the more you share with others, the richer you will be. Your character and behavior are fine, and your parents are happy because of this. Your parents have told me that you care for them down to the tiniest details, and that you care for others close to you as well. Your parents are happy to have such a filial daughter. But your parents are even happier because you and your brother know enough to care for everyone, know enough to engage in charity, and together with your friends donate pocket money to help children in distress. Your parents gave you two your bodies and spirits. And the thought crossing my aging mind is that with two such children, and with two such parents as Thủy and Hằng, who should be happier, you or they?

In the very long stretch of life that remains to you, there will be moments when you will be hesitant in the face of difficulties and obstacles, and moments when you will feel cold and lonely . . . I think that at such moments, the thoughts of your father that I record in this book will help to warm your heart, make you feel more confident, and help you see that life, though bitter, is not lacking in sweetness—this depends on one's personal will and perception.

I hope that when you close this book, your love, gratitude, and admiration for your parents will be even greater. This will please your parents, but you will gain something greater still: perfect goodness of character. Only that is important, my child!

Though these pages concern your family, I think that when your friends and the people of your generation read these stories about your father, though their responses may differ, they will surely find in them things of great benefit to the spirit—if they are inclined in that direction—as they pursue the long journey of their lives.

—Lê Thanh Dũng, coauthor

Final Words

If we should write something, what should it be? "Memoirs" would not be right, and we didn't like the word either. Just write some things from your life for fun. Don't define it—whatever it is, who cares, as long as it's true. Anyway, the main thing is to record these stories so they will not be forgotten or drop by the wayside, and so they can be read for pleasure and profit by friends, and by our children and grandchildren . . .

Yes, the story is very long and open-ended, and the book can tell only part of it.

And the child who began to make the acquaintance of films and pictures at the age of thirteen grew up to be a young man of twenty-five staggering back from the Northwest and knocking timidly on the door of a film school, and has now left his mark on Vietnamese cinema in the form of dozens of films that have won prizes at international film festivals.

What will he do next? A man of his passionate temperament will surely not be content to rest—and perhaps the friends who trust him won't give him "permission" to rest.

The stories that grew up between the two of us will perhaps go beyond the realm of personal exchange and reach various other people, both inside and outside the country. When that occurs, the various things that can be seen happening in this little book will have turned into the past, and many of the personages involved will perhaps have returned to dust.

Trần Văn Thủy is a human being, too, and has feelings of happiness, anger, love, and hate like the rest of us. He is also an artist, and like an artist in any field, he is sensitive and easily to be moved by what goes on around him. He has recounted his past as if he were conversing with himself after his long trek on the road of life, and, as he observes, there were a great many instances of coincidence, and of good and bad fortune, in that story. But one may say in summation that his sorrows were numerous, and his joys very few.

In a book of this nature, it is hard to avoid certain areas that some people may find depressing, and even repugnant, but what can be done about this? Life is not meant to be easy, and if things occur in a particular way, they should be recounted truthfully, just as they are.

Every person may have a different way of looking at bygone events. This is an entirely ordinary phenomenon; people often use the expression "nine people, ten ideas!" (a diversity of views). The things that are bared in this book amount also to a point of view. And I think it is a straightforward, good-natured, and sincere point of view.

A country in which everyone can say what he thinks is a blessed and happy country; even if it is still poor, it has something that can be called civilized.

Food to eat, clothes to wear, education, land, social justice, and a sense of national pride . . . are all among the basic, essential needs of human beings. But it is even more essential, more basic, to be able to say what you actually think, because if you have that, you will have everything!

It is true that Thủy's life was full of setbacks and uncertainty, but in the final analysis, his destiny was fortunate. Many people have worked with even greater dedication, and have contributed even more, but have endured even greater hardship and wretchedness. They live in silence, and depart from life in silence . . .

Life is an impermanent realm. To live is to reside abroad; to die is to return home.

The Buddha teaches this.

I'm a boarder in the mortal realm;
In a hundred years I'll return to the distant place on the horizon.

Trịnh Công Sơn sings this.

Though life is an impermanent realm, we are nevertheless immersed in life, so how can we be indifferent to it?

Yet life is still a cold, impassive stream that flows on to oblivion.

The sweet, the bitter . . . all of this will pass away.

—Lê Thanh Dũng, coauthor

A Note from the Translators

In the second half of 2013, the publication of a remarkable book, *Chuyện Nghề của Thủy* (*Thủy's Craft*), coauthored by Lê Thanh Dũng and Trần Văn Thủy, became the talk of the town in Vietnam's book market. The book immediately sold out. The book market was then flooded by pirated copies, and the publisher, Phương Nam Books, had to respond by printing a second edition.

Phương Nam Books then organized a series of book-launch events in major cities across Vietnam: Hồ Chí Minh City, Nha Trang, Đà Nẵng, Huế, and Hanoi. These events were well covered by local media and blogs, and offered a good opportunity for the authors to interact with the audience, which included not only well-known intellectuals and artists in the community but also people who appeared in Trần Văn Thủy's films and this book.

Why was the book so well received? Why did it become a best seller as soon as it hit the stands? The answer may be found in the turbulent adventures of the internationally famous documentary film director Trần Văn Thủy, whose life was a saga of continuous—and ever-changing—hardship and danger. But what attracted readers was not only the story itself but also the unprecedented candor with which it was told. Above all, the book showed the author's sincere respect for truth and his appreciation for his readers.

The book was what readers needed but could find only erratically in the publishing culture of Vietnam, an environment that has seen some remarkably frank literature published since the official encouragement of socially critical literature that was part of the *đổi mới* (renovation) policy of 1986, which admonished writers not to "bend their pens" and to "write what they think," but whose parameters seem to be arbitrarily enforced (on one day a particular work is published with no problem; on another, an equally provocative work will be censored or brutally edited according to coded and uncoded bans, including crude cuts or the distortion of facts, sometimes with no explanation). This keeps recurring, on and off, even now. Thủy has said that this book was written with his own blood and sweat, because all that he relates in it were the brute realities of his own life, realities that caused him suffering, bruising blows, and harassment.

Yet it is important to note that the book has been published officially in Vietnam, cleared by the state censorship authority, with due registration and permission for distribution. At one of the book-launch events, a well-known intellectual said, "*Is it true that we can say and write anything we want? Am I having an illusion or not? . . .*" One young reader has exclaimed after reading the book, "*What a good book! But why wasn't it banned?*"

It might be a bit too early to say that from now on new publications that speak the truth in an honest and candid manner will easily reach readers. However, the publication of this book is an indication that a new paradigm for the management of art and culture is needed and appreciated by the public in Vietnam. Perhaps a more open climate and a new approach can be expected in the new process of greater global integration. In the last few years, the Internet and the blogosphere have brought about a phenomenal change in the fringe media, while mainstream publications are still under draconian control and censorship.

In an article published in the last issue of the controversial *Saigon Marketing* weekly just before its closure (in February 2014), Trần Văn Thủy commented, "We are born equally with one mouth, a mouth that has the right and duty to say truthfully what we think. Right or wrong, it is our own expression. There is no reason why this mouth, granted by god, should say utter nonsense to please others . . ."

It is a challenge and pleasure to translate and share with readers this touching story that has so captivated us.

—Eric Henry and Nguyễn Quang Dy

Awards Presented to Trần Văn Thủy for His Films

The People of My Homeland (Những Người Dân Quê Tôi)
Thủy's first film, shot in the southern war zone
Silver Dove Award at the Leipzig International Film Festival, 1970

Betrayal (Phản Bội)
Concerning the border war between Vietnam and China
Golden Award for Best Director at the Vietnam Film Festival, 1980

Hanoi in Whose Eyes (Hà Nội Trong Mắt Ai)
Banned from 1982 to 1987
Golden Award for Best Film Script, Best Directing, and Best Camerawork at the 1988 Vietnam Film Festival

The Story of Kindness (Chuyện Tử Tế)
Completed in 1985 and described in the foreign press as "a bomb from Vietnam"; viewing rights purchased by ten large broadcasting stations throughout the world, and shown widely in Europe, Japan, Australia, and the United States
Silver Dove Award at the Leipzig International Film Festival, 1988

A Story from the Corner of a Park (Chuyện Từ Góc Công Viên)
Golden Award at the Festival of the Cinema Association, 1996

The Sound of a Violin at Mỹ Lai (Tiếng Vĩ Cầm Ở Mỹ Lai)
Golden Award at the 43rd Meeting of the Asia Pacific Film Festival, 1999

Awarded the "Witness to the World" prize by the International Cinema Conference in New York, 2003

Acknowledgments

I wish first of all to thank the editors of *Tạp chí Điện ảnh Việt Nam* (*Journal of Vietnamese Cinema*) for allowing me to include in chapter 6 my reminiscences of the filmmaker Nguyễn Giá that appeared in their publication in 1985.

Secondly, I wish to express my affection and gratitude to my American friends in the William Joiner Center, and in particular to Kevin Bowen, and Nguyễn Bá Chung. I wish to state in all sincerity and from the bottom of my heart, to these friends that all of you are dedicated emissaries working in the cause of establishing peace between nations, are people whose joys and sorrows arise from the prosperity or decline of Vietnam, the people of Vietnam, and the future of Vietnamese-American relations.

Nguyễn Bá Chung put great quantities of time into this, and did not shrink from the trouble of accompanying me to many places, meeting many people, participating in many conferences and film showings . . . Without holding anything back, he also explained to me many consequences of the war and many historical mistakes. He has lived far from Vietnam ever since the '50s of the last century but nevertheless thought of his old country with pain and concern.

And I must say in addition that Chấn, Nguyễn Bá Chung's wife, was an endlessly hospitable woman, with the compassion and faith of a true Christian. Chung and his wife had me live in their house, and introduced me to many Vietnamese intellectual friends who would ordinarily have been very difficult for me to contact.

Thus, my first trip to the United States and the ones that followed were due entirely to invitations that came from the United States from people like Kevin Bowen and Nguyễn Bá Chung—they had nothing whatsoever to do with some intervention of "the party and government of communist Vietnam," as was claimed by various Vietnamese expatriates living in the United States.

Finally, I would like to express my admiration and gratitude for the contributions to my films made by a number of cherished colleagues.

When my colleagues and I were embarking on the film *The Sound of a Violin at Mỹ Lai,* Nguyễn Văn Nhân and Lê Mạnh Thích were two people who believed in us and gave their wholehearted support to the film. Since there was little time for the project, we had no film script, and hadn't obtained a decision from the Department of Cultural Affairs, we also had decisions with regard to personnel, or an estimated budget, but in spite of this, those two gentlemen still supplied us with movie cameras, money, and letters of introduction, and we set out for Quảng Ngãi. I have to say that these two people were men of feeling, devoted to their work and to their colleagues. We are grateful from the bottom of our hearts to such people. When I meet with difficulties and obstacles in my work, I am sometimes discouraged, but when I think of the bonds of feeling between us, I try harder. Thus it would appear that when people believe in each other, life can be more toilsome than ever.

And then there were my colleagues Hồ Trí Phổ, Vương Khánh Luông, Lê Huy Hòa, Đặng Trần Anh, and Phan Minh Hưưng, who dealt with technical matters, film printing, economics, and finance. Each of them made noteworthy contributions.

Before he accepted my invitation to work with me, anh Hồ Trí Phổ was working in a studio making scientific films that also belonged to our company. He was a person equally able to think, write, and act. I often said that he was like a kitchen cleaver: whatever business came to him, he did it, and did it well. When we worked together, he would on his own initiative plan out everything the film crew had to do in a detailed and attentive manner, including highly specialized matters and the arrangement of such things as meals and lodging. We would surely have more excellent films if a person of his vast experience, so full of the stuff of life, so resourceful, and with so many latent abilities, had been methodically trained. Thinking of Hồ Trí Phổ, I feel intense regret that the film studio failed to assess him at his true value and did not make a fitting use of his gifts and abilities. Nevertheless, he made many contributions to three films of ours: *The Story of Kindness, A Story from the Corner of a Park,* and *The Sound of a Violin at Mỹ Lai.*

When I invited Vương Khanh Luông to be my cameraman for *The Sound of a Violin at Mỹ Lai,* I had confidence in his competence and care, his ability to capture arresting images, and his years of experience as a news photographer. Luông had created many filmed interviews, and had accompanied many prominent personages on their trips to meet leaders of other countries. He followed in the footsteps of the news photographer Phan Trọng Quỳ; both he and Quỳ were skilled practitioners, experts in the art of capturing scenes that occur only once, even only in a single instant—an art that not just any news photographer can lay claim to. Later on, Vương Khanh Luông made many documentary films of which he was the principal director. Those documentary films are very genuine in content, very dramatic, and attractively structured.

Among the various cameramen who have worked with me, there was also Nguyễn Như Vũ. He made many films and did fine work both before and after he worked with me on *A Story from the Corner of a Park.* The directors of the studio, and his colleagues as well, valued him very much. He was peaceful and taciturn by nature—as was the case with his father, the cameraman Nguyễn Như Ái. Vũ was truly in love with his profession, knew how to listen, and also had views concerning the political aspects of his work. I always felt totally at ease when I worked with Vũ.

When I made *The Story of Kindness,* it was not by chance alone that I invited Lê Văn Long to be my chief cameraman. Among the cameramen working for the documentary film studio at that time, Long was not especially skilled or well known. But when I began that project, it seemed to me that *The Story of Kindness* would at times require daring, and the capacity to skim quickly over situations, not just care and competence. I felt that Long had that quality. He was not concerned about face, or about the impression he made on others; he liked to speak truthfully and directly, and was willing to take risks. This impression was greatly strengthened later when I reflected that if someone else had been my cameraman for *The Story of Kindness,* the film would perhaps have lacked the long episode dealing with former days—the episode in the boyhood of the future cameraman in which he is put in charge of a herd of ducks, crawls into a hut to sleep, receives a black mark on his record, and then had a fine mathematics teacher who later became a vegetable vender... The attractiveness and usefulness of Long lay in these things.

Twenty years ago, I invited the cameraman Đỗ Khánh Toàn to be my main cameraman in the film *A Spiritual World*. Like nearly all of my films, it was made on 35-millimeter celluloid film. We traveled throughout Vietnam to make the film, spending the longest time in Huế. Due to this, the scenes in the film were extremely varied in character. Đỗ Khánh Toàn did his work very painstakingly, and was careful in arranging the details of every scene, never showing any sign of weariness. Since he was trained in the Democratic Republic of Germany, he was accustomed to doing his work in a "Western" manner, and it was perhaps for this reason that in 1989 I invited him to work with me on a long film shot in western Europe, including Germany, France, Italy, England, and Belgium. Đỗ Khánh Toàn had a way of living and working that was easy to venerate, for he was always sincere and selfless, and placed weight on the bonds of obligation.

I also have indelible memories of two sound engineers, Mai Thế Song and Lê Huy Hòa, who in former days belonged to the Central Documentary Film Studio. I have long held very clear ideas about the use of sound in my profession, and especially in documentary films with modern subjects. I have spoken about this as well with my younger colleagues and students, both in Vietnam and in other countries. Sound is really able to make a film come alive, and endow it with truth and seductive power. I don't lie when I say that sound may account for fifty percent of the soul and value of a film. But it is very important to have modern sound equipment and a skilled sound engineer with equipment especially adapted for films. Mai Thế Song and Lê Huy Hòa were people of this sort, and contributed more than a little to the success of films made by the Central Documentary Film Studio, which included projects in which I participated. They were both people who had received methodical training and who loved their profession. It should also be noted that dealing with sound in films shot with celluloid is far more complex than integrating sound with videotaped films.

My experience with these two gentlemen makes me reflect that when you work with colleagues of such stature, you have to ask yourself if your own contributions are worthy to be matched with theirs.

And, in a professional spirit, I would like to draw the attention of younger directors to the fact that films are products made by teams of people working together; they are products of the pooled intelligence and achievements of these teams. A film director is like an orchestral conductor; he must know, respect, and understand the people who make up his band before he can exploit their talent and intellect.

And I want to say a few words to express my gratitude to Nguyễn Sĩ Chung. He studied at film school with me back in 1965, and later studied with me in the Soviet Union in the 1970s. Then he returned to Vietnam and worked along with me in the documentary film studio until he retired. Chung's main profession was script writing, but later he also directed many films. His film *The Countryside,* which he made in 2001, won a Golden Award at the Asia-Pacific Film Festival in Jakarta. Together with me and some other colleagues, including the cameraman To Thu and the sound engineer Cao Huy, Chung made a film in the Soviet Union in 1986. Chung had a rich fund of experience in his life and professional work, and there was nothing we didn't recount to each other. Then, from 2009 to 2011, Chung worked with me, Phung Lê Anh Minh, and Nguyễn Sĩ Khoa—his youngest son—on the film *Songs Resounding for a Thousand Years.* Before that, I had worked with his eldest son Nguyễn Sĩ Bằng on a four-part film concerned with the early journalist, translator, and activist Nguyễn Văn Vĩnh titled *A Barbarian of Modern Times.* This friend of mine is a modest man who knows much, says little, and shares his feelings in a calm, composed manner, so he is much cherished by his friends, and by . . . women.

I can't refer to all of the colleagues whom I value; I only wish to add that I am deeply conscious of the fact that it is only due to my association with all of these dedicated and talented people that I have been able to make films that have been enthusiastically received both within Vietnam and elsewhere.

—Trần Văn Thủy

Notes

Introduction / A Friendship

1. In the narrative, Trần Văn Thủy tends to use this term to describe his side of the war, adopting a convenient terminology that has become common in modern Vietnam in spite of the fact that "Viet Cong" was used only by the Republic of Vietnam and American forces, during the war, to describe the (Southern) National Liberation Front fighters. The regular army, to which Thủy belonged, properly the People's Army of Vietnam, was called the NVA (North Vietnamese Army) by those forces.
2. Trần Văn Thủy, *If You Go to the Ends of All the Seas* (Westminster, CA: Thời Văn, 2003), 157.

1. The Swimmer

1. After World War II, the French, who had colonized Vietnam in the nineteenth century, sent troops to reestablish their control of Vietnam. During the war, the country was ruled by the Vichy French government that collaborated with the Axis powers, and the Japanese; Hồ Chí Minh and the Vietnamese Communists had fought against them in alliance with the United States.

    But in 1945, as part of the American doctrine of containing communism, the United States refused to recognize Hồ's government and supported the return of French forces, which led to the French-Indochinese War of 1949–54.
2. These words, and Auntie Nhuận's story, ended the film *There Was a Village* (1993), which Thủy made for Japanese television.
3. "Homeland" here is the equivalent of "hometown." Thủy further explains: "When I returned to my home village after many years in faraway places, I no longer saw the names of all the villages as they had been in former days. I was very sad. History records that during the tenth year of emperor Minh Mạng's reign (1829), when Nguyễn Công Trứ, the dinh điền sứ (magistrate in charge of the lands), together with our founding ancestor Trần Trung Khánh, built the dikes, reclaimed the sea and expanded the land, to establish the district of Ninh Nhất, they named the new villages Cửu An (Nine Villages at Peace), including An Lạc (At Peace with Happiness), An Phú (At Peace with Wealth), An Lễ (At Peace with Ceremony), An Phong (At Peace with Tradition), An Nhân (At Peace with Humanity), An Nghĩa (At Peace with Rectitude), and An Đạo (At Peace with Morality), et cetera. . . . The people of those days thus established a moral foundation and expected future descendants to follow the

core values in the names of these villages. But now their 'civilized and reformist" descendants have simplified these names to Village 1, Village 2, Village 3, and so on, as if they were military barracks. The former names are gradually fading in the recollection of the elders. It is a great pity."
4. The famine of 1945 in Vietnam was largely caused by the occupying Japanese Army's order that farmers in the North grow jute (a plant with industrial uses needed for military purposes by the Japanese) instead of rice. As a result, over two million people died of starvation.
5. The Land Reform Campaign, i.e., the forced collectivization of privately owned farmland, was implemented when the Communist government in North Vietnam was strongly influenced by Mao's doctrines in China. Somewhere between 53,000 and 172,000 people indiscriminately labeled as "class enemies" because they owned land, employed others, or were simply denounced by opportunistic neighbors were slaughtered in a self-inflicted "class war." The Vietnamese leadership, under Hồ Chí Minh, later declared that the policy was a mistake and implemented a "rectification" campaign, but grave damage had already been done.
6. A child who can swim will not drown, but one who climbs may fall.
7. Streets in the ancient quarter of Hanoi were named after the goods sold on each.

2. The Measuring Stick and the Mirror

1. The provinces were Lai Châu, Sơn La, and Nghĩa Lộ. This occurred in 1963.
2. "Kinh people" means the mainstream majority group living in the lowlands of Vietnam; that is, the Vietnamese. They are here said to resemble "jungle demons" because of their paternalistic attitude and aggressiveness, which can create havoc among ethnic minority peoples who in Thủy's romantic view live more humbly and naturally. The word *Kinh* literally means "terrible."

3. Do You Feel Honored?

1. Evacuation sites are areas where civilians, especially children, were brought to be safe from American bombing.
2. At the 1954 peace conference in Geneva, at the end of the war with the French, it was decided to divide Vietnam temporarily at the 17th parallel, with the North under president Hồ Chí Minh and the Communist Party, and the South a republic under prime minister Ngô Đình Diệm, with elections about reunification to follow. The elections were never held. Quảng Trị Province was just south of the so-called Demilitarized Zone dividing the country; it was one of the most fought-over areas of the war.
3. That is, members of the Communist Party. Without that membership, a person would not be considered trustworthy to perform such politically delicate work as being a war correspondent.
4. People such as Thủy who came from what would be considered a "bourgeoisie" family, and were thus part of the class to be struggled against by Communists, were often denied decent education and career possibilities.
5. That is, going to the war. Ironically, this was the same phrase used by American marines, who were usually "sent south" to Vietnam from training bases in Okinawa.

4. Going South

1. Đặng Thùy Trâm (b. 1942) was a civilian doctor killed by American forces in Quảng Ngãi in 1970. She became famous when her wartime diary was returned to her mother by an American veteran and published in 2005.
2. This is a very different interpretation from the way Trâm's diary has been presented, both in Vietnam and upon its translation into English and publication in the United States. Trần Văn Thủy and Thanh Thảo both criticize the romanticization of Trâm's wartime experience, and find in her words evidence that she was criticized for not being politically pure enough, and that a person of her integrity would have a hard time in postwar Vietnam.

5. Rebirth

1. Baseball-size bombs containing hundreds of razor-sharp flechettes; they explode when picked up, often by farmers in their fields or by children at play.
2. The Republic of Korea was one of the allies fighting with the United States in the Vietnam War. Others were Thailand and Australia. Presumably, Teacher Niên did not know Korean, and so was translating the pamphlets into Mandarin with the idea that the latter was a lingua franca the Koreans would understand.
3. Army of the Republic of Vietnam; soldiers of the Vietnamese Southern Republic.

6. The Beauty and the Bullet

1. The account that follows is excerpted from a newspaper article that Thủy published in September 1985.
2. The start of the famous Tết Offensive, when National Liberation Front (Việt Cộng) and People's Army soldiers attacked every major city and base in South Vietnam. While the coordinated attacks by a force supposedly almost defeated was a major propaganda victory, turning public opinion in the United States against the war, it was ultimately a military disaster, particularly for the NLF, which lost hundreds of thousands of fighters.
3. Lai Xá is a place in the Hanoi area known as a "photography village."

7. Carrying the War Home

1. An expression of close friendship meaning that the two women had carried out a formal, but personal, ceremony acknowledging each other as sisters.
2. What the Americans called the Hồ Chí Minh Trail, and the Vietnamese called the Trường Sơn trails, was a network of paths, trails, and roads extending from North to South Vietnam in the jungles of the Trường Sơn mountain range on the western border of Vietnam, and the eastern border areas of Laos and Cambodia. The highly organized system of moving soldiers and material into the battle zone, and—as in Thủy's case—back north of it, included base areas and way stations providing resupply, guides, and medical assistance, when possible.
3. On the twentieth anniversary of the William Joiner Center for the Study of War and Social Consequences at the University of Massachusetts Boston, on January 10, 2002.

4. The Bến Hải was the river along the 17th parallel that was the demarcation between North and South Vietnam.

8. An Uneasy Homecoming

1. Here Thủy refers to the duty of an eldest son to take care of his parents (and younger siblings), a filial duty that had to be painfully subordinated to the greater duty owed to the nation. By writing "Yet I had to grit my teeth and go" he is saying that he had no choice about leaving his parents (and girlfriend), not because he was being "heroic" or "hated the enemy" but because he was ordered (or perhaps felt the social pressure) to go. He implies this was the case for many people, though later they may have put on a mantle of patriotism.

9. Letters from the Fire

1. The National Liberation Front was the umbrella organization for South Vietnamese insurgents fighting the (South Vietnamese) government of the Republic of Vietnam and the Americans. NLF fighters were called Việt Cộng (Vietnamese Communists or, in the military phonetic alphabet, Victor Charlie, or sometimes just Charlie) by Americans. See note 1 in the introduction on Trần Văn Thủy's usage of "Việt Cộng." Note also that in the text here, "homeland" refers specifically to the speaker's region in southern Vietnam. Although one of Hanoi's major goals in the war was the reunification of the country, there are differences of culture and language usage between the two parts of the country (much the same as exists between various regions of the United States).
2. Đặng Thùy Trâm (see chapter 4).
3. This is an allusion to the famous poem "Sound of Autumn" (Tiếng Thu) by the poet and writer Lưu Trọng Lư (1912–1991), one of the founders of the New Poetry Movement in Vietnam.

10. The Trans-Siberian Express

1. Evacuation points were areas where civilians were evacuated during American bombing raids.
2. Lập Thạch was the evacuation destination for several offices under the Ministry of Culture.
3. Meaning there was very little sense in filming smaller stories (such as a minor clash along the border at Bắc Luân Bridge or how people of Chinese origin were leaving Vietnam like refugees) while the real big story (the imminent invasion of Vietnam) was not being covered.
4. *Pilots in Pajamas* is an East German propaganda film about American pilots imprisoned in the facility that came to be known as the Hanoi Hilton (Hỏa Lò Prison).

11. Hanoi in Whose Eyes

1. Hoàng Đạo Thúy (1900–1994) was a cultural activist and social historian. He led the Vietnamese Boy Scout movement in the North during the colonial period. He

was the author of more than half a dozen books, including several on the scenes and history of Hanoi.
2. The Huy Văn Palace (more of a shrine than a palace) was built in 1496 by emperor Lê Thánh Tông to commemorate his mother. The Bộc (or Sùng Phúc) Pagoda (near Gò Đống Đa, another historic site) was associated with emperor Quảng Trung, who in 1789 fought a victorious battle here against the invading Qing troops; Quán Thánh Temple (near the West Lake) was an eleventh-century temple dedicated to Trấn Vũ, a Daoist deity. Nguyễn Trãi (1380–1442) was a wise scholar and statesman who helped found the Lê dynasty. Chu Văn An (1292–1370) was a scholar, physician, and official of the Trần dynasty. Ngô Thời Nhậm (1746–1803) was a scholar and official of the Lê dynasty who supported emperor Quảng Trung and the Tây Sơn dynasty. The Temple of Literature was built in 1070 during the reign of Lý Nhân Tông and housed the Quốc Tử Giám, or Imperial Academy, Vietnam's earliest national university. Đoàn Thị Điểm (1705–1748) was a woman poet, best known for "Lament of a Soldier's Wife" (Chinh Phụ Ngâm), a Vietnamese translation of a poem in Chinese by Đặng Trần Côn (c. 1705–1745). Bà Huyện Thanh Quán (1805–1848) was a woman poet celebrated for classical verses evoking beautiful scenes in Hanoi and other landscapes. Hồ Xuân Hương (1772–1822) was a woman poet celebrated for subtle and witty verses with double meanings full of sexuality. A selection of her verses, translated by John Balaban, has been published under the title *Spring Essence* (Port Townsend, WA: Copper Canyon Press, 2000).
3. Nguyễn Vĩnh Phúc (1926–2012) was the author of many books on the history of Hanoi and coauthored the well-known book *The Streets of Hanoi* (Đường Phố Hà Nội) with Trần Huy Bá.
4. Many people at the time suspected that the reference to the "Lê Mạt" dynasty was a veiled reference to Lê Duẩn, a party chief during the war years (translators' note).
5. This is an allusion to an episode in the Chinese "Saga of Wú and Yuè" (translators' note).
6. "Nôm" refers to an adaptation of Chinese characters used in traditional times to write Vietnamese texts.

13. The Story of Kindness

1. Bạch Mai had been almost totally destroyed in Nixon's Christmas bombing of 1972.
2. Dean Wilson is a lecturer in film at the University of Social Sciences and Humanities in Hanoi. He has been consultant to the Film Studies Program at the Vietnam National University, Hanoi, for the Ford Foundation's Vietnam cinema and television initiative, as well as consulting for USAID and the Motion Picture Association of America. Michael Renov is professor of Critical Studies and Vice Dean for Academic Affairs at the University of Southern California. He is the author of *Hollywood's Wartime Woman: Representation and Ideology* and *The Subject of Documentary*.

14. Kindness Repressed

1. This story of smuggling a film from one Communist country not to the West, but to another Communist country may seem strange to the Western reader, but as the author suggests, it was symptomatic of the role artists took in allowing viewers to see

what they knew to be true about their societies but that they had never seen expressed. It can be said that this book fulfills that same function, which is one reason it was so popular in Vietnam.
2. The Hàn River is a north-flowing river leading to the Bay of Đà Nẵng in Central Vietnam.

15. Kindness Abroad

1. From a verse fable about a cicada and an ant by Jean de La Fontaine (1621–1695). The Vietnamese translation was by the journalist, translator, and social activist Nguyễn Văn Vĩnh (1882–1936).
2. This refers to the much-publicized case of two sisters arrested in Vietnam for drug smuggling; one was sentenced to death, and the other to twenty years in prison. The *tâm thư* was written in prison by the second sister.

16. A Violin at Mỹ Lai

1. No more pressures or losses than those inflicted on any other American infantry unit; in fact, many other units suffered far worse casualties without massacring civilians.

17. A Letter

1. A tree with mimosa-like branches and leaves and delicate pink or orange blossoms, often seen in Southeast Asian school yards.

18. A Birth

1. Nguyễn Mộng Giác (1940–2012) was a Vietnamese author who escaped from Vietnam by boat in 1981 and settled in California in 1982. He is best known for his long novel *Mùa Biển Động,* or "The Choppy Sea Season."
2. Diane Fox's memory of the trip—or of the geography it encompassed—was somewhat different: she drove Thủy only from the University of Washington to Portland State University, a three-hour trip.
3. Diane actually first came to know about Thủy through a mutual friend, her landlady, who was a friend of Thủy's.
4. She was then a graduate student working on her PhD.
5. Wayne Karlin, Trương Vũ, and Lê Minh Khuê, eds., *The Other Side of Heaven: Post-War Fiction by Vietnamese and American Writers* (Willimantic, CT: Curbstone Books, 1995).

20. Immense Sorrow Is Forbidden

1. *Văn Nghệ (Literature and Art):* the most well-known literary magazine in Vietnam.
2. This was a spoken drama written in 1983 by Lưu Quang Vũ (1948–1988) based on a folktale in which Trương Ba, a cultivated man, dies in an accident, after which his soul enters the body of a pork vender. The tale served as a subject for *chèo* theater throughout traditional times. The play was performed in the Hanoi opera house under the direction of Nguyễn Đình Nghi, the son of the poet and dramatist Thế Lữ. It won

the Vietnamese National Drama Award in 1990. In 2002, it was performed in London under the title *The Butcher's Skin*, thus becoming the first Vietnamese spoken drama to receive international attention. Lưu Quang Vũ and his wife, the poet Xuân Quỳnh, were both killed in a traffic accident in 1988.
3. Xuân Diệu, poet (1916–1985); Nguyễn Tuân, writer (1910–1987); Chế Lan Viên, poet (1920–1989); Văn Cao, composer (1923–1995); Trần Văn Cẩn, painter (1910–1994); Nguyễn Sáng, painter (1923–1988); Bùi Xuân Phái, painter (1920–1988) are among the best-known intellectuals and artists of modern times.
4. Võ Nguyên Giáp was the founder of the People's Army of Vietnam, and its leader in the victories against the French, the Americans, and the Republic of Vietnam.
5. Thủy writes, "Later on, I had the good fortune to have occasion to visit the general's family many times. Sometimes I went to shoot an interview, and sometimes I went with friends from other countries who were visiting him. In particular, I had a French friend, Orso Delage, who did charitable work in Vietnam and had long harbored a wish to meet the general, whom he deeply revered. I took Orso and his friends to see the general and his family on three different occasions. They met in a very cordial manner, like friends who had known each other for a long time. Later Orso suggested the idea to me of building a kindergarten and a preschool in Mường Phăng, a place where the general had had his headquarters during the Điện Biên Phủ campaign, or perhaps in Lệ Thủy, Quảng Bình Province, the general's homeland."
6. The use of "Labyrinth" here indicates a wrong path—chosen out of all of the other possible paths in a maze—that has been blindly followed by people lost in outdated ideology, from which extrication is difficult.

21. The Language of My Land

Epigraph: Trần Văn Thủy, interview with Michael Renov and Dean Wilson, August 13, 2011, Hanoi, Vietnam.

1. This passage is drawn from Christopher E. Goscha, "The Modern Barbarian': Nguyễn Văn Vĩnh and the Complexity of Colonial Modernity in Vietnam," *European Journal of East Asian Studies* 3, no. 1 (2003): 135–69.
2. Thủy's Vietnamese readers would get the irony here: the police station once belonged to the regime Thủy's army fought to overthrow.
3. Nguyễn Cao Kỳ (1930–2011) was an air force chief and prime minister of the Republic of Vietnam.
4. The author here uses a Vietnamese slang expression of contemptuous dismissal.
5. Nođar Đumbatze (1928–1984) was a popular Georgian novelist during the Soviet era. His *Rules for the Ages,* also known as *The Law of Eternity*, appeared in 1978.
6. These lines are from the song "Tình Ca" (Love of Country), the melody and lyrics of which were both written by Phạm Duy (1921–2013) in 1953.

Index

Note: Throughout this index TVT refers to the author, Trần Văn Thủy.

abstract painting, 187
Agent Orange, 156–57
Agfa color film, 27, 61–66
ai ("who"), meanings and associations of, 95
American bombing, 15
American soldiers, 31
ammo boxes as film canisters, 35–36, 62–63
An Phú village, Hải Hậu (childhood and ancestral home of TVT), 4–6, 20
Andreotta, Glenn, 124, 131
anthropology: introducton to, 9; activities in, 13
Anvares, Santiago (documentary film director), 106–7
Army of the Republic of Vietnam (ARVN), 23, 31, 41–42
"Ashokan Farewell" (piece played annually on the violin at Mỹ Lai by Mike Boehm), 126, 133
attempts to escape from Vietnam by boat (of Nguyễn Hữu Đính), 149–50
Auntie Nhuận, 3–6, 140
awards for films, xix, 195–96 (list); Red Carnation (USSR), 74; Silver Dove, 122; Best Documentary, 129, 131

"B quay" (derisive term; "making a U-turn to go back north"), 22, 49, 63, 66

Ba Đình Square (Hanoi), 95
Bà Huyện Thanh Quán (early Hanoi poet), 86
Bà Market (also called Núi Bà Market), 29, 38
Babak, Marian (Russian filmmaker), 75–76
Bạch Mai Hospital, 104–5
bags, tubular, 49
Baikal-Amur Railway Line (Siberia), 74–76
ballet, 187
Bàn Thạch Market, 28, 37
Ban Thống Nhất (Unification Department), 55–56, 60
Ban Tổ Chức Trung Ương (Central Organization Department), 55–56
banana leaves, uses of, 15, 33–34
bánh chúng (sticky rice cakes for Tết), 60
bánh cuốn (steamed rolls), 15
Barbarian of Modern Times (film), 201
"Bauxite Vietnam" (webpage), 154
Bảy (government interrogator), 177–78
bears, gall bladder juice of (as treatment for cancer), 99–100
Bến Hải River (separating North from South Vietnam), 54
Bến Tre Province, 145
Betrayal (film), 78–79, 84

Blind Teachers Examining an Elephant (*Thầy Mù Xem Voi;* film directed in Europe by TVT), 200
bobbins (devices used in rolls of movie film), 44–45
Bộc Pagoda (Hanoi), 86
Boehm, Mike, 83, 124–33; playing the violin at Mỹ Lai, *illus.*
"Born in the North to die in the South" (war slogan), 144
bourgeois, petty (as a social classification and term of abuse), 23–24, 163
Bowen, Kevin (director of William Joiner Center), 198
Buddha, 191
Bùi Đình Hạc (film studio director), 91–92, 114–15
Bùi Xuân Phái (artist, famed for Hanoi street scenes), 94, 171
burial caskets, 6
burial sites and incense smoke (as a theme in TVT's films), 170–71

Ca Lê Thuần (chief of group traveling to the USSR), 72
Cẩm Nâm River (south of Hội An), 45
cameras: Admiral (Czechoslovakia), 18; Bolex, xiii; Paya Polex, 27, 44
canisters (for holding film), 112, 116, 129
Cao Nghị (government functionary), 114–18, 122–23
cắp tráp (playing a subordinate role in a film production), 78
career as a filmmaker, TVT's reflections on, 5
cassava, 52
cave shelters, 32
CBS (TV network), 127–28
censorship and repression, 89–90, 92–93, 95–96, 106–23, 132, 153, 175, 182–83, 192–93
Central Party Congress in Việt Bắc (the Northern War Zone; 1950), 60
Chấn (wife of Nguyễn Bá Chung), 197
Châu Giang River, 37–38
Chế Lan Viên (poet), 171

Chị Tú (younger sister of the musician Văn Cao's wife, Thúy Bằng), 47
Chiêm Sơn Bridge (over the Thu Bồn River), 28, 35
"Chiều" ("Dusk"; a song), 141
childhood schoolmates and teachers of TVT and Nguyễn Hữu Đính, 140–41, 144–45
Children's Palace, The (venue for sports and performances in Hanoi), 7, 40, 90, 92
Chinese traditional novels, 141
Chử Đồng Tử (mythical figure), 38, 40
Chu Văn An (historical figure), 86
Chuyên (unit commander), 22
cinema, nature and potentialities of, 14
Cinema Academy (Hanoi), 15–18, 73–74
Cinema Association, 47
Cinema Department, 16, 47, 60, 130, 132
Colburn, Larry, 124, 127, 132
colleagues of TVT (working in such areas a technology, film printing, economics, and finance), 198
College of Fine Arts (Hanoi), 66
communication between North and South, limits placed on, 141–42
Countryside, The (film), 201
crab (cooked by stealth to avoid starvation), 51–52
crossing the West German frontier (to get to Frankfurt am Main), 118–19
Cù Huy Cận (poet), 97
cyclo drivers, 58–59, 100–101, 150

Đặng Thùy Trâm, 21–25
Đặng Trần Sơn (a sharer in some of TVT's early adventures), 10–12, 14–15, 57
Đặng Văn Drum, 87
Đặng Xuân Thiều (Ministry of Culture director), 9
Đào Trọng Khánh (scriptwriter), 85
Davis, Peter (film director), 153
Day in Hanoi, A (film), 70
death anniversaries, 6
Decornoy, Jacques (French journalist), 122

"Đêm Đông" ("Winter Night"; song by Nguyễn Văn Thương), 141
Đèo Văn Long (Thái chieftain), 10–11
Department of Culture and Arts, 171, 182
Department of Ideology and Culture, 154–55
"đi B" (going to the South), 20
Điện Biên (aka Điện Biên Phủ; a village), 15, 75
Điện Hồng (village), 43
Đinh Anh Dũng (filmmaker), 176
Đỗ Ba (a child rescued at Mỹ Lai), 126–28, 131
Đỗ Khánh Toàn (cameraman for *A Spiritual World* and *Wise Blind Men Examining an Elephant*), 200
Đoàn 559 (army battalion in charge of the Hồ Chí Minh Trail System), 53–54
Đoàn Chuẩn (songwriter), 8
Đoàn Thị Điểm (eighteenth-century poet), 86
documentary cinema, nature of, xv, xx
documentary film history in Vietnam, 106
Documentary Film Studio (Hanoi), 77, 200
Đỗ Mười (general secretary of the Communist Party), 169
đổi mới ("renovation"; government policy beginning in 1986), 82, 192–93
Đồng Xuân Thuyết, 99–100
Đồng Sĩ Nguyên (commander of Đoàn 559), 53–54
Duy Xuyên District, 28, 41, 65, 69

educational tour for young American film students, xii, xviii–xx
Eternal Gardens, The (cemetery in Westminster, California; the burial site of many well-known expatriate Vietnamese), 170–71
ethnic minority peoples, 12–13, 17, 52–53, 73–74

famine of 1945, 5–6
film, protection of in wartime conditions, 33–36, 40, 49–50

film festival delegates, 83
film festivals: Dà Nẵng (1988), 68, 106–10, 114; Leipzig International Film Festival (1970), 71; (1988), 107–9, 111, 113–18, 121–23; (1989), 123
filmmaking methodology, 86, 100–101
filmmaking technique, 95, 201
"Five City Gates of Hanoi, The" (film proposed to promote tourism in Hanoi), 85–86, 89
folk sayings, 7
Fox, Diane (anthropologist), 156–60
Frankfurt am Main, 119
French border guard, 119–20
French public phones, 120

gear, management of in wartime, 28–31, 40
German customs officials, 118–19
guild-streets of Hanoi, 7–8

Hà Mậu Nhai (director of the Liberation Film Company), 65–66
Hà Xuân Trường, 92, 182
Hai Hường (wife of Mr. Tý), 29, 38–39, 70
Hải Phòng (northern seaport city), 100, 144, 169
hand grenades, 31, 70
Hằng (TVT's wife), 56–58, 71–72, 125, 189
Hàng Bún Street, no. 52 (former residence of TVT), 111–12, 180–81
Hanoi in Whose Eyes (film) xvii, 81–82, 84–98, 110, 152, 171–72, 174–75, 180–81, 183
hatred and prejudice (as divisive elements in society), 133, 137–39, 152–56, 177
helicopter gunners (particularly feared by combatants on the ground), xi–xii, xviii, xx
Hemingway, Ernest, 94
Heynowski, Walter (German filmmaker), 78
hill farming (to grow military "self-reliance" crops), 26–27, 66

Hồ Chí Minh, 60, 90, 106, 121
Hồ Chí Minh trails (Trường Sơn trails), xii–xiii, 48
Hồ Trí Phổ (scriptwriter and filmmaker, close colleague of TVT), 100, 198–99
Hồ Xuân Hương (early nineteenth-century poet), 86
Hoà Bình Province, 20, 22, 26
Hoàng Đạo Thúy (writer), 85
Hoàng Giác (songwriter), 143
Hoàng Khởi Phòng (expatriate Vietnamese writer), 152, 170
Hoàng Minh Giám (professor; subject of film by TVT), 182
Hoàng Ngọc Hiến (invitee of the William Joiner Center), 154
Hoàng Trần Doãn (friend and "sworn brother" of TVT), 181–82
"Hoàng Trưu" (verse narrative), 5
Hoàng Tùng (bureaucrat in charge of propaganda and ideology), 182
Hoàng Xuân Hãn (scholar residing in France), 179
Hội An (seaside resort town in Central Vietnam), 45
Hồng (wife of Nguyễn Hữu Đính), 147–50
Huệ Chi (invitee of the William Joiner Center), 154
Hùng (younger brother of Hồng, Nguyễn Hữ Đính's wife), 149
Huy (policeman, son of an old schoolmate of Hằng, TVT's wife), 180–81
Huy Văn Palace (Hanoi), 86
Huỳnh Thúc Kháng (anti-colonialist; associate of Phan Chu Trinh), 176–77

If You Go to the Ends of All the Seas, 6, 137, 154, 187
international delegations at film festivals, 107–10
inversive development (film development technique), 63–64

Japanese broadcasting station (sponsor of a film by TVT), 164

K25 Rehabilitation Camp, 55
Karlin, Wayne, xi–xv, xvii–xx, 158–59; as helicopter door gunner during the war, *illus.*
Karmen, Roman (Russian documentary film director, TVT's teacher), 66–67, 73–75, 77, 109
Khổng Minh Dụ (chief of Cultural Security in the Ministry of Public Security), 168–69
Kiệt. *See* Thanh and Kiệt
Kinh (name used to distinguish ethnic Vietnamese from other ethnicities in Vietnam), 12, 52–53
Korean troops (as participants in the war), 27

La Fontaine (seventeenth-century French fable poet), 120
Lai Châu (northwestern outpost in the Thái-Mèo Autonomous region), 10–11, 14, 17, 19
Lai Xá (Hanoi district known as "Photography Village"), 43
Lake Baikal, 72, 157
Land Reform policy (1954), 5–6
Lao Động ("Labor"; a newspaper), 124
Laos, 22, 48
Lê Bá Huyến (film director; defector to the South), 21
Lê Cảnh Hưng (emperor), 87
Lê Đình Điều (expatriate journalist), 171
Lê Duẩn (Vietnamese politician), 77
Lê Đức Thọ (politician), 93
Lê Huy Hòa (sound engineer), 200
Lê Lợi (emperor), 88
Lê Mạnh Thích (filmmaker and deputy director of the Documentary Film Studio), 124, 170, 198
Lê Mạt (later Lê) dynasty, 87
Lê Minh Khuê (writer), xi–xii, 159
Lê Tâm (female friend of Nguyễn Hữu Đính), 146–47
Lê Thanh Dũng (coauthor), 163, 187–88; with TVT, *illus.*
Lê Văn Chiêu (mathematics teacher), 102–3

Lê Văn Long (cameraman), 101–2, 111, 199–200
lepers, treatment of, 103
Liberation Film Company, 65
Light in the Jungles (book by Roman Karmen), 75
Lò Minh (friend of TVT), 181
Long Biên Bridge (formerly Paul Doumer Bridge, in Hanoi), 6, 35
Ludemis (Greek poet), 95
Lương Quy Nhân (chief of Lai Châu's Department of Cultural Affairs), 10, 14–15
Lưu Hà (cameraman), 90
Lưu quảng Vũ (playwright and poet), 98, 208n
Lưu Xuân Thư (Documentary Film Studio director), 84–85, 90
lý lịch (personal record or resumé), malign role played by, 20, 102
Lý Thái Bảo (director of the Documentary Film Studio, Hanoi), 77–78
Lý Thái Tổ (emperor), 94

Mạc (TVT's brother-in-law), 58–60
Mai Lộc (friend of Roman Karmen), 58–60
Mai Thảo (expatriate writer), 170
Mai Thế Song (sound engineer), 200
Maison, Blanche (French ambassador), 177
malaria, 49, 62
Ministry of Culture, 9, 179
Ministry of Public Security, 168, 178
minority peoples in Vietnam, 12–13
movies, early impressions of, 7–8, 14, 143
Mount Dựng, 31–34, 41
Mường Lay (place in the far northwest), 10
Mường Mô (mountain in the far northwest), 12
Mường Tè (a remote place in the far northwest), 12
Mr. Hy (fellow military man), 65, 69
Mr. Tý (also known by his pen name, Triều Phương), 28–34, 43, 65, 68–70

Mrs. Hảo (wife of the musician Nguyễn Văn Thương), 48, 69
Ms. Nhanh (Mỹ Lai survivor), 127–29
Ms. Nhung (Mỹ Lai survivor), 127–29
Muội (aka "chị Mạc"; TVT's elder sister), 58–60, 143
Mỹ Lai, 124–33

Nam Định (city close to An Phú, the ancestral home of TVT), 5, 60, 142, 144
National Economics Exhibition (USSR), 76
National Institute of Cinema (Moscow), 67, 72, 76, 108
National Movie Center (Hanoi), 129
National Training Academy for Cadres (Vũng Tàu), 145–47
negatives (artistic use of in films), 66–67
Nghiêm Hà (secretary to Trần Độ), 173
Ngô Bích Hạnh (filmmaker), xvii
Ngô Đình Diệm, 32
Ngô Thời Nhậm (historical figure), 86
Ngọc Lan (expatriate singer), 171
Ngọc Linh (artist), 112
ngụy ("puppet"; northern regime's term for members of the southern regime), 151
Nguyễn, Rosemary (American Vietnamese speaker), 158
Nguyễn Bá Chung (writer, translator), 197
Nguyễn Cảnh Chân Meeting Hall (in the compound of the Communist Party Central Committee), 97
Nguyễn Cao Kỳ (politician), 180
Nguyễn Đình Thi (writer), 75, 97
Nguyễn Đức (secretary of the Cinema Academy's party executive committee), 18–19
Nguyễn dynasty, 87–88
Nguyễn Giá (wartime filmmaker), 41–46, 197
Nguyễn Huệ (aka emperor Quang Trung), 87–88
Nguyễn Hữu Đính (longtime friend of TVT), 139–51, 187
Nguyễn Hữu Thái (younger brother of Nguyễn Hữu Đính), 142–43

Nguyễn Khắc Viện (scholar, intellectual), 97
Nguyễn Khoa Điềm (minister of culture), 130
Nguyễn Khuyến School (Nam Định), 140–42
Nguyễn Mạnh Lân (friend of TVT; Russian-Vietnamese interpreter), 73
Nguyễn Mộng Giác (expatriate Vietnamese writer), 156
Nguyên Ngọc (writer and editor), 138, 171
Nguyễn Như Vũ (filmmaker and cameraman for *A Story from the Corner of a Park*), 199
Nguyễn Quang Phan Bình (filmmaker), xvii
Nguyễn Sa (expatriate poet), 170
Nguyễn Sáng (artist), 171
Nguyễn Sĩ Bằng (worked with TVT on *A Barbarian of Modern Times*), 201
Nguyễn Sĩ Chung (filmmaker and scriptwriter; worked together with his son for TVT in the film *Songs Resounding for a Thousand Years*), 201
Nguyễn Tiến Năng (secretary to Phạm Văn Đồng), 179
Nguyễn Thế Đoàn (filmmaker and film technician), 60–65, 71
Nguyễn Thị Phương Khanh (childhood classmate of TVT and Nguyễn Hữu Đính), 140–41, 144–45
Nguyễn Tiến Dũng (TVT's brother-in-law), 116, 118, 122
Nguyễn Trãi (Lê dynasty statesman), 85–86, 88
Nguyễn Trãi School (Saigon), 144–45
Nguyễn Trung Hiếu (ARVN sergeant), 23–24
Nguyễn Trung Hiếu (cameraman), 103
Nguyễn Tuân (writer)
Nguyễn Văn Hạnh (deputy director of the Department of Culture and Art), 113
Nguyễn Văn Linh (politician), 96–98, 171, 175
Nguyễn Văn Nhân (director of the Documentary Film Studio), 124, 130, 198

Nguyễn Văn Thương (songwriter), 48
Nguyễn Văn Vĩnh (early twentieth-century journalist and reformer), 154, 176–77, 201, 208n
Nguyễn Việt Dũng (bureaucrat), 90
Nguyễn Vĩnh Phúc (scholar), 86
Nội Bài Airport (Hanoi), xix, 187
Nông Ích Đạt, 16–17
nuns, Catholic, compassion of, 82, 104, 172
nước mắm (fermented fish sauce), 34

Odessa (Ukraine), 77
official opposition to TVT's films, xiv–xv
Orange County, California (home of "Little Saigon"), 152
orange juice packets, 49
ORWA (type of film), 61–63, 95

Parade (Polish film), 123
Pain That Belongs to No One in Particular (Russian book of poems by Simonov), 75
Paris Peace Accords, 77
Party, the (Vietnamese, Communist), 19–20, 163–64, 167–69
Party, the (USSR, Communist), 76
patriotism, nature of, xiv, 165–66, 176–77
"people," use of the word in government parlance, 172
People of My Homeland (film), 27, 41, 68, 71
personal connections (as a key element in government), 179
Peterson, Pete (U.S. ambassador to Vietnam), 129
Phạm Chuyên (Hanoi police chief), 180
Phạm Đình Chương (musician and songwriter), 171
Phạm Duy (songwriter), lyrics quoted, 184
Phạm Hà (film director; elder colleague of TVT), 181
"Phạm Tải and Ngọc Hoa" (verse narrative), 5

Phạm Văn Đồng, 91–93, 175, 178–79
Phạm Văn Khoa (friend of Roman Karmen), 73
Phan Chu Trinh (early twentieth-century scholar and patriot), 154
Phan Huỳnh Điểu (songwriter), 66
Phan Thanh Hảo (friend of TVT), xvii–xviii
Phan Trọng Quỳ (news photographer), 199
Phan Văn Đỗ (friend of Mike Boehm), 125
Phan Văn Khải (former prime minister of Vietnam), 104
pháo bầy (coordinated artillery barrages), 26, 32–33
phi lao (seaside pines), 37, 39
photojournalists, mission of in wartime, 40
Phúc (filmmaker; husband of TVT's younger sister), 117
Phương Đình Pháp (mandarin in court of Lê Cảnh Hưng), 87
Phương Nam Books (publisher of the original Vietnamese edition of this book), 192
Pilots in Pajamas (film), 78
Place Where We Lived, The (film), 74
popular and rural music (Vietnamese), 5, 8, 70, 140–41
Portland, Oregon, 158–59
"Prayer" (piece played annually on the violin by Mike Boehm at Mỹ Lai), 126, 133
publication of *Chuyện Nghề Của Thủy* ("The Professional Career of Thủy," the original version of this book), 81, 192–93

Quán Thánh Temple (Hanoi), 86
Quảng Bình Province (just north of the DMZ), 20
Quảng Đà Province, 29, 41–42, 45
Quảng Nam Province, 22
Quảng Ngãi Province (location of Mỹ Lai), 25, 70, 128, 130–31, 198
Quảng Văn Temple (Hanoi), 86–87

Quy Hoà Leprosarium, 103–4, 172

Railway Department (Vietnam), 110
reeducation camps, 148–49, 159–60
religion, social value of, 104
rentrer (Vietnamese "dinh-tê"; to return from a liberated area to a French-occupied city), 8
Resistance War (against France, 1946–1954), 3, 5–7
rice-hulling, 11–12
Rising Wind, The (*Nổi Gió*, a film), 21
Rugerd (cultural attaché with the East German embassy in Vietnam), 109, 111–13
rural folk verse (lullaby), 3
Russia, film training in, 41

salary as a photo journalist, 64
Scheumann, Gerhardt (German filmmaker), 78
scripts, relation of to filming, 76
self-satire (in *The Story of Kindness*), 105
Simonov, Konstatin (Russian poet), 75
singing (of TVT's childhood classmates and teachers), 140–41
social injustices and inequities, 82, 85, 99, 164
Sơn (teacher from Hải Phòng, a war casualty), 29
"Sơn Nữ Ca" ("Song of the Mountain Girl"; song), 141
Song of the Stork (film), xvii
Songs Resounding for a Thousand Years (film), 8, 180, 183–84, 201
"Sound of Autumn" ("Tiếng Thu"; poem by Lưu Trọng Lưu), 70
Sound of a Violin at Mỹ Lai, The (film), 25, 83, 124–33, 198–99
Southern Vietnamese, character traits of, 110
Soviet Culture (USSR newspaper), 75
Spiritual World, A (film), 164
Story from the Corner of a Park, A (film), 157, 199
Story of Kindness, The (film), xiv, 82–83, 98, 143, 171–72, 175, 183–84

streets of Hanoi, 7–8
suffocation (in unventilated tunnels), 26, 29–31
suicide attempts (of Nguyễn Hữu Đính), 147–48
sweep operations, 29, 41–42
swimming, 7, 40, 50–51
symphonic music, 187

Tạ Ngọc Phách (real name of Trần Độ), 174
Talib, Abu (Tagestan poet), 88
tâm thư (letter from the heart) incident, 121, 208n
Tạp chí Điện ảnh Việt Nam (Journal of Vietnamese Cinema), 197
taro (plant), 51
Teacher Niên, 27–29
Temple of Literature (Hanoi), 86
Tết offensive, 1968 (Tết Mậu Thân), 42–45, 62
Thai Hằng (singer and actress, wife of the songwriter Phạm Duy), 171
Thái Nguyên (northern province), 72
Thái-Mèo Autonomous Region, 10–13
Thanh and Kiệt (young Vietnamese expatriate couple), 159–60
Thanh Thảo (poet from Quang Ngãi), 23–25
Thanh Thiên (member of the Vietnamese Association in France), 121
There Was a Village (film), 164, 203n
"Thiên Thai" ("The Other World"; song by Văn Cao), 141
Thompson, Hugh, 124, 131–32
"Thu" ("Autumn"; song), 141
Thu Bồn River, 28, 35–37, 43
Thủ Đức Officer Candidate School, 145
Thu Hương (TVT's daughter), 187–89
"Tống Trân and Cúc Hoa" (verse narrative), 5
trailing and interrogation by police, 110–13, 177–80
Trầm Tử Thiêng (expatriate songwriter), 171
Trần Độ (broad-minded politician), 98, 113, 117, 163, 165, 171–75, 177

Trần Đức (narrator in *The Story of Kindness*), 105
Trần Đức Hình (deputy director of Cinema Department), 16–17, 71
Trần Hải Hạc, 120–22
Trần Hữu Nghĩa (cousin of Mr. Tý), 68
Trần Hữu Ngoạn (director of the Quy Hoà Leprosarium), 103–4
Trần Huy Bá (scholar), 86
Trần Nhật Thăng (TVT's first son), 71
Trần Thế Dân (film director, wartime comrade of TVT), 47–48, 70
Trần Văn Cẩn (painter), 171
Trần Văn Thủy: A Story of Unkindness (a book written by a Vietnamese expatriate attacking TVT), 156
Trần Văn Vĩnh (TVT's elder brother), 6–7, 56
Trần Văn Vỵ (TVT's father), 6–7, 60, 72
Trịnh Công Sơn (songwriter), 163, 188, 191
trứng vịt lộn (fertilized duck eggs), 39
Trường (defector to the South), 21
Trương Bá's Soul in the Butcher's Skin (a drama by Lưu Quang Vũ), 171
Trường Chinh (prominent politician), 9, 93
Trương Huy (director of academic affairs at the Cinema Academy, later chief of the editing division in the Documentary Film Studio), 17, 85
Trường Sơn Mountains (Hồ Chí Minh trail area), 27, 48, 52–53
Trường Vũ (ARVN veteran), 158–59
truth-telling (versus dishonesty), 24–25
"Từ Thức Meets an Immortal" ("Tư Thức Gặp Tiên"; traditional tale), 142
tunnels and underground shelters, 29–31, 39–43
TVT's mother, 56, 117

Unification Department. *See* Ban Thống Nhất
Unification Park (Hanoi), 54–55
USSR historical issues (TVT's former ignorance of), 76

Văn Cao (songwriter), 47, 171
Văn Nghệ (*Literature and Art*, a Vietnamese journal), 171
Văn Phác (minister of culture), 47, 92, 182
Văn Thị Xoa, xii, 36–37, 65
Văn Vượng (guitarist), 94
Viễn (childhood friend of TVT), 141, 151
Việt Cộng (used by TVT throughout this book to refer to all soldiers on the Communist side, both People's Army of Vietnam and Southern Liberation Front), xiii, 28–29
Việt Linh (film director), 181
Việt-Xô (Vietnamese-Soviet) Hospital, 57, 63
Vietnam on the Road to Victory (film by directed by Roman Karmen), 75
Vietnamese Association in France, 117, 120–23
Vĩnh, "little" (a child), 51–53
Vĩnh Trinh Dam (Dam at Vĩnh Trinh), 32–33
Võ Hoàng Khả (party cell secretary), 19–20
Võ Nguyên Giáp (famous general), 165, 174–75
Võ Văn Kiệt (politician), 175
"voluntary" shops, 12
Vũ Hạ (expatriate playwright)

Vũng Tàu, 145–48
Vương Khanh Luông (filmmaker, and cameraman for *The Sound of a Violin at Mỹ Lai*), 199

water (as a motif in the life of TVT; water-related travels), 157–58
Wild Game Hunters of Mount Đak Sao (film), 48
William Joiner Center (University of Massachusetts Boston), 137, 197–98
Wilson, Dean (film scholar), 105
Woman's Association of Quảng Ngãi, 130

Xoè (Thái ethnic dance), 11
xôi (sticky rice), 15
Xuân Diệu (poet), 171
Xuân Thủy (negotiator in the Paris Peace Accords), 77
Xuyên Châu (village), 36
Xuyên Thanh (village), 33–34
Xuyên Trường (village south of the Chiêm Sơn Bridge over the Thu Bồn River), 28, 33–34, 43

"yellow music" (a pejorative term used by the government for sad café music), 8
Yevtushenko, Yevgeni, 75
younger sister of TVT, 20, 117, 164

Trần Văn Thủy, a People's Army veteran of the American war, is a well-known independent filmmaker in Vietnam. He is the two-time winner of the Silver Dove Award in the Leipzig International Film Festival and has won the Golden Award for Best Director, Best Filmscript, and Best Camerawork at several Vietnam Film Festivals, as well the Golden Award at the Asia Pacific Film Festival and the "Witness to the World" Award at the International Cinema Conference in New York.

Lê Thanh Dũng, coauthor of *Chuyen nghe cua Thuy* is a writer, a translator (Chinese to Vietnamese), and an expert in communications technology. He served in the military for two years, after which he studied at the Nanjing Telecommunication Institute in Nanjing (China) and later graduated with a doctoral degree from the Hungary Science Academy in 1974. He has worked at Vietnam Posts and Telecommunications Group (VNPT) and received, with Trần Văn Thủy, the Best Book of 2013 award from the Institute of Research into Educational Development.

Wayne Karlin, a USMC veteran of the Vietnam war, is the author of seven novels and three nonfiction books, and edited a series of novels and short story collections of authors from Vietnam in translation, as well as other anthologies. Several of his books have also been translated into Italian, Dutch, Swedish, Norwegian, and Vietnamese and published abroad. He is the recipient of several Maryland State Arts Council Awards for Fiction, two National Endowment for the Arts fellowships, the Paterson Fiction Prize, and the Vietnam Veterans of American Excellence in the Arts Award.

Eric Henry served in the U.S. Army in Vietnam. He is a former senior lecturer in the Asian Studies Department of the University of North Carolina at Chapel Hill, and is literate in Chinese, Vietnamese, Korean, Japanese, French, Italian, and Russian. The author of a book on classical Chinese drama and numerous academic articles and essays, he has received the University of North Carolina Favorite Faculty Award and the Yale University Price Fellowship in East Asian Studies.

Nguyễn Quang Dy graduated from the Diplomatic Academy in Hanoi with a BA in English and international relations. Dy worked in the foreign service for over three decades, doing different jobs and assignments in Vietnam and overseas (as English translator/editor, press officer/secretary, researcher, and analyst.), having extensive experience in government and public relations. He retired in 2004 to work as a senior consultant for training programs. From 1997 to 2000, Dy worked as a lecturer at the Diplomatic Academy, teaching English and communication, and served as associate editor for *World Affairs Weekly* in Hanoi. After retirement, he worked as a senior advisor for the Fulbright school in Hồ Chí Minh City (run by Vietnam Program at Harvard) and for a public policy training program in Hanoi.

www.ingramcontent.com/pod-product-compliance
Lightning Source LLC
Chambersburg PA
CBHW020649230426
43665CB00008B/359